MW00772409

The French at Waterloo: Eyewitness Accounts

The French at Waterloo: Eyewitness Accounts

Napoleon, Imperial Headquarters and I Corps

Andrew W. Field

Pen & Sword

MILITARY

AN IMPRINT OF PEN & SWORD BOOKS LTD.
YORKSHIRE - PHILADELPHIA

First published in Great Britain in 2020 by
PEN & SWORD MILITARY
An imprint of
Pen & Sword Books Ltd
Yorkshire – Philadelphia

ISBN 9781526768469

A CIP catalogue record for this book is available from the British Library

Typeset in 10.5/13 Ehrhardt by Vman Infotech Pvt. Ltd.
Printed and bound in the UK by TJ International Ltd, Padstow, Cornwall.

Pen & Sword Books Ltd incorporates the imprints of Pen & Sword
Archaeology, Atlas, Aviation, Battleground, Discovery, Family History,
History, Maritime, Military, Naval, Politics, Social History, Transport,
True Crime, Claymore Press, Frontline Books, Praetorian Press,
Seaforth Publishing and White Owl
For a complete list of Pen & Sword titles please contact

PEN & SWORD BOOKS LTD
47 Church Street, Barnsley, South Yorkshire, S70 2AS, England
E-mail: enquiries@pen-and-sword.co.uk
Website: www.pen-and-sword.co.uk

Or

PEN AND SWORD BOOKS
1950 Lawrence Rd, Havertown, PA 19083, USA
E-mail: Uspen-and-sword@casematepublishers.com
Website: www.penandswordbooks.com

Contents

Dictated to his secretary, Fleury de Chaboulon, at Laon, two days after the battle and published in the *Moniteur Universel* in Paris on 21 June.

This book was based on long and exhaustive discussions of the battle that General Gourgaud, Napoleon's senior orderly officer at Waterloo, had with Napoleon during the emperor's exile on St Helena. It was possibly even dictated to Gourgaud by the emperor and was published by Gourgaud on his return to France in 1818. This book develops the idea that Marshals Ney and Grouchy were responsible for the loss of the battle.

Anonymously published in 1820, but generally accepted as being dictated by Napoleon to General Bertrand during his exile on St Helena. In these memoirs, Napoleon clearly shifts the blame for the loss of the battle onto Marshals Ney and Grouchy.

Jardin Aîné was Napoleon's equerry at Waterloo, responsible for the Emperor's horses. This is the English translation of Aîné's journal.

Throughout the Waterloo campaign, Mameluke Ali filled the post of Napoleon's personal servant. It is probably well-known that he was not a Mameluke at all, but a Frenchman called Louis Étienne Saint-Denis. Ali inevitably offers us little detail on the battle, although he gives the impression that the arrival of the Prussians was a surprise. He gives an interesting account of the capture of Napoleon's carriages.

During the Waterloo campaign March and served as *Premier Valet de Chambre* (senior personal servant) to Napoleon. March and tells a similar, though no less interesting story to Ali. Once again, we see that an eyewitness appears to have been surprised by the appearance of the Prussians. March and clearly points the finger of blame for the defeat at Grouchy.

Fleury de Chaboulon served as Napoleon's secretary during the Waterloo campaign, but not as secretary to his cabinet as he claims. De Chaboulon clearly follows Napoleon's accounts of the battle; he speaks of Napoleon's expectation that Wellington would have retired during the night, prior knowledge of the Prussian approach and suggests that Napoleon's whole plan was predicated on Grouchy's move against the Prussian rear. Like most French accounts, he falsely gives Wellington's army a numerical advantage over the French. The battle itself, to which he was not an eyewitness, follows Gourgaud's account almost exactly, including the claim that the British were defeated before the decisive intervention of the Prussians. Napoleon's accusations against Ney's commitment of the cavalry are repeated. It is only after the battle has ended that de Chaboulon returns to some interesting personal experiences.

Coignet served during the 1815 campaign as the wagon-master to Napoleon's headquarters. His participation in the Waterloo campaign was limited by his role; it is probable that he saw nothing of the battle and his account seems to be based on what he must have read in later years. His story of being sent on reconnaissance is likely to be included to give him some role in the action; it seems unlikely that the baggage master would be tasked with such an important task, even given his considerable experience. He speaks nothing of his key duties in the headquarters.

Coignet's account is very pro-Napoleon and therefore promotes the idea that Grouchy was expected to arrive on the battlefield during the day and his failure to do this was the reason for the defeat. His suggestion that the Allied artillery fired at him, a single horseman, is unlikely to say the least. Given that his post was with the headquarters at le Caillou, much of what he describes towards the end of the battle is almost certainly hearsay.

Flahaut was one of Napoleon's personal aides-de-camp during the Waterloo campaign. Flahaut was appointed as aide-de-camp to Napoleon on 20 March 1815, the day Napoleon entered the Tuileries, and served as such throughout the campaign. The following was written in response to Marshal Marmont's critical comments in volume seven of the marshal's memoirs. Marmont was widely accused of having betrayed Napoleon by surrendering his corps to the Allies in 1814, an act which precipitated Napoleon's first abdication. He was therefore hated by all of Napoleon's adherents and it is no surprise that he fled Paris with Louis XVIII when Napoleon returned in 1815 and was very critical of the emperor's handling of the campaign.

In 1815 Gourgaud served in Imperial Headquarters as colonel and senior *officier d'ordonnance* (senior orderly officer) to Napoleon. We have already read Gourgaud's full account of the campaign and battle that is widely accepted to either have been dictated by Napoleon, or a reflection of his views, opinions and thoughts on the battle that had long been discussed with Gourgaud during the emperor's exile on St Helena. In the following account, Gourgaud describes his own experiences during the battle which give it not only a more authentic feel, but also indirectly challenges some of what had appeared in his campaign overview. It is noticeable that, like Napoleon's initial account of the battle, he gets La Haye Sainte mixed up with Mont-Saint-Jean. It is also interesting that his account of the deployment and actions of the guard differ substantially from his account of the campaign written after his return from St Helena; although lacking detail, as this is his personal recollection, it is likely to be a more accurate description than that put to him by Napoleon. He was nominated *maréchal de camp* three days after the battle.

During the 1815 campaign, Ney served as commander of the left wing of the French army until Waterloo, when he commanded I and II Army Corps and the 3rd and 4th Cavalry Reserve Corps under the overall command of Napoleon. After Waterloo, Ney quickly left the army and returned to Paris. Addressing the Chamber of Representatives, he did nothing to cover the disaster and almost exaggerated it; this destroyed any chance Napoleon had of clinging on to power. This account was recorded from his address.

What is significant about Ney's short account is that once again (a trend we shall see in many accounts), despite Napoleon declaring that he was aware of the Prussian presence and threat long before they actually appeared on the battlefield, one of his most senior commanders describes their appearance as a surprise.

At Waterloo Colonel Heymès served as the senior aide-de-camp to Marshal Ney. Heymès did not write on his own adventures at the battle but wrote with the emphasis on the participation of his chief on the campaign in an effort to counter the criticism that Napoleon and his adherents had raised against Ney. Like Napoleon, Heymès underplays both the scale of the disaster suffered by d'Erlon's corps and the effect of the British cavalry counter-attack. However, like many other French witnesses he appears to have been surprised by the appearance of the Prussians. He admits that Ney made a mistake in committing the cavalry, but says that Napoleon could have stopped them, but didn't. He is also one of only a few Frenchmen that describe the British use of rockets.

At Waterloo, Levavasseur served as aide-de-camp to Marshal Ney. Levavasseur's account is largely self-serving but does include some interesting personal vignettes. He makes much of his own participation and contribution, although there is little to challenge in his narrative. His loyalty is clearly to Marshal Ney first and Napoleon second. What is of interest, and which contradicts many histories of the battle, is his claim that Marshal Ney used his senior aide-de-camp, Crabbé, to command a composite force, composed of a squadron from each of the cuirassier regiments (probably of just Watier's division) to support the left flank of d'Erlon's assault. This was the force that was attacked and defeated by Somerset's Household Brigade. He too appears surprised by the intervention of the Prussians, apparently having been taken in by the subterfuge that the firing from that flank was from Grouchy.

At Waterloo, Drouot served as the *Aide-Major-général* of the Imperial Guard, effectively the overall commander of the Guard. This is a largely uncontroversial, even sterile, account which follows the generally accepted phases of the battle.

Baudus served at Waterloo as aide-de-camp to Marshal Soult and was thus part of imperial headquarters. Whilst he does not give many personal anecdotes, his comments on the battle are incorporated into his two-volume study on Napoleonic warfare, he does include some interesting facts and insights. Baudus concentrates on the arrival of the Prussians and tells us that Soult had always been worried about their appearance, whilst Napoleon seemed unconvinced that they could have an impact on the battle. He is very critical of Napoleon's decision to inform the army that the Prussian arrival was actually that of Grouchy. Once more we have a credible witness undermining Napoleon's accounts that say that he was fully aware of the Prussian threat.

In 1815 Petiet served as *adjutant-commandant* (staff colonel) attached to the *Grand-quartier general* (general headquarters) under the orders of Marshal Soult. As one of Soult's staff officers, it is unlikely that Petiet saw much of the battle, and yet offers us considerable detail. Despite his privileged position which must have given him a good understanding of the strategic situation and overview of the battle, there can be little doubt that much, if not all, of the detail of the battle must have come from hearsay and what he subsequently read. He makes the claim that an order had been sent to Grouchy on the evening of the 17th informing him of the imminent battle; this is the same claim made by Napoleon in his memoirs, a claim that has been widely disputed. As we can see that Petiet wrote these lines after reading the accounts of others, it is likely that this claim is made on the basis of Napoleon's account rather than something he knew for himself. Despite all this, Petiet's is an interesting and well-written account.

General Drouet d'Erlon commanded I Army Corps at Waterloo. D'Erlon's account of Waterloo is rather superficial and unsatis-fying; it comes from a pamphlet he wrote in which he says his aim was not to write his memoirs but merely to correct some mistakes of his biographers. Only 119 pages long, it briefly covers the outline of his career but gives little detail. Disappointingly therefore, it does not touch on the more controversial aspects of the battle on which he might have enlightened us, not least the thinking behind his use of large, divisional columns in his main attack on the Allied ridge.

At Waterloo, Fleuret was *Adjutant* of the 1st Battalion of the 55th *de ligne*, which formed part of the 1st Brigade (Charlet) of the 1st Infantry Division (Quiot) in I Army Corps. In most histories, Charlet's brigade (Charlet commanded the 54th *de ligne*, but had been promoted to command the brigade as the appointed brigade commander (Quiot) had been given command of the division because of the absence of its nominated commander, Allix.) were responsible for the attack on the farm of La Haye Sainte. It is therefore odd that Fleuret does not mention this and describes that his battalion attacked the main Allied line. Also of interest is how the remains of his regiment were formed into a single battalion and moved to the right flank to fight with the Young Guard against the Prussians.

Captain Pierre Duthilt 100

In the 1815 campaign, Captain Duthilt served as aide-de-camp to General Bourgeois, who commanded the 2nd Brigade of the 1st Division (Quiot vice Allix). In contrast to Fleuret's account above, Duthilt appears to claim that it was his brigade, the 2nd, that was ordered to assault La Haye Sainte. However, the attack he describes clearly by-passes the farm and although he later says it was captured, he does not tell us by whom.

Private Louis Canler 106

During the Waterloo campaign Canler was a private in the 28th *de ligne*. This regiment was part of the 2nd Brigade (Bourgeois) of the 1st Infantry Division (Quiot vice Allix), part of I Army Corps. Canler's account is full of interest, mainly because he gives a clear and atmospheric description of what it was like to be in the midst of one of d'Erlon's huge columns and restricts himself solely to what he saw and experienced for himself. According to Duthilt's account (above), Canler's regiment, as part of the same brigade, was to have attacked La Haye Sainte, but Canler does not mention this. Canler's adventures after the repulse of d'Erlon's attack are also of great interest.

Maréchal de Camp **Antoine Noguès** 111

During the Waterloo campaign, Noguès commanded the 2nd Brigade of the 3rd Infantry Division (Marcognet) in I Army Corps. Noguès' account tells us of Napoleon's wish to attack the Allied army on the evening of the 17th and makes the unusual and unsubstantiated claim that d'Erlon's attack went in with no skirmishers in front.

Lieutenant Jacques-François Martin 113

Jacques-François Martin served as a lieutenant in the 45th *de ligne*; part of the 2nd Brigade (Grenier), 3rd Infantry Division (Marcognet), part of I Army Corps. Martin's account is particularly useful because of how soon after the battle it was written. We can therefore be confident that both the more mundane and dramatic events that he describes were still fresh in his memory and that there were few pressures on him to tell anything other than the exact truth. Rather like Canler's account, this is written solely from the point of view of what he experienced and saw for himself and, also like Canler, paints a vivid picture of his experiences in one of d'Erlon's massive columns. He was later to publish a book covering his interesting, if relatively short, military career (*Souvenirs d'un Ex-Officier (1812-1815)* [Paris: Librairie Cherbuliez, 1867]). As can be seen, the book was published much later and contains many details on Waterloo that he could not have known at the time, thus exposing a natural tendency to add detail that must have been read later. It is also interesting as it is the first account from a junior rank that accuses some of treason; perhaps an understandable reaction to the defeat and an attempt to find an explanation for the inexplicable.

Lieutenant General Baron Pierre Durutte

Durutte served as the commander of the 4th Infantry Division, part of I Army Corps. Durutte's account tells us that the battle had already started as his division took its position in line. He is clearly critical of the handling of d'Erlon's corps, though he seems to make clear that his column was not broken by the counter-attack of the British heavy cavalry. It is also interesting to note his comments on the French use of the lance. Although he talks of deploying skirmishers and then two battalions towards Frischermont, this was to counter a threat from this direction, leaving one to wonder which French troops actually attacked La Haie and Pappelotte as described by the Allied forces posted there. By the end of the battle, Durutte tells us that his whole division had been sent to the centre despite the growing pressure from the Prussians on the French right.

Captain Chapuis

Chapuis commanded a grenadier company in the 85th *de ligne* (Colonel Masson). This regiment was part of the 2nd Brigade (Brüe), 4th Infantry Division (Durutte), part of I Army Corps. Chapuis gives us a detailed and interesting account of the battle from his regiment's perspective and how it was left out of d'Erlon's attack in order to protect the artillery. He speaks disparagingly of his divisional commander, Durutte, who he could not forgive for failing to take a more active role at Ligny on the 16th and wondered if Durutte was implicated in the desertion of his chief-of-staff and aide-de-camp on the same day. He does not mention a movement to support the centre as Durutte claims; perhaps the 85th were left behind as they had been during d'Erlon's attack.

Chef de Bataillon Joseph-Marcelin Rullière

Rullière commanded the 2nd Battalion of the 95th *de ligne*. This regiment was part of the 2nd Brigade (Brüe) of the 4th Infantry

Division (Durutte), part of I Army Corps. Rullière's account is of particular interest, not least because I am unaware of its use, or any part of it, in any other English language book on Waterloo. I have therefore taken the liberty of presenting it in full and not restricting myself just to the day of the 18th, in the hope that this will be of interest to readers. Rullière's account is the only one that seems to describe in detail the formation of d'Erlon's corps for its attack on the Allied left centre and he also speaks of its weaknesses. Like Chapuis, he makes no mention of his regiment moving to the French centre late in the battle.

During the 1815 campaign Bro commanded the 4th Lancers which were part of the 2nd Brigade (Gobrecht) of the 1st Light Cavalry Division commanded by General Jacquinot. This division was part of I Army Corps (d'Erlon).

Bro gives an interesting account of his regiment's counter-attack against the charging British cavalry in which he was wounded and forced to leave the battlefield. He also describes the death of General Ponsonby.

During the Waterloo campaign, Colonel Marcellin Marbot commanded the 7th Hussars. The regiment belonged to the 1st Brigade (Bruno) of the 1st Light Cavalry Division (Jacquinot), attached to I Army Corps (d'Erlon).

Marbot's memoirs end with Napoleon's first abdication in 1814 so we have no detailed account by him of the Waterloo campaign. However, two letters written to Marshal Grouchy give some interesting detail on his role at Waterloo. The first says little of the battle but has some interesting observations on the morale of the army after the defeat; the second enters into more details on the role of his regiment during the battle. In the years after the publication of Gourgaud's history and Napoleon's memoirs, Grouchy wrote copiously to counter the accusations of Napoleon that he was responsible for the loss of the battle and had no doubt sought evidence from Marbot to help his case. In particular, Marbot describes his role on the right flank of the army which seems to confirm Napoleon's claim that he was truly expecting Grouchy to arrive in time to take a decisive role in countering the arrival of the Prussians. However, we must take a cautious approach in taking

Marbot's word for this. His memoirs are not generally accepted as the unadulterated truth (showing a tendency to stretch the truth in order to tell a good story) and as an ardent supporter of Napoleon, he seems inclined to support Napoleon's claims about the battle. For example, he describes skirmishing with the advanced Prussian cavalry and yet Prussian accounts are all adamant that they approached the battlefield unobserved and without any contact with the French. Marbot's account clearly supports Napoleon's claim that he was expecting Grouchy to arrive on the battlefield, but some historians believe that his account was deliberately falsified to give credence to Napoleon's version of events.

During the Waterloo campaign, Victor Dupuy served as a squadron commander in the 7th Hussars (Marbot). The regiment belonged to the 1st Brigade (Bruno) of the 1st Light Cavalry Division (Jacquinot), attached to I Army Corps (d'Erlon).

Dupuy might be considered a more dependable witness than Marbot, his commanding officer. However, he supports Marbot's claim that his mission was to meet Grouchy rather than scout the Prussians.

List of Plates

Napoleon wrote three accounts of the battle. Although followed by his closest supporters, they have been largely ridiculed by more serious historians.

Marshal Ney wrote nothing of the battle before his execution, but his verbal account to the Chambers that was recorded put a deliberately discouraging slant on the battle.

Along with Marshal Ney, Napoleon laid much of the blame for the failure of the campaign on Marshal Grouchy's failure to prevent the Prussians reaching the battlefield. History has judged him rather better.

Gourgaud was Napoleon's senior *officierd'ordonnance* (orderly officer). His published history of the campaign is widely credited to Napoleon, but he did write his own, more personal account of the campaign.

Flahaut was one of Napoleon's personal aides-de-camp. He does not give a full account of the battle, or his own part in it, but does give some interesting insights to Napoleon's actions during the day.

A near-contemporary map of the battlefield showing its topography.

Drouot served as the *Aide-Major-général* of the Imperial Guard and one of Napoleon's closest confidantes. Like Ney, he did not write of the battle but his account delivered to the Chambers was recorded.

D'Erlon commanded I Corps during the campaign. His account is not long but includes some interesting insights to the battle.

Captain Duthilt served as aide de camp to General Bourgeois, who commanded the 2nd Brigade of the 1st Division (Quiot vice Allix) in d'Erlon's corps. He gives a detailed and interesting account of the battle as it affected his brigade.

Durutte served as the commander of the 4th Infantry Division, part of I Army Corps. He gives a rather short, but interesting, account of his division's part in the battle.

Colonel Bro commanded the 4th Lancers which were part of the 2nd Brigade (Gobrecht) of the 1st Light Cavalry Division commanded by General Jacquinot.

This division was part of I Army Corps and protected the right flank of the corps. He was heavily involved in the repulse of the Union Brigade and was wounded.

An artist's impression of one of d'Erlon's columns at Waterloo. Much criticised with the benefit of hindsight, early descriptions did not give them such a bad press. Neither d'Erlon, nor any of his commanders gave any explanation for their unusual formation.

Rather like the battle for Hougoumont, the fight for La Haye Sainte cost much French effort and blood. However, unlike Hougoumont, it did eventually fall to the French and offered Napoleon a springboard for an assault on the very centre of Wellington's line. Unfortunately, d'Erlon's corps had suffered so much in their main assault that they were unable to fully exploit the opportunity its fall offered.

Introduction

Many of the printed accounts of eyewitnesses have been . . . influenced so much more by warm feelings than by sober judgement, that in the difficulty of discerning between truth and imagination, the mind is frequently led into the medium of placing a superficial value on the whole.[1]

Unlike the British, the French did not write prolifically about Waterloo. This should not be surprising. Immediately after the battle, the French army was in complete disarray, spread across the countryside of southern Belgium and northern France, exhausted and demoralised. Many did not return to the army and realising Napoleon's dream was over, went back to their homes and families. In the immediate aftermath of the catastrophe there was not the time, the means or the inclination to reflect on the biggest humiliation of French arms during Napoleon's reign. Nor when time was available, after the dust had settled or in their retirement, after the disbandment of the army and the restoration of the monarchy, was there the political or social appetite to rake over the coals. In later years, no French equivalent of Siborne appeared to encourage people to finally take up their pen. Two hundred years later, this relative paucity of French accounts is a great frustration to both the amateur enthusiast and professional historian who wants to try to establish the truth of what happened that day.

Unfettered by the political or social climate of France and keen to protect his own reputation at the expense of others, Napoleon, in his exile on St Helena, was one of the first to give his own account of the campaign and battle: few followed him. It was only after the collapse of the monarchy that the accounts of both officers and men began to follow.

Many readers will be familiar with my four-volume series of books looking at the Waterloo campaign from the French perspective. The first of these, *Waterloo, the French Perspective*, concentrated on the major battle of the campaign and drew heavily on the individual French eyewitness accounts of the battle. Whilst French accounts generally break the battle down into similar phases to Allied accounts – the attack on Hougoumont, d'Erlon's attack, the great cavalry charges, the appearance of the Prussians, the attack of the Imperial Guard, the rout – it is perhaps inevitable that they put a somewhat different interpretation on the importance and outcome of each of those phases.

When reading the individual accounts of a battle by those who took part in it, there is an initially alarming level of disagreement evident between them. Surely, if they were present at the same battle, their recollections would be similar in many details? Not so; when studying first-hand accounts it soon becomes clear that hardly any two accounts do agree and that individuals, although observing the same events, do not interpret them in the same way, and this highlights the fact that each participant sees only a miniscule part of the whole, restricted by their own particular role in the battle, their place in the chain of command, where they were actually located on the battlefield and what restrictions there were on their ability to observe what was going on around them (the lay of the ground, smoke, etc.). This makes life very difficult for a historian who tries to base his narrative of events on the accounts of those who were there, even if the theory that these accounts are likely to be the most accurate is a worthy one. The many other reasons why eyewitness accounts vary so much are explored in the first chapter of this book, as it is vital for the reader to understand why such accounts can vary so much in detail before trying to interpret them for themselves. The author is therefore left to read all the conflicting accounts, balance them against the accounts of the opposition, read the official reports and communications and then apply his own intellect, best judgement, logic, common sense and military experience (if he has any), to decide what is the most likely interpretation of each particular event. This, ultimately, is very much an individual interpretation that can inevitably be credibly challenged by others with a different viewpoint.

This is certainly what I found as I wrote my four books, and whilst ready to argue my own interpretation, which I have had to do on numerous occasions, it is clear that other interpretations are perfectly credible and backed up by equally credible evidence. I was soon forced to accept that my books were *my* interpretation and that there were others that were perhaps equally credible, and whilst some interpretations are more likely to be accurate than others, it is almost impossible to declare authoritatively that any interpretation based on the same evidence as another interpretation is 'wrong'.

In my previous books, I inevitably chose what to include and what to edit out of each account. Not only, therefore, were these my own decisions, but they inevitably took those paragraphs out of the context in which the writer intended them and this, given the inevitable contradictions and errors the accounts included, left me open to the accusation that I only presented evidence that supported my own thesis; and this is inevitably true. I therefore determined that now was the time to publish the full accounts of each of the eyewitnesses I have been able to track down, many of which have not been available before in English, in order to share the whole with those who are interested. This is what I have attempted to do in this and a following volume. These two books will serve a double goal; firstly, for enthusiasts to read the whole of the French accounts to get the full French perspective on this battle which generations of French historians have struggled to come to terms with; and secondly, to allow enthusiasts to make their own interpretation based on their own analysis and judgement on the trustworthiness of the full account of each witness. I have therefore tried to avoid giving my own opinions and interpretations, but feel that for some, it would be useful to identify themes and prejudices that run through some French accounts, point out what are clear errors, deliberate or otherwise, and help readers who do not have a thorough knowledge of the battle to put the accounts into perspective and understand why some of these prejudices might have appeared in them.

The translations that follow are therefore the whole passage on the battle from each contributor and in the few examples where I have cut something out, I have explained in outline what was covered. This is almost inevitably a description of what was happening elsewhere than on the battlefield, where the author could not possibly have seen things for himself and was therefore repeating something he had read in someone else's account.

One of my challenges has been to make a judgement on whether an account should be included or excluded. One or two of those included are very short, but I have felt them worthy of inclusion because of a point of interest; some very short ones have been excluded because they add nothing to our understanding of the battle. Otherwise I have generally included all the accounts that I have available to avoid any self-imposed censorship. The accounts from more senior officers tend to cover the whole battle, because their role or location made them privy to a much wider observation and understanding of what went on, and often include an eloquent, if often very biased, critique on the handling of the battle; whilst those, regrettably much fewer, accounts from more junior ranks give much greater low-level detail on tactics and personal experiences, but are restricted to their own, much narrower, viewpoints. Both add considerably to our understanding of what happened and why it happened in a particular way, whilst unfortunately and frustratingly leaving many questions and quandaries unanswered.

I have also chosen to include, where possible, quite comprehensive biographies of the contributors. Apart from the intrinsic interest in the backgrounds of the Frenchmen who fought at Waterloo, this adds considerable context to their accounts and also helps to put their contributions into perspective. These make clear the incredible battlefield and campaign experience of many of Napoleon's senior commanders and cannot help but make the reader question how the battle could have gone so horribly wrong for the French. For those who have a good knowledge of the personalities, or perhaps no interest in them, I trust it will be no inconvenience to skip over their background and move directly to their accounts.

Finally, a word on translation: I am not a professional translator and have therefore spent many, many hours translating the accounts that follow; a large majority are entirely my own. I take full responsibility for any mistakes, but have tried hard to retain *what I believe* is the true meaning of what each contributor was trying to say rather than stick rigidly with a literal translation, which often, in English, does not always make things clear. As far as possible I have also tried to retain the feel of the original and this has inevitably involved my own interpretation rather than just strict translation. This will not satisfy everyone, but I trust all those with a fascination for this famous battle will find something new and of interest in my work.

The second volume of this book will cover eyewitness accounts from II and VI Corps, the cavalry reserve, the Imperial Guard and the medical services.

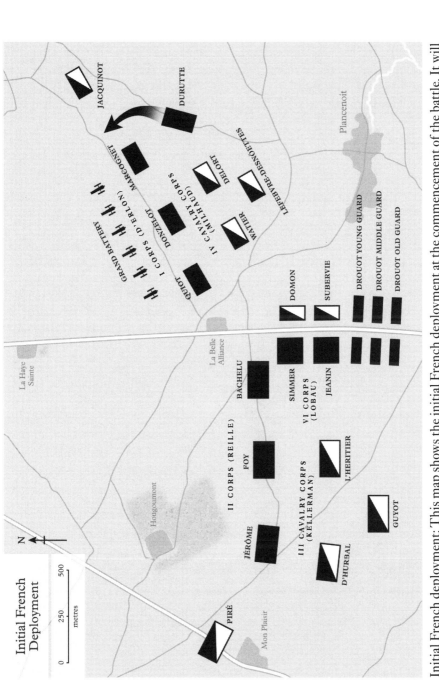

Initial French deployment: This map shows the initial French deployment at the commencement of the battle. It will be noted that Durutte's division of d'Erlon's I Corps was still moving into its allocated position when the battle started.

Chapter 1

Using Eyewitness Accounts

If ever the truth lies at the bottom of a well, she does so immediately after a great battle, and it takes an amazingly long time before she can be lugged out.[1]

In the Introduction I have already highlighted the extent to which most eyewitness accounts of Waterloo contradict each other and touched on why we need to approach such testimony cautiously if we are trying to use it to get to the truth of what really happened in the battle. Whilst first-hand accounts often add colour and atmosphere to our impression of the fighting, it is vital to understand when and in what context each eyewitness wrote if we are to decide what credibility we can give to them. Thus, a letter written the day after the battle or event it is describing has more value than an account drawn fifty years afterwards. However, an account drawn from a journal or diary written day by day over the events or travels that it describes could have the same value as a letter written immediately after the event, even if it was written many years later.

General Histories of the Campaign and Battles

We must be particularly wary of the early general histories of the battle as these must have been based on official correspondence and reports, and the earliest letters and accounts from those who were present. Although correspondence will generally be dependable on what orders and direction were given, any interpretation on what the situation was and what the enemy was doing was just that, an interpretation, and, depending on the accuracy of the intelligence upon which it was based, quite likely to be inaccurate or at best only partially accurate. Official reports were even more likely to vary from the truth, as the writer, presumably someone fairly senior in the originating headquarters, if not the commander himself, had some incentives, whether things had gone badly or well, to write up the situation and the part they had played in it. There are plenty of examples of this and it is only natural for a commander to exaggerate to some degree his own performance and that of the troops he commanded, whilst blaming others, overwhelming odds or something else over which he had no control (such as the weather) for any setbacks. As we have already seen, there are plenty of reasons why an eyewitness would not tell the whole truth, especially in regards to their own contribution to the action. For all these reasons, histories written by authors who were not present relied on the accounts of others and it therefore follows that there were many that challenged their interpretations. As we shall see, Napoleon's own accounts are a prime example of this.

Many early histories were motivated by an understandable (if not historically politically correct) national pride, national prejudice or even for their use as propaganda in a subsequent conflict to establish some sort of racial, military or cultural supremacy in order to boost national morale. All too often, restricting one's account purely to fact was not a criterion for a serious history. In more recent times, however, there has been a discernible and most welcome shift towards a more objective and even-handed approach to writing history, based on thorough research and questioning what was once accepted as established fact. As a result of this trend, many previously accepted historical accounts are being challenged and many have been exposed as riddled with inaccuracies and myths; myths that have been repeated as fact solely on the basis that they have been constantly recycled over the years and their origin has not been robustly challenged.

Having introduced the French perspective of the Waterloo campaign in my own series of books, along with Paul Dawson who has taken a similar approach, it now seems time to look at as many full French eyewitness accounts as possible and allow others to make their own interpretations. This is no mean challenge, as any re-appraisal of the battle from a French viewpoint must fully comprehend how cataclysmic this battle was, and still is, in the French historical and military psyche. Even in more recent interpretations, some French historians find it difficult not to follow Napoleon's line that the British army was beaten and the battle lost only due to the intervention of the Prussians; this perspective is noticeable in many of the accounts which follow.

Perhaps inevitably, British readers are more likely to feel British accounts are the most accurate, whilst the French accounts have been disregarded on the basis that they were trying to excuse their momentous defeat. Furthermore, many French histories have drawn heavily, although unsurprisingly, on Napoleon's own accounts of the campaign. Unfortunately, as we shall discuss in the next chapter, these have been largely discredited and therefore accounts that have drawn on them have had their own credibility undermined.

The major failing of French general historical accounts is their lack of objectivity; they are either unapologetically pro- or anti-Napoleon, and this lack of objectivity seriously detracts from their value as a true historical analysis. M.A. Thiers, perhaps France's most famous military historian of that era, wrote a massive twenty-volume history of Napoleon's campaigns of which the last one covers the campaign of 1815. However, Thiers was an unashamed and unrepentant admirer of Napoleon and can be little trusted as a wholly objective recorder of history, despite his eloquence and apparent attention to detail. His account was challenged by a number of eyewitnesses who wrote specifically to contradict his interpretation and some of his 'facts'. Even more modern French historians, such as Lachouque, set out to enhance the Napoleonic legend rather than our understanding of what really happened, and like many British accounts repeats already much recycled myth. French historians also seem least likely to identify their sources, throwing fresh doubt on the dependability of their accounts. In the absence of a victory, many French historians have judged the outcome of the battle on *la gloire*, in which they feel free to give Napoleon's army a considerable lead! It is for these reasons that I will restrict myself to presenting only eyewitness accounts.

The situation is not helped by the fact that few of the most senior commanders on the French side left detailed accounts of their own actions or the campaign as a whole, and most of the accounts and correspondence that do exist were generated in response to the criticisms of others, primarily Napoleon himself who, in exile on the island of St Helena, dictated his own accounts of the campaign which heaped much of the blame for his defeat on his two lieutenants, Marshals Ney and Grouchy.

Eyewitness Accounts

When considering the veracity of eyewitness accounts the historian must question whether the author had any personal agenda that was likely to colour his judgement and it might be useful to look at these before we explore the accounts themselves.

Each eyewitness will have had a unique and very personal view of the battle, but actually saw only a miniscule part of the whole, restricted by their particular role, their place in the chain of command, where they were on the battlefield and what restrictions there were on their ability to observe what was going on around them; in the context of the whole battle, each participant's experience must have been rather like viewing the battle through a drinking straw! Their own interpretation is therefore very much influenced by what was going on in their immediate vicinity rather than being able to see or appreciate the bigger picture and we must remember that most of the accounts we shall read were by officers whose concentration was very much on those areas or men for which they had responsibility and they rarely had an opportunity to casually observe what was going on beyond this. Indeed, one French eyewitness of Waterloo admits that he was convinced that the battle was won right up to the very moment the army disintegrated around him.

What we cannot unfortunately tell is when many of these accounts were actually written and what they were based on; a journal/diary, notes or just memory immediately after, or often many years after, the events in question. Unless stated in the accounts, we are often left with the date they were published rather than when they were actually written. We must therefore be careful of first-hand accounts written long after the battle in which the authors speak with apparent authority on episodes or strategy to which they were not a party and therefore unlikely to know at the time. We must give credit only to those things they saw or did for themselves, and those things which their post or position gave them direct access to. Too many participants who wrote their memoirs much later in life often included much information which could certainly have been false (deliberately or not) that had been included in the books of others that they had subsequently read and taken as fact; not least Napoleon's own accounts of the battle. Many accounts are also interlaced with comment and criticism; once more, this is almost inevitably present in those accounts that were written much later and swayed by all the benefits of hindsight and without fully understanding the circumstances in which those they have chosen to criticise faced when they took the decisions they did, or wilfully ignoring them in order to strengthen their own arguments. Once more, Napoleon's later accounts are a good example, but he is certainly not alone in this; many senior officers were critical not only of Napoleon, but also of others, in order to give the impression that they were half-hearted supporters of the emperor or dragged into serving him almost against their will.

The best French eyewitness accounts are certainly those that only describe their own personal experiences in detail; but if this was our only criteria for presenting French accounts, there would be few enough of them. The need for the French to explain and come to terms with their defeat encouraged many more to put pen to paper, even if their accounts were more an analysis of the battle than a true record of their own experiences.

So let's quickly look at some of the reasons why our eyewitnesses may have coloured their accounts of the battle. The first must surely be simple exaggeration. Youngsters in particular, perhaps especially those who were in their first battle, are probably far more likely to exaggerate than very experienced senior officers; yet even the latter, in an attempt to promote their own or their formation's contribution to the battle, may well exaggerate to a certain extent and this is quite evident in some of the accounts that follow. It is difficult to be sure, especially if one has not experienced something similar in one's own life, the extent to which another might recall events in detail; no doubt some people's memories are better than that of others. A battle that was as cataclysmic as Waterloo was quite likely to be ingrained into the memory of many of those who were present, and particularly more so if it was the only battle they fought in.

Aged forty-nine and after a long career in the infantry, my last operational tour was in Afghanistan. Out of the six months I spent there, most time was spent in the headquarters of which I was a part and I saw only a few weeks of action on the ground during which I experienced the nearest thing to close combat that I was involved in throughout my whole career. However, these few weeks and the firefights I was involved in will remain clear in my memory until my death. And yet, in the conversations with many of the young soldiers with whom I was privileged to share those experiences, I often wondered whether we were actually at the same place at the same time, so much did our interpretations of what happened and where vary! Whilst I would tend to forgive them their enthusiastic recollections, there is no reason why young soldiers of 200 years ago were not partial to the same tendencies as those of today, and whilst the basic context and situation of the action were entirely accurate, the details of the actual fighting, due to the adrenalin, excitement and a certain amount of fear, no doubt distorted their memory and perspective. And who am I to say categorically that my own interpretation is the accurate one? However, the often graphic accounts by the few younger eyewitnesses we shall read later display an innocent naivety that almost demands giving them the benefit of doubt as to their authenticity, whilst they rarely pretend to have any knowledge of what happened beyond their own very personal and localised experiences.

Self-promotion is certainly one of the most prominent reasons for exaggeration, although once more, this is probably a forgivable human trait as long as it does not go as far as deliberately taking credit from others. The French army of this period was very much a meritocracy that offered promotion, or rewards such as the coveted *légion d'honneur*, to those who excelled on the battlefield. There can be little surprise then that many soldiers, officers or other ranks, were prepared to stretch the truth to gain promotion, and the realistic hopes of people with even the humblest of backgrounds of reaching high rank no doubt encouraged this. More senior commanders, writing with the benefit of high rank and after the fear of persecution by a royalist government had passed, were no doubt keen to justify their own performance in light of the catastrophe.

However, it must be admitted that in the almost unique circumstances of Napoleon's return and the Waterloo campaign, there were also a significant number who wished to play down what they did by not promoting themselves. After the emperor's second abdication and the restoration of the monarchy there were many who wished to ingratiate themselves with the new government and were very happy to downplay their own part in the fighting and enthusiasm for Napoleon's return. The restoration of the Bourbons and the ensuing 'White Terror' inevitably generated a climate which did not encourage the publication of memoirs and accounts glorifying the campaign and those who took part in it. All this is particularly true of the senior officers who had most to lose.

But some people wrote not to promote themselves, but others. Whilst this, of course, did not necessarily include distorting their own actions or experiences, the general tone of an account, and certainly any personal comment or criticism, could go some way towards countering negative criticism of some by others. The most obvious target was Napoleon himself. We have already examined how

Frenchmen generally fell into one of two parties, pro- or anti-Napoleon, and it can be seen in some of the following accounts how this coloured the authors in their description of the campaign. Evidence seems to suggest that the vast majority of junior officers and other ranks almost hero-worshipped their emperor, whilst more senior officers resented Napoleon's return and the way it forced them to commit themselves either way. The way he is portrayed in their writings therefore reflects this. That said, a number of French accounts were written in defence of both Ney and Grouchy who, as we have already discussed, were criticised by Napoleon and blamed by him for the defeat. Sons of both marshals went into print to defend their fathers and both wrote to senior and headquarters officers to request their version of events. This has given us a number of accounts which might not otherwise have appeared and these are presented in these two books.

Some accounts were also written that promoted a writer's regiment or under-played its failure(s) in order to maintain regimental pride, although in the latter case this was perhaps more by omission rather than by lies. Individuals went a long way to promote the achievements of their regiments and then to enjoy the reflected glory. This is particularly true with a number of British regiments vying to credit themselves alone with the glory of having repulsed the Imperial Guard with no help from any other regiments, whilst the French Guard strove to find reasons for the repulse beyond the abilities or courage of the regiments themselves. Indeed, when comparing the accounts of this particular phase of the battle, it is impossible to reconcile those of the different British regiments, so much do they contradict, and even challenge, each other. French accounts complement each other to a much greater degree, but then contradict all the contradicting British accounts!

The final error we must mention is that of a fading memory. Many of the accounts we shall read were written in retirement, long after the events they describe. Although it is fair to argue that one's memory is likely to be keen on such life-changing experiences, this is probably only true for those who had few similar experiences. As many of the biographies make clear, many, indeed most, of the writers had considerable battlefield experience and had fought in a significant number of major battles. After twenty or thirty years, and much longer in some cases, it must have been extremely difficult to unravel an overwhelming number of both exciting and traumatic experiences that must inevitably rather have morphed into a confusing mass over time.

We must therefore be wary of those accounts that were written long after the events that they describe. Those based on diaries or notes kept at the time may safely be assumed to be relatively accurate, but when this is not the case we must treat them with a little more caution. Later accounts often draw on histories of the battle or personal accounts of others. When a junior officer describes events that he could clearly not have seen for himself because of his own position on the battlefield we must be especially wary as these have often been based on less authoritative accounts. This tendency, however forgivable, is much in evidence in many of the French accounts.

As a writer's age and memory affect their ability to recall their experiences accurately, it is perhaps inevitable that they use things they have read to fill in the gaps in their memory. Reading other accounts before writing their own and including events they heard about from others rather than observed for themselves, and after the lapse of many years, may actually have led to some believing that they had experienced these things for themselves. Ensign Leeke of the 52nd Light Infantry wrote exhaustively on his regiment's role in the repulse of the Old Guard and solicited many officers to give their own account of events. He complained of '. . . the impossibility which some officers find to distinguish, after the lapse of many years, between what they recollect to have seen, and what they have read of, or have heard from others'. In some of the accounts we shall look at later, the witness describes events which he could not have seen for himself, so must have either got the information second-hand from someone else that might have been present, or read about in a subsequent history.

I am no apologist for any of the French writers that are presented in this or the following book. I have generally presented their accounts in full and my own interpretation goes no further than to point out general themes, leaving the reader to decide on the dependability and usefulness of each narrative. But whatever credibility we each choose to give the following accounts, we must be very wary of dismissing those of one side or the other just because they may contradict those of our own nation. All accounts of those that fought at Waterloo, whichever side they fought on, contradict to a greater or lesser extent those of all others, even those of their own nation. Therefore, serious history demands that we consider each individual account objectively and with a full understanding of the context and possible distortions that are inevitably present in virtually all of them, without this needing to distract from their intrinsic value or interest.

Chapter 2

Napoleon's Own Accounts

The victor will never be asked if he told the truth.[1]

To put all the other French accounts of Waterloo into perspective, and to start to understand why French soldiers and historians have struggled to come to terms with the catastrophe, it is vital to look at Napoleon's own accounts of that momentous battle. One of the main reasons for this is that his accounts were some of the first to be published and therefore the first to be read, thus shaping French perceptions of the battle, even after convincing evidence was presented that challenged his interpretation, such was the grip that he had on the imaginations of many of his fellow countrymen, let alone his diehard supporters. Indeed, even many modern historians have found it difficult to shake off his influence and particularly his claims that at one stage the battle was won, which inevitably, and understandably, feeds the vanity of many who believe(d) in his invincibility and French military dominance.

Napoleon himself is credited with three accounts of the battle. The first was his official report that was dictated to his secretary, Fleury de Chaboulon, at Laon, two days after the battle. The second was la Campagne de 1815, ou relation des opérations militaires qui ont eu lieu en France et en Belgique, pendant les Cents Jours, écrite à Ste Hélène, par général Gourgaud *which may have been written by Gourgaud, as suggested in the title, but was based on long and exhaustive discussions of the battle that Gourgaud recorded he had with Napoleon during the emperor's exile on St Helena; indeed, some claim that the account was dictated to Gourgaud by the emperor to be published on the former's return to France. Finally there is* Mémoires pour servir à l'histoire de France en 1815, *anonymously published in 1820, but generally accepted as being dictated by Napoleon to General Bertrand during his exile.*

Perhaps unsurprisingly, many French histories of the battle were based on Napoleon's accounts, and consequently, foreign commentators have attached little credibility to them. Primarily, this is because Napoleon was famous for twisting the facts in his reports: his rewriting of the official account of the battle of Marengo is perhaps the most famous example, and it was from this tendency that the catchphrase 'to lie like a bulletin' originated. Secondly, they were seen as pieces of propaganda rather than a serious attempt to describe the battle accurately and it is fair to say that all three appear to have been used by Napoleon as a vehicle to lay the blame for the disaster on a number of marshals and generals, rather than on himself. Furthermore, much of his analysis is clearly based on all the advantages of hindsight. However, it is in the interpretation and analysis of the fighting, rather than the sequence or even results of the fighting, that the two sides differ fundamentally; and it is here that I contend that through a failure to examine any, yet alone all, of the French evidence beyond Napoleon's own accounts, or histories based on them, that most British historians have failed to be truly objective.

These three accounts were written without reference to any documents or correspondence and we must assume they were dictated or discussed from memory. It is therefore not surprising that they contain a number of verifiable errors. Napoleon's detractors, both contemporary and modern, have also been quick to accuse him of selective memory and out-and-out lies, recorded to protect his own reputation and deflect criticism onto others; primarily Marshals Ney and Grouchy. In particular, it is true to say that in relation to the actions of Grouchy, Napoleon's accounts cannot be depended on as a true and balanced record of events.

Fleury de Chaboulon tells us that the first of these accounts, le bulletin de Mont-Saint-Jean, *was drafted at Philippeville the day after the battle, completed at Laon on the 20th and published in the* Moniteur *in Paris on the 21st. In his account of the campaign, de Chaboulon wrote of the bulletin at Laon:*[2]

Then the emperor retired into another room with M. de Bassano and I. After having sent new orders to Marshal Soult on the movements and rallying of the army, he put the finishing touches to the bulletin of Mont-Saint-Jean, already sketched out at Philippeville. When he had finished, he called for the Grand Marshal, General Drouot and the other aides-de-camp. 'Here', he said to them, 'is the bulletin of Mont-Saint-Jean; I want it read out to you; if I have omitted some essential facts, you are to recall them for me; my intention is to miss nothing out. It is necessary, as after Moscow, to reveal the whole truth to France! I could', continued Napoleon, 'blame much of the misfortune of this day on Marshal Ney, but what is done, is done; it is not necessary to speak any more of it.' I read this latest twenty-ninth bulletin; several minor changes proposed by General Drouot were agreed by the emperor; but I do not know by what bizarre reason he did not want to admit that his carriages had fallen into the hands of the enemy. 'When you pass through Paris', M. de Flahaut said to him, 'they will soon notice that your carriages have been taken. If you hide it, they will accuse you of hiding the important truth and it is necessary to either tell them everything or nothing'. The emperor, having thought of various options, accepted this advice.

I then made a second reading of the bulletin and everyone having agreed on its accuracy, M. de Bassano sent it to Prince Joseph by a special courier.

We see here that Napoleon's accusations against Ney have already started. Despite the claim that this was to be the whole truth, needless to say the bulletin is a piece of propaganda that, despite admitting of defeat, is designed to persuade the people of France that the situation was far from being beyond repair. The detail of the fighting is inevitably superficial, and thus of little use in helping us to fully understand the true ebb and flow of the battle. But what is of particular interest is his introduction of a number of themes that are repeated in his subsequent accounts and which were often taken up and reinforced in later accounts by other authors. The emphasis of these seems to be to cover up a number of fundamental mistakes or to find excuses for the defeat. They are:

- *The claim that there was early identification of the approaching Prussians.*
- *The French army was outnumbered by the Anglo-Dutch army.*
- *The under-playing of the catastrophic defeat of the whole of d'Erlon's corps.*
- *The mistiming of the commitment of the cavalry.*
- *The deployment of the Middle Guard to protect the cuirassiers rather than to break the Anglo-Dutch line.*
- *That the battle against Wellington was won.*
- *The Guard was defeated by British cavalry.*

It will be noted that throughout this first account, Napoleon mixes up Mont-Saint-Jean with La Haye Sainte, but this mistake is rectified in his subsequent accounts.

Le Moniteur, 20th June 1815

[On the 17th] At ten o'clock in the evening, the English army occupied Mont-Saint-Jean with its centre, finding itself in position in front of the Soignies forest; it would have been necessary to have three hours for an attack, so we were obliged to wait until the next day.

The emperor's general headquarters was established at the farm of Caillou, near Planchenoit. The rain fell in torrents. Thus, during the 16th the left, right and reserve were all engaged across a distance of a little under two leagues.

The Battle of Mont-Saint-Jean

At nine o'clock in the morning, the rain having eased a little, I Corps started its movement and placed itself, the left on the Brussels road opposite the village of Mont-Saint-Jean, which appeared to be the centre of the enemy's position. II Corps had its right on the Brussels road and its left on a small wood a cannon's range from the English army. The cuirassiers moved into reserve to the rear on the heights. VI Corps with the cavalry of d'Aumont [Domon], under the orders of Count Lobau, was designated to move to the rear of our right to oppose a

Prussian corps which appeared to have evaded Marshal Grouchy with the intention of falling on our right flank, an intention that we had been informed of by our reports and by a letter of a Prussian general that was being carried by an orderly officer taken by our scouts.

The troops were full of enthusiasm. We estimated the strength of the English army at 80,000 men; we supposed that the Prussian corps, which would be in a position to intervene towards evening, to be 15,000 men. The enemy forces were thus more than 90,000 men. Ours were less numerous.

At midday, all the preparations being complete, Prince Jérôme, commanding a division of II Corps, and destined to form the extreme left, moved against the wood of which the enemy occupied a part. The cannonade began; the enemy supported with thirty guns the troops which he had sent to guard the wood. We also had artillery deployed on our side. At one o'clock, Prince Jérôme was master of the whole wood, and the whole English army retired behind a curtain [the crest of the ridge?]. Count d'Erlon attacked the village of Mont-Saint-Jean and supported his attack with eighty guns. There was engaged a terrible cannonade which made the English army suffer much. All the shots struck on the plateau. A brigade of the 1st Division of Count d'Erlon seized the village of Mont-Saint-Jean; a second brigade was charged by a body of English cavalry which caused it heavy casualties. At the same moment, a division of English cavalry charged the battery of Count d'Erlon by its right and disorganised several pieces; but General Milhaud's cuirassiers charged this division, of which three regiments were broken and cut to pieces.

It was 3pm. The emperor had the Guard advanced to deploy it into the plain to replace I Corps which had occupied it at the beginning of the action; this corps was already further forward. The Prussian division, whose movement had already been reported, then started to engage with Count Lobau's skirmishers, extending its fire along the whole of our right flank. It was necessary to deal with this attack before undertaking anything elsewhere. To this end, all the means of the reserve were ready to move to the support of Count Lobau and to destroy the Prussian corps when it advanced.

This done, the emperor planned to make an attack on the village of Mont-Saint-Jean, which we hoped to be decisive; but by a movement of impatience so frequent in our military annals, and which had often been so unfortunate for us, the reserve cavalry having noticed a retrograde movement made by the English to shelter from our batteries, from which they had already suffered much, crowned the heights of Mont-Saint-Jean and charged the infantry. This movement, made at the right time and supported by the reserves would have decided the day, was made in isolation and before the outcome of the affairs on the right were terminated, became disastrous.

Not having the ability to countermand the order, the enemy showed many masses of infantry and cavalry and the two divisions of cuirassiers were engaged, all our cavalry rushed at that moment to support their comrades. There, for three hours, were made numerous charges which broke several squares and captured six colours of the English infantry, advantages out of all proportion to the casualties suffered by our cavalry from canister and musketry. It was impossible to commit our infantry reserves until we had repulsed the flank attack by the Prussian corps. This attack continued to prolong our right flank perpendicularly [to our main front]. The emperor sent General Duhesme there with the Young Guard and several reserve batteries. The enemy was contained, repulsed and fell back; he had exhausted his strength and we no longer had anything to fear. This was the moment that the attack on the enemy centre was to have taken place. As the cuirassiers suffered from the canister fire, four battalions of the Middle Guard were sent to protect the cuirassiers, hold the position and if that was possible, to disengage some our cavalry and pull it back into the plain.

Two other battalions were sent to hold *en potence* on the extreme left of the division that had manoeuvred on our flanks, in order to ensure we had no concerns on this side; the rest were deployed in reserve; part to occupy the angle behind Mont-Saint-Jean, part on the plateau behind the battlefield which covered our line of retreat.

As things stood, the battle was won; we occupied all the positions that the enemy had occupied at the beginning of the action; our cavalry having been poorly engaged too early, we could not hope for a decisive success. But Marshal Grouchy, having learnt of the movement by the Prussian corps, marched on the rear of this corps and this would have assured us of a dazzling success the next day. After eight hours of the fire and charge of infantry and cavalry, the whole army saw with satisfaction that the battle was won and the battlefield was in our hands.

At 8.30, the four battalions of the Middle Guard which had been sent onto the plateau beyond Mont-St-Jean to support the cuirassiers, having been hampered by canister fire, marched with the bayonet to take the batteries. The day was ending; a charge made on their flank by several English squadrons put them into disorder; the fugitives re-crossed the valley, the neighbouring regiments who saw some troops belonging to the Guard disband, thought that they were of the Old Guard and ran off: the shouts, 'all is lost, the Guard is repulsed!' were heard; soldiers even claimed that at several points badly intentioned individuals shouted, '*sauve qui peut*!' [save yourselves] A great panic spread all at once on the whole battlefield, all ran in the greatest disorder down the line of communications, soldiers, gunners, caissons struggled to get on there: the Old Guard who were in reserve were assailed and even they were driven away.

In an instant, the army was just a confused mass, all arms were mixed together and it was impossible to reform a unit. The enemy, noticing this astonishing confusion, sent off columns of cavalry; the disorder increased, the confusion of the night prevented the troops rallying and to show them their error.

Thus a battle ended, a busy day, of false measures repaired, of great success for the next day, all was lost by a moment of terrified panic. Even the service squadrons, ranged close by the emperor, were broken and disorganised by these tumultuous waves and nothing remained but to follow the torrent.

* * *

The second account, based on discussions between Napoleon and General Gourgaud on St Helena during his exile (if not actually dictated), gives us a far more detailed description of the battle.

The very first sentences Gourgaud writes in this account are, 'The Emperor Napoleon having deigned to make known to me his opinion on the principle operations of the campaign of 1815, I profit from this favourable circumstance and of my recollections of the great catastrophe which I witnessed, to write this account'. We can therefore be sure that the particular interpretation and bias in the following account is surely Napoleon's. Frankly, if considered objectively, it is relatively uncontroversial and the sequence and phasing of the fighting is in general agreement with other national histories, but still fails to lay any emphasis on key phases of the battle, striving instead to put a positive slant on French progress until the sudden and overwhelming appearance of Blücher with Ziethen's corps.

Note how in some instances, the themes identified in the bulletin have been developed and new reasons for the defeat have been introduced:

- *The identification of the Prussians was made before the main attack made by General d'Erlon and two cavalry divisions were immediately deployed to oppose them. Lobau was ordered to reconnoitre the ground to the right.*
- *The French army was outnumbered by the Anglo-Dutch army.*
- *The destruction of d'Erlon's attack by British cavalry is again significantly underplayed, but much is made of the French cavalry counter-attack.*
- *Lobau's VI Corps was deployed to the right and the Prussian advance onto the battlefield was 'routed'. However, the size and significance of the Prussian force is increasing.*
- *At the time of the Prussian attack, the Anglo-Dutch army had been defeated.*
- *Ney becomes responsible for the premature commitment of the cavalry.*
- *There is a growing emphasis on the failure of Grouchy to prevent the arrival of the Prussians.*
- *The Anglo-Dutch army has been defeated, but the arrival of the Prussians encourages them to re-take their positions.*
- *The remainder of the Guard is now formed up for a decisive attack on the Anglo-Dutch line. This attack has to be cancelled to allow the Guard to meet a new*

> *Prussian attack. The Guard supporting the cavalry on the ridge are broken by British cavalry.*
> - *Traitors, malcontents and deserters are responsible for encouraging the rout.*
> - *The absence of a cavalry reserve (the Guard cavalry having been committed without Napoleon's orders) means the Allied cavalry cannot be stopped.*

Gourgaud, *The Campaign of 1815 or, a Narrative of the Military Operations which took place in France and Belgium during the Hundred Days* (London: James Ridgway, 1818), pp. 88–112.

In 1815 Gourgaud served in general headquarters as colonel and premier officier d'ordonnance *(senior orderly officer) to Napoleon. Three days after the battle, Napoleon nominated him* maréchal de camp. *He accompanied Napoleon to St Helena and remained there until March 1818 before returning to France to publish the following account of the battle.*

On the morning of the 18th the weather was extremely cloudy; it had rained throughout the whole of the night, and even at day-break the rain had not abated. The reports of the night, and the observations that were made, removed all doubt respecting the presence of the Anglo-Belgic army. Its force amounted to between eighty-five and ninety thousand men, and two hundred and fifty pieces of artillery. The French army, having only sixty-seven or sixty-eight thousand men, was of course inferior in numbers, though it was superior with regard to the quality of its troops. The Belgic and German soldiers could not be placed on an equality [*sic*] with the French; among the latter were the Imperial Guard and the four divisions of cuirassiers. The French artillery, including the reserve batteries of the Guard, was nearly as numerous as the enemy's artillery; it amounted to two hundred and forty pieces of cannon. Victory appeared far from doubtful, and with that victory there was every reason to hope for the destruction of the English army, owing to the position it had assumed. At break of day, the emperor, while at breakfast, observed, 'We have eighty chances out of a hundred in our favour'. At that moment, Marshal Ney, who had come from inspecting the line, presented himself: 'No doubt Sire', said the marshal, 'if Wellington had been simple enough to remain there; but I come to inform you that they are actually retreating, and that, if you are not speedy in attacking them, they will escape us.' The emperor did not attach much importance to this report: he thought it evident that since the Duke of Wellington had not attempted his retreat before day-break, he had determined to encounter the risk of a battle. About eight o'clock, the weather began to brighten up: the emperor reconnoitred the enemy's line: he was of the opinion that the troops might manoeuvre in the surrounding grounds. He despatched orders for the battle to the different commanders of the army corps: all was now in motion.

The English [army] had the forest of Soignies in its rear and only one high road for its communications with Brussels; this position rendered its retreat extremely difficult. It occupied a fine level height. Its right was appuyed [*sic*; meaning 'anchored on' or 'supported by'] on a ravine, on the other side of the Nivelles road, and extended as far as Braine-la-Leud: its left crowned the heights of La Haie, and its centre, occupying on the left the farm of La Haye Sainte, and on the right that of Hougoumont, was in front of the village of Mont-Saint-Jean, at the junction of the two roads leading to Nivelles and Charleroi, which this line cut. It was ascertained that the enemy had raised no redoubts or works of any other kind and that there were few or no natural obstacles in his front. The height was slightly concave in the centre and the ground, descending with a gentle declivity, terminated by a ravine of no great depth which separated the two armies.

The French army was ranged in the following order. General Reille, with II Corps, his right on the road from Charleroi to Brussels, his left on the Nivelles road, having in his front the wood of Hougoumont, and his light cavalry stationed on the other side of the high road. General d'Erlong [*sic*], with his left on the Charleroi road and his right on a line with the left of the English, facing the village of La Haie; his light cavalry on his right, sending out parties on the Dyle. General Kellerman's corps of cuirassiers, in second line, behind II Corps: General Milhaut's [*sic*] behind I Corps. VI Corps was Count Lobau's, formed in close column on the right of the Charleroi road: by this means it was in reserve behind the left of I Corps, and in potence [*en potence*] behind the centre of the first line. The Imperial Guard, in third line, formed a general reserve, having the infantry in the centre, General Lefebvre-Desnouëttes' division of cavalry on the right, and the division of horse grenadiers and dragoons on the left.

These arrangements sufficiently indicated the emperor's design, which was to penetrate the centre of the English army, to force it back on the high road and, on reaching the outlet of the forest, to cut off its retreat on the right and left of the line. The success of this attack would have rendered all retreat impracticable and must have occasioned the destruction of the English army: at all events, it would have separated it from the Prussian force.

About eleven o'clock, General Reille commenced a cannonade to drive the enemy from the wood of Hougoumont. The engagement soon became warm on that point. Prince Jérôme with his division took possession of the wood: he was driven out; but a new attack once more rendered him master of it. The enemy had, however, kept possession of the large house in the centre of the wood. Battlements had been formed on it, which rendered it a post of tolerable strength and at the same time secured it against a coup de main. The emperor ordered General Reille to establish a battery of howitzers and to set fire to the house. It was observed with satisfaction that the best English troops were on that point; among the rest, General Cooke's division of the Guards. At this moment a corps of five or six thousand troops, of various descriptions, was perceived in the distance, on the side of Saint-Lambert. This was at first supposed to be Marshal Grouchy's corps; but in a quarter of an hour after a party of hussars took prisoner a Prussian orderly officer with a dispatch, which proved that the troops which had been observed were the advance-guard of Bülow's corps. The Major-General (Soult) dispatched an officer to Marshal Grouchy to inform him of this circumstance; he even sent him the intercepted dispatch. The staff officer, who was fully sensible of the importance of his mission, was expected to reach the Marshal in less than two hours. Great advantages were anticipated from the Marshal's coming upon the rear of Bülow's corps. But, as that corps appeared to be not more than two short leagues from the field of battle, it became necessary to send off a force to oppose it. Marshal Grouchy might delay crossing the Dyle, or might be prevented by unforeseen obstacles. Lieutenant-General Domont [*sic*] was therefore sent forward with his light cavalry, and Subervick's [*sic*] division of Pajol's corps of cavalry, making altogether a force of nearly three thousand cavalry, to meet Bülow's advance-guard; his instructions were to occupy all the passes, to prevent the enemy's hussars from attacking our flanks, and to send off couriers to meet Marshal Grouchy. Count de Lobau, with both divisions of his corps (seven thousand men), proceeded to reconnoitre his field of battle, in the rear of General Domont's cavalry, so that, in case General Bülow's movement should not be stopped by Marshal Grouchy, he might advance against the Prussians, and protect our flanks. Thus the destination of this corps was changed.

The emperor, having adopted every precaution for opposing Bülow's corps, directed Marshal Ney to commence the intended attack with I Corps, reinforced by batteries of reserve, and to take possession of La Haye Sainte, on the Charleroi road, which was the point of appuy [the anchor or support] for the enemy's centre. Attacked in his centre, the enemy would be induced to make counter movements on his wings, which would clearly explain the state of the battle, to deploy all his forces, and expose all his plans. A battle, like a drama, has a beginning, a middle and a denouement. The beginning occasions counter movements on the part of the enemy, and gives rise to incidents, which must be surmounted, and which have an influence on the last movement by which the battle is decided.

The French troops were full of enthusiasm; the emperor inspected the whole line, and such were the acclamations of joy, that they interrupted the manoeuvres, and prevented the orders from being heard. The emperor stationed himself on an eminence near the farm of La Belle Alliance, from whence he could command a view of everything; the enemy's wings as well as those of the French army. He was therefore in a situation to form a judgement on all the movements which the enemy might make on finding his centre threatened; and His Majesty had at hand all the reserves, in order that he might dispose of them with the utmost rapidity, or place himself at their head, and remedy any unexpected manoeuvres on the part of the enemy.

It was noon, when eighty pieces of artillery commenced their fire. In about half an hour, the enemy's batteries, which were opposed to us, fell back, and were reinforced by new batteries from different points of their line. All the enemy's sharpshooters withdrew from the bottom of the curtain. The enemy stationed his masses behind the crests of heights to protect them, and to diminish the loss occasioned by our artillery. Our infantry advanced. Some movement was now observed on the Brussels road: all the carriages and baggage wagons of the right and left, which were at a distance from the road, hurried in disorder onto it, on the approach of the fire, with the view of reaching Brussels. The enemy's line however made no manoeuvre; it maintained its immobility. His cavalry made several successful charges on the flank of one of the columns of the first corps, and about fifteen of our pieces of artillery, which were advancing, were driven back into a hollow road. One of Milhaut's [*sic*] brigades of cuirassiers advanced against this cavalry, and the field of battle was soon covered with their slain. When the emperor perceived that the enemy did not attempt to make any great movement on his right, and that some disorder prevailed on ours, he proceeded thither at full gallop. Milhaut's cuirassiers, and behind them in second line the cavalry of the Guard, presented a formidable appearance. The emperor soon restored order: the cannonade was maintained with fury, and a new attack on La Haye Sainte rendered us masters of that important point.

The enemy attached great importance to the post of Hougoumont on his right: he sent off fresh troops to reinforce the brigade of the Guards. On the other hand, General Reille supported the attack of Jerome's division, by Foi's [*sic*] division. The howitzers had set fire to the house, and almost entirely destroyed it. Three fourths of the woods and orchards were in our possession. The field of battle was strewed with the English Guards, the flower of the enemy's army. It was half past four o'clock, and the most vigorous fire was still kept up on every side. At this moment, General Domont informed His Majesty, that he observed Bülow's corps in movement, and that a division of from eight to ten thousand Prussians was debouching from the woods of Frischenois [*sic*. Frischermont: These woods are generally referred to as the Paris woods]: that no tidings had been received of Marshal Grouchy: and that reconnaissances, which had been sent in the directions in which it was supposed he might be moving, had not met one of his couriers. [At half past four, Lobau's corps of 7,000 men advanced against the Prussians, which reduced the force opposed to the Anglo–Belgic army to 60,000 men.] Count Lobau's corps advanced in three columns to the positions which he had reconnoitred. By this movement this corps had changed its front, and placed itself *en potence* on the extremity of our right. The first Prussian brigade, being vigorously attacked, was soon routed: but it was immediately supported by the second brigade, and in half an hour after the whole remains of Bülow's corps arrived and formed, constantly extending itself beyond the right of Count Lobau's corps; so that, though Bülow did not gain ground upon the latter, he still maintained his fire on our rear. VI Corps was drawn up in order of battle, parallel with the road opposite to the point where the emperor had stationed himself.

Napoleon, observing that the Prussians continued to outflank the right of VI Corps, sent General Duhesme's division of the Young Guard, with two batteries, to that point. Thus our line was prolonged till it came even with the front troops of Bülow's left. At the same time a division of I Corps, which formed our right, and which was in reserve, advanced rapidly on the extreme left of the Anglo-Belgic line, took the village of La Haie, and thus cut off the communication between the Anglo-Belgic army and IV Prussian Corps. We every moment hoped for, and impatiently awaited the arrival of Marshal Grouchy on the rear of this corps, which would have been cut off from all means of retreat. It was six o'clock, and no account of the Marshal had yet been received. However, all our dispositions were attended with the greatest success. The impetuosity of the Young Guard had occasioned great loss to the enemy; and the capture of the village of La Haie, which turned Bülow's right, stopped his progress, and he ceased to act on the offensive: nothing more was to be feared from him. As soon as the emperor had perceived that Bülow's attack was actively proceeding, and that though it was nearly four o'clock this corps was not stopped by Marshal Grouchy, he ordered Marshal Ney to establish himself at La Haye Sainte, to fortify it and to station several battalions there; but to make no movement until he saw the issue of the manoeuvres of the Prussians. Half an hour after, about five o'clock, at the moment when the Prussians were attacking us with the greatest vigour, the English attempted to retake La Haye Sainte. They were vigorously repulsed by the fire of our infantry, and by a charge of cavalry; but Marshal Ney, borne away by excess of ardour, lost sight of the orders he had received; he debouched on the level height, which was immediately crowned by two divisions of Milhaut's cuirassiers, and the light cavalry of the Guard. The officers, who surrounded the emperor, observing this movement, the success of the charges, the retreat of many of the English squares, and the cessation of the fire of part of the enemy's batteries, shouted victory, and made every demonstration of joy. The emperor did not share in this exultation; he observed to Marshal Soult, 'This is a premature movement, which may be attended by fatal consequences'. Soult expressed himself with considerable warmth [in this he means anger rather than friendliness] respecting Ney and said, 'He is compromising us, as he did at Jena'. The emperor directed Kellerman's cuirassiers to support our cavalry on the height, lest it should be repulsed by the enemy's cavalry, which, in the present state of affairs, would have occasioned the loss of the battle: for it was one of those critical moments in which a very trivial incident may give rise to the most important result. This movement of the cavalry, who galloped forwards exclaiming '*Vive l'Empereur!*' overawed the enemy, encouraged our troops, and prevented them from being alarmed by the Prussians continuing their fire on our rear.

About six o'clock we found that the Prussians had engaged their whole force: they ceased to act on the offensive, and their fire became stationary. Half an hour after they began to fall back, and our troops advanced. The balls of the Prussians no longer reached the high road, nor even the first position which the troops of Duhesme and Count de Lobau had occupied: these troops had now advanced. The extreme left of the Prussians wheeled round on the rear, and proceeded to replace itself in line with the first brigade. Our cavalry maintained its station on the height, notwithstanding the fire to which it was exposed. They penetrated many of the enemy's squares, took three standards, and destroyed a great number of batteries, the guns of which, without their trains, fell into our hands. Consternation and stupor prevailed throughout the enemy's line: the fugitives had already reached Brussels: to retreat in good order was impossible; and their whole army seemed threatened with destruction. During the last half hour the situation of the French army had completely changed: the enemy was not threatening us at any point: we were masters of his field of battle, and in an offensive position on his centre. We had gained the advantage, not only over the Anglo-Belgic army, of eighty-five thousand men, but likewise over Bülow's corps of thirty thousand Prussians. Still no account had been received of Grouchy. Thus, between sixty-five and sixty-eight thousand French troops had beaten a hundred and fifteen thousand English, Belgians, Prussians etc. At half past seven, Marshal Grouchy's cannonade was at length heard: he was supposed to be at the distance of about two leagues and a half on our right. The emperor was of opinion that this was the moment for making a decisive attack, and determining the fate of the day. For this purpose he ordered back several battalions and batteries of the Guard, which had been dispatched towards Planchenoit. At this moment the enemy's army received intimation of the arrival of Marshal Blücher, with the first Prussian corps, which had left Wavres in the morning, and was coming by way of Ohain to join the left of the Anglo-Belgic army. This was not the only reinforcement the enemy received; two brigades of English cavalry, amounting to six regiments, which had been placed in reserve on the Ohain road, and which were now rendered disposable by the arrival of the Prussian troops, were observed to enter the line. These events revived the spirits of the Anglo-Belgic army; it gained courage and resumed its position.

At this critical moment, three battalions of the second line of our right fell back in good order upon the Imperial Guard, which the emperor had just been collecting. This movement, for which it was impossible to assign a cause, weakened our line. The emperor hastened to inquire the reason for it: the men replied, that they had not been forced, but that the retrograde movement had been ordered. The emperor addressed them and they returned to their post.

The cavalry, which from the height on which it was stationed commanded a full view of the field of battle in front, on its right, and on its rear, observed this retrograde movement of the three battalions: they also perceived Blücher's I Corps, which had just advanced on a line with the village of La Haie, and the two fresh brigades of cavalry, which were preparing for a charge: they imagined they were about to be cut off and several regiments fell back.

The emperor was then forming his Guard into columns, for the projected attack; but observing the hesitation of the cavalry, he concluded that they had been overcome by circumstances, and that, without waiting until all the columns should be formed, it would be necessary to immediately to support the cavalry, and to make some movement to rally the spirits of the troops, and to stop the inclination that they manifested to retreat. He marched with his first four battalions to the left of La Haye Sainte, and directed General Reille to concentrate the whole of his corps on his extreme left, and to form it into attacking columns. When the emperor arrived at La Haye Sainte he found part of Ney's troops retreating: he sent his aide-de-camp Labedoyère to inform them, with a view to restore their courage, that Marshal Grouchy's corps was approaching. At the same time he consigned to Marshal Ney the four battalions of the Guard that he then had under his own direction, ordering the marshal to march forward and maintain the position of the height. This produced the desired effect; the troops halted, and returned to their former position. A quarter of an hour after, the other eight battalions arrived on the brink of the ravine: the emperor formed them in the following order: one battalion in order of battle [i.e. line], having two in close column on its flanks, a formation that united the advantages of the narrow and the deep order. Two of these brigades thus ranged, and marching at battalion distance formed a first line, behind which the third brigade was posted in reserve. The batteries were stationed in the intervals. General Reille on his part, concentrated the whole of his corps in the vicinity of Hougoumont, crossed the ravine, and attacked the enemy's position.

Meanwhile, the four battalions of the Middle Guard were engaged with the enemy; they repulsed all before them, and stood undaunted under the fire of a considerable portion of the enemy's line. General Friant, commander of the infantry of the Guard, having received a wound in the hand came to tell the emperor, that everything was going well on the height, and that upon the arrival of the Old Guard we should be masters of the whole field of battle.

Between half past seven and eight o'clock, a cry of alarm was heard on our right. Blücher, with the whole of Ziethen's corps, had attacked the village of La Haie, which was instantly carried. A general feeling of astonishment pervaded the whole right: we were thus cut off from Count Lobau's corps. The traitors and malcontents who were in the army, together with the deserters, did everything in their power to augment the confusion, which spread instantly throughout the whole line. The eight battalions of the Guard, among which were those of the Old Guard, instead of marching forward as they did to support the four battalions engaged with the enemy, should have proceeded to the right, to serve as a reserve, and to rally the troops driven from La Haie: they might have formed barriers by each battalion resolving into a square: the whole extremity of our right might still have rallied behind them. The sun had set: there was no reason to despair; when the two brigades of the enemy's cavalry, which had not yet been engaged, penetrated between La Haye Sainte and General Reille's corps. They might have been stopped by the eight squares of the Guard; but perceiving the great disorder which prevailed in our right, they turned them. These three thousand fresh cavalry rendered all attempt to rally impossible. The emperor ordered his four service squadrons to charge them. These squadrons were not sufficiently numerous: the whole division of the reserve cavalry of the Guard would have been requisite; but by a misfortune, corresponding with other fatalities of the day, that division, consisting of two thousand horse grenadiers and dragoons, all picked men, was engaged on the height, without the emperor's orders. There was now no means of rallying the troops: the four squadrons were overwhelmed, and the confusion every moment increased. The corps of cavalry and the four battalions of the Guard, which, on the level height, had for several hours opposed nearly the whole of the English army, were now overcome. Their artillery had expended all its ammunition: they beheld from the heights the fire of our squares in their rear: they likewise began to retreat, and the victory was lost to us. The height being abandoned, all the Anglo–Belgic army moved forward, and posted itself in the position which we had so long occupied. In the state of disorder into which the French army was thrown, it happened, as it frequently does in such circumstances, that our infantry and cavalry engaged with each other by mistake. The eight battalions of the Guard, which were in the centre, after having withstood for a long time all the attacks of the enemy's infantry and cavalry, and contended for every foot of ground, were finally completely disorganised by the mass of fugitives, and overwhelmed by the numbers of the enemy that surrounded them. These brave grenadiers fought to the last, and dearly sacrificed their lives. Cambrone [*sic*], when called upon to surrender, made the following truly French reply: 'The Guard dies, but does not surrender!'

The emperor proceeded to the left of Planchenoit, on a second position, where a regiment of the Guard with two batteries was in reserve. Here he renewed his endeavours to stop and rally the fugitives; but, on the one hand, the darkness of the night, which prevented the fugitives from seeing the emperor, and, on the other, the extreme confusion, which everywhere prevailed, rendered it extremely difficult to restore order. At this moment the Prussian cavalry, supported by some battalions of light infantry, and the whole of Bülow's corps, resumed the offensive, and, advancing by the right of Planchenoit, so greatly increased the confusion, that all thoughts of rallying were at an end. The emperor, finding that all his efforts were vain, that the enemy was already on the high road, and that not the slightest hope remained, yielded to necessity. He took the road to Charleroi . . .

The final account that appeared in 1820 was translated into English the same year and, although published anonymously, was even then attributed to Napoleon himself. The original English edition is very rare, but a later translation appeared in 1945 edited by Somerset de Chair and was reprinted again in 1986. These memoirs give a similar account of the battle to that of Gourgaud, but the main difference is that Napoleon gives a more detailed analysis of his own movements and decisions, despite complicating things by writing in the third person.

Although displaying his usual intellect, this is essentially a justification of his performance heavily, and in places clumsily, clouded by all the advantages of hindsight. I hope readers will forgive me for using de Chair's translation that presents the narrative in the first person, rather than the third in which it was written, as I believe it is important for us to understand that it is Napoleon's own viewpoint that we are reading rather than that of a more objective commentator.

In this final account, we see how the themes we have already examined have become far more explicit:

- *There is now much more detail on Napoleon's orders to Grouchy, reinforcing the Marshal's failure to prevent the Prussian irruption onto the battlefield which led directly to the French defeat.*
- *The first sighting of the Prussians is thought to be a detachment of Grouchy's, reinforcing the idea that Grouchy should already be on his way.*
- *The French army was outnumbered by the Anglo-Dutch army.*
- *The whole emphasis of this account has Napoleon's focus being on the Prussian advance and his moves to counter it. However, he specifically seems to play down any anxiety he felt to put the emphasis on his expectation that Grouchy would attack their rear.*
- *The overwhelming defeat of d'Erlon's attack gets even less attention and emphasis.*
- *Napoleon bemoans the commitment of the Guard heavy cavalry commanded by Guyot.*
- *The battle was won after the repulse of Bülow and the success of the French cavalry who only awaited the arrival of the Guard to complete the victory.*
- *The sudden arrival of Blücher swung the odds back into the Prussian favour and broke the French right flank; he specifically blames Durutte's division for a poor defence.*

Napoleon's Memoirs, edited by Somerset de Chair (London: The Soho Book Company, 1986), pp. 517–36.

During the night the rain continued to fall, which made all the flat country more or less impassable for artillery, cavalry and even infantry. During the day of the 17th and even the night of the 17th to 18th, the right flank of the French army reported that they were in touch with Marshal Grouchy's troops, who had been pursuing Marshal Blücher all day without anything of importance happening. At nine in the evening, General Milhaud, who had marched with his corps to maintain the communications with Marshal Grouchy, reported that he had received information of a column of enemy cavalry which had fallen back on Wavres in all haste from Tilly. A corps of 2,000 horse was making for Hal, threatening to turn the right of the forest of Soignies and to move on Brussels. The Duke of Wellington, alarmed, sent the 4th Infantry Division there. During the night the French cavalry returned to camp. The English division remained in observation and was pinned down during the battle.

I was camped in front of Planchenoit, astride the main Brussels highway, and four and a half leagues from this great town, with I, II and VI Infantry Corps, the Guard, a light cavalry division of Pajol's, and the two cuirassier corps of Milhaud and Kellerman, in all 68,900 men and 242 guns, with the Anglo-Dutch army in front of me 90,000 strong, with 250 guns, and with its head-quarters at Waterloo. Marshal Grouchy, with 34,000 men and a hundred and eight guns, ought to have been at Wavres; but he was in fact in front of Gembloux, having lost sight of the Prussian army, which was at Wavres. Its four corps were assembled there, 75,000 strong.

At ten o'clock in the evening, I sent an officer to Marshal Grouchy whom I supposed to be at Wavres, in order to let him know that there would be a big battle next day; that the Anglo-Dutch army was in position in front of the forest of Soignes, with its left resting on the village of La Haye; that I ordered him to detach from his camp at Wavres a division of 7,000 men of all arms and sixteen guns before daylight, to go to Saint-Lambert to join the right of the Grand Army and co-operate with it; that, as soon as he was satisfied that Marshal Blücher had evacuated Wavres, whether to continue his retreat or to go in any other direction, he was to march with the bulk of his troops to support the detachment which he had sent to Saint-Lambert.

At eleven o'clock in the evening, an hour after this despatch had been sent off, a report came in from Marshal Grouchy, dated from Gembloux at 5pm. It reported that he was at Gembloux with his army, unaware as to which direction Marshal Blücher had taken, whether he had gone towards Brussels or Liège; that he had accordingly set up two advance guards, one between Gembloux and Wavres, and the other a league from Gembloux in the direction of Liège.

Thus Marshal Blücher had given him the slip and was three leagues from him! Marshal Grouchy had only covered two leagues during the day of the 17th.

A second officer was sent to him at four in the morning to repeat the order which had been sent to him at ten in the evening [Grouchy denies that either of these two officers arrived]. An hour later, at five o'clock, a new report came in, dated from Gembloux at 2am; the Marshal reported that he had learned at 6pm, that Blücher had moved with all units on Wavres; that, in view of this, he had wanted to follow him then and there, but that, the troops having already made camp, and prepared their meal, he would only be starting at daylight, in order to arrive early in front of Wavres, which would come to the same thing, and that the men would be well rested and full of dash.

During the night, I gave all the orders necessary for the battle next day, although everything seemed to show that it would not take place. During the four days since hostilities had begun, I had, by the most skilful manoeuvres, surprised my enemies, won a smashing victory, and divided the two armies. It added considerably to my glory, but had not yet sufficiently improved my position. The three hours delay which the left had suffered, during its movement, had prevented my attacking the Anglo-Dutch army, as I had intended, during the afternoon of the 17th, which would have crowned the campaign with success! It was, in fact, probable that the Duke of Wellington and Marshal Blücher were taking advantage of the very night to cross the forest of Soignes and join up in front of Brussels. After that junction, which would be effected before nine in the morning, the position of the French army would become extremely delicate. The two armies would be reinforced with everything that they had in their rear. Six thousand English had disembarked at Ostend within the last few days: they were troops returning from America. It would be impossible for the French army to risk crossing the forest of Soignes in order to encounter, on emerging, forces nearly twice as strong, joined up and in position; and yet, in less than a few weeks, the Russian, Austrian and Bavarian armies, etc., would cross the Rhine and move towards the Marne. The 5th Corps, on the look-out in Alsace, was only 20,000 strong.

At one o'clock in the morning, much pre-occupied with these weighty thoughts, I went out on foot, accompanied only by my Grand Marshal. My intention was to follow the English army in its retreat and to attempt to engage it in spite of the darkness of the night, as soon as it was on the march. I went along the line of the main defences. The forest of Soignes looked as if it was on fire. The horizon between this forest, Braine-la-Leud, the farms of the Belle-Alliance and La Haye, was aglow with the fires of bivouacs. The most profound silence prevailed. The Anglo-Dutch army was wrapped in a profound slumber, following on the fatigues which it had experienced during the preceding days. On arriving near the woods of the Château of Hougoumont, I heard the noise of a column on the march;

it was half past two. Now, at this hour, the rearguard would be leaving its position, if the enemy were in retreat; but this illusion was short-lived.

The noise stopped; the rain fell in torrents. Various officers sent out on reconnaissance and some secret agents, returning at half past three, confirmed that the Anglo-Dutch were showing no signs of movement. At four o'clock, the despatch riders brought me a peasant who had acted as a guide to an English cavalry brigade which had gone to take up a position on the extreme left at Ohain. Two Belgian deserters, who had just quitted their regiment, told me that their army was preparing for battle, and that no retreating movement had taken place; that Belgium was offering prayers for my success; and that the English and the Prussians were both equally hated there.

The English general could do nothing more at variance with the interests of his cause and his country, to the whole spirit of this campaign, and even to the most elementary rules of war, than to remain in the position which he occupied. He had behind him the defiles of the forest of Soignes. If he were beaten any retreat was impossible.

The French troops were bivouacked in the middle of the mud. The officers considered it impossible to give battle during the day. The artillery and cavalry could not manoeuvre on the ground, so drenched was it. They calculated that it would require twelve hours of fine weather to dry it up.

The day began to dawn. I returned to my headquarters thoroughly satisfied with the great mistake which the enemy general was making and very anxious lest the bad weather should prevent my taking advantage of it. But already the sky was clearing. At five o'clock I perceived a few rays of that sun which should, before going down, light up the defeat of the English army: the British oligarchy would be overthrown by it! France was going to rise, that day, more glorious, more powerful and greater than ever!

The Anglo-Dutch army was in battle position on the road from Charleroi to Brussels, in front of the forest of Soignes, standing on a fairly good plateau. The right, composed of the 1st and 2nd English Divisions and the Brunswick Division, commanded by Generals Cook and Clinton, rested on a ravine beyond the Nivelles road. It occupied the château of Hougoumont, in advance of its front, with a detachment. The centre, composed of the 3rd English Division and the 1st and 2nd Belgian Divisions, commanded by Generals Alten, Collaert and Chassé, were in front of Mont-Saint-Jean. The left rested on the Charleroi road, and occupied the farm of La Haye Sainte with one of its brigades. The left, made up of the 5th and 6th English Divisions and the 3rd Belgian Division, under the commands of Generals Picton, Lambert and Perponcher, had its right resting on the Charleroi road and its left behind the village of La Haye, which it occupied with a strong detachment. The reserve was at Mont-Saint-Jean, at the intersection of the roads from Charleroi and Nivelles to Brussels. The cavalry, drawn up in three rows on the heights of Mont-Saint-Jean, lined the whole rear of the army's battle front which covered a distance of 2,500 *toises* [a *toise* was about 2m].

The enemy's front was protected by a natural obstacle. The plateau was slightly hollow at its centre and the ground sloped away gently to a deep ravine. The 4th English Division, commanded by General Colville, occupied, as right flank, all the exits from Hal to Braine-la-Leud. An English cavalry brigade occupied, as left flank, all the exits from the village of Ohain. The units which the enemy revealed were of varying strength; but the most experienced officers estimated them at 90,000 men, including the flanking corps, which tallied with the general information received. The French army numbered only 69,000 men, but victory appeared no less certain on that account. These 69,000 men were good troops; and, in the enemy army, only the English, who numbered 40,000 men at most, could be counted as such.

At eight o'clock, breakfast was brought to me, in which I was joined by several generals. I said, 'The enemy army exceeds ours by nearly a quarter; but the odds are nine to one in our favour'.

'No doubt', said Marshal Ney, who came in at this moment, 'if the Duke of Wellington were simple enough to wait for Your Majesty; but I come to inform you that, already, his columns are in full retreat. They are disappearing into the forest.'

'You have not seen right', I replied. 'There is no longer time, he will expose himself to a certain defeat. He has thrown the dice, and our number has turned up!'

At this moment some artillery officers, who had been all over the plain, announced that the artillery could manoeuvre, although with some difficulty, which, in an hour's time, would be considerably lessened. I mounted my horse at once and went to the skirmishers opposite La Haye Sainte; reconnoitred the enemy line again; and told the engineer General Haxo, a reliable officer, to get nearer to it, in order for him to satisfy himself as to whether they had erected some redoubts or entrenchments. This general returned promptly to report that he had seen no trace of fortifications.

I reflected for quarter of an hour, dictated the battle orders, which two generals, seated on the ground, wrote down. The aides-de-camp carried them to the different army corps, who were standing to arms, full of impatience and ardour. The army moved off and began to march forward in eleven columns.

It had been arranged that, of these eleven columns, four were to form the first line, four the second and three the third.

The four columns of the first line were: the first, that on the left, formed by the cavalry of II Corps; [the next, by three divisions of II Corps;] the [third], by three infantry divisions of I Corps; the fourth, by the light cavalry of I Corps.

The four columns of the second line were: that of the left formed by Kellerman's corps of cuirassiers; the second, by the two infantry divisions of VI Corps; the third by two light cavalry divisions, one of the VI Corps commanded by the divisional general Daumont [*sic*], the other detached from Pajol's [1st Cavalry] Corps and commanded by the divisional general Subervic [*sic*]; the fourth by Milhaud's corps of cuirassiers.

The three columns of the third line were: that of the left, formed by the division of mounted grenadiers and the dragoons of the Guard, commanded by General Guyot; the second, by the three divisions of the Old, Middle and Young Guard, commanded by Lieutenant-Generals Friant, Morand and Duhesme; the third by the mounted chasseurs and the lancers of the Guard, under Lieutenant-General Lefebvre-Desnouëttes. The artillery marched on the flanks of the columns the parks and the ambulances at the tail.

At nine o'clock, the heads of the four columns forming the first line, arrived at the point where they were to deploy. At the same time, the other seven columns could be seen not very far off debouching from the heights. They were on the march, the trumpets and drums summoning them to battle. The music resounded with airs which brought back to the soldiers the memories of a hundred victories. The very soil seemed proud to support so many brave men. This was a magnificent spectacle; and the enemy, who were situated in such a way that every man was visible, must have been struck by it. The army must have seemed to them twice as big as it really was.

These eleven columns deployed with such precision that there was no confusion; and each man took up exactly the place which had been planned for him in the very mind of his leader. Never had such huge masses moved about with such ease.

The light cavalry of II Corps, which formed the first column of the left in the front line, deployed in three lines astride the road from Nivelles to Brussels, more or less on a level with the first woods of Hougoumont park, with a view, on the left, of the whole plain with large numbers of guards at Braine-la-Leud and its light artillery on the Nivelles highway.

II Corps, under the orders of General Reille, occupied the area between the Nivelles and Charleroi roads, a stretch of between 900 and 1,000 *toises*; Prince Jérôme's division, holding the left near the Nivelles highway and the Hougoumont wood, General Foy the centre; and General Bachelu the right, which reached the Charleroi road near the farm of la Belle Alliance. Each infantry division was in two lines, the second thirty *toises* from the first, with its artillery in front and its parks in the rear near the Nivelles road.

The third column, formed from the first corps, and commanded by Lieutenant-General Count d'Erlon, rested its left on la Belle Alliance, on the right of the Charleroi road, and its right opposite the farm of La Haye where the enemy's left were. Each infantry division was in two lines; the artillery in the gap between the brigades.

Its light cavalry, which formed the fourth column, deployed on its right in three lines, watching La Haye, Frischermont, and throwing outposts at Ohain, in order to observe the enemy's flank. Its light artillery was on its right.

The front line was scarcely formed up before the heads of the four columns of the second line reached the point where they were to deploy. Kellerman's cuirassiers established themselves in two lines thirty *toises* from each other, resting their left on the Charleroi road. They covered an area of eleven hundred *toises*. One of their batteries took up position on the left, near the Nivelles road; the other on the right, near the Charleroi road.

The second column, under Lieutenant-Général Count de Lobau, moved up to fifty *toises* behind the second line of II Corps; it remained in columns, drawn up by divisions, occupying a depth of about a hundred *toises*, along and on the left of the Charleroi road, with a distance of ten *toises* between the two divisional columns, and its artillery on its right flank.

The third column, its light cavalry, under divisional general Daumont [*sic*], followed by General Subervic's [*sic*], placed itself in column drawn up by squadrons, with the left resting on the Charleroi road, opposite its infantry, from which it was only separated by the roadway; its light artillery was on its right flank.

The fourth column, Milhaud's corps of cuirassiers, deployed in two lines thirty *toises* apart and a hundred *toises* behind the second line of I Corps, the left resting on the Charleroi road, the right in the direction of Frischermont; it covered about nine hundred *toises*, its batteries were on its left, near the Charleroi road, and in its centre.

Before this second line had formed up, the heads of the three reserve columns arrived at their deploying points. The heavy cavalry of the Guard placed itself one hundred *toises* behind Kellerman, ready for action in two lines, thirty *toises* apart, the left on the side of Charleroi, with the artillery in the centre.

The central column, composed of the infantry of the Guard, deployed in six lines, each of four battalions, ten *toises* from each other, astride the Charleroi road and a little in front of the farm of Rossomme. The artillery batteries belonging to the different regiments placed themselves on the left and right, those of the reserve, both foot and mounted, behind the lines.

The third column, the mounted chasseurs and lancers of the Guard, deployed in two lines thirty *toises* apart, a hundred *toises* behind General Milhaud, the left on the Charleroi road, and the right in the Frischermont direction, with its light artillery in its centre. At half past ten, which seemed incredible, the whole manoeuvre was complete, all the troops were in their positions. The most complete silence reigned over the field of battle.

The army was drawn up in six lines, forming the figure of six V's: the first two, of infantry, having some light cavalry on the wings; the third and fourth, cuirassiers; the fifth and sixth cavalry of the Guard, with six lines of infantry of the Guard, placed at right angles at the head of the six V's, and VI Corps, drawn up in columns, at right angles to the lines taken up by the Guard. The infantry was on the left of the road, its cavalry on the right. The Charleroi and Nivelles roads were clear, being the means of communication whereby the artillery of the reserve could reach the different points of the line quickly.

I passed along the ranks; it would be difficult to express the enthusiasm which animated all the soldiers: the infantry raised their shakos on the ends of their bayonets; the cuirassiers, dragoons and the light cavalry, their helmets or shakos on the ends of their sabres. Victory seemed certain; the old soldiers who had been present at so many engagements admired this new order of battle. They sought to divine what aims their general had in mind; they argued about the point at which, and the manner in which, the attack would take place. During this time, I gave my final orders and went . . . on the heights of Rossomme, and dismounted; from there I could see both armies; the view extended far into the distance to right and left of the battlefield.

A battle is a dramatic action, which has its beginning, its middle and its end. The order of battle that the two armies take up, the opening moves to come to grips, are the exposition; the counter-moves, which the attacked army makes, form the crux which imposes new dispositions and brings on the crisis; from which springs the result, or dénouement. As soon as the attack by the centre of the French army was revealed, the enemy general would make counter-moves, either with his wings, or behind his line, in order to provide a diversion, or rush to the support of the point attacked; none of these movements could escape my experienced eye in the central position which I had taken up, and I had all my reserves under control to send them according to my will or wherever the pressure of circumstances should demand their presence.

Ten artillery divisions, including three divisions of twelve[-pounders], came together, the left resting on the Charleroi road on the hillock beyond La Belle-Alliance and in front of the left hand division of I Corps. They were intended to support the attack on La Haye Sainte, which two divisions of I Corps and two divisions of VI Corps were to make, at the same time as the two other divisions of I Corps were moving on La Haye. By this means, the whole of the enemy would be turned. The light cavalry division of VI Corps, drawn up in close formation, and that of I Corps on its wings, were to take part in this attack, which the second and third lines of cavalry would support, as well as the whole Guard, both foot and mounted. The French army, master of La Haye and Mont-Saint-Jean, would cut the Brussels road along the whole right of the English army where its principal forces were.

I had preferred to turn the enemy's left, rather than his right, first, in order to cut it off from the Prussians who were at Wavres, and to oppose their joining up again, if they had intended doing so; and, even if they had not intended doing so, if the attack had been made on the right, the English army, on being repulsed, would have fallen back on the Prussian army; whereas, if made on the left, it would be separated there from and thrown back in the direction of the sea; secondly, because the left appeared to be much weaker; thirdly and finally, because I was expecting every moment the arrival of a detachment from Marshal Grouchy on my right, and did not want to run the risks of finding myself separated from it.

While everything was going forward for this decisive attack, Prince Jérôme's division, on the left, exchanged shots at the Hougoumont wood. Soon the firing became very brisk. The enemy having unmasked close on forty guns, General Reille moved forward the artillery battery of his 2nd Division, and I sent orders to General Kellerman to have his twelve light guns moved up. Soon the cannonade became really hot. Prince Jérôme carried the Hougoumont wood several times, and was several times turned out of it. This was defended by an English guard's division, the enemy's best troops, which I was glad to see on his right, which made the attack on the left all the easier. Foy's division supported Prince Jérôme's, and both sides performed prodigies of valour. The English guards covered the woods and avenues of the Château with their dead, but not without selling their lives dearly. After various vicissitudes, which took up several hours of the day, the whole wood remained in French hands; but the château, where several hundred stout fellows were embattled, put up an unbreakable resistance. I gave orders to assemble a battery of eight field howitzers which set fire to the barns and roofs, and made the French masters of this position.

Marshal Ney received the honour of commanding the big attack in the centre. It could not have been entrusted to a braver man, nor one more accustomed to this kind of thing. He sent one of his aides-de-camp to announce everything was ready and that he waited only for the signal. Before giving it, I wanted to cast a final look over the whole battlefield, and perceived in the direction of Saint-Lambert a cloud which looked to me like troops. I said to my chief-of-staff, 'Marshal, what do you see towards Saint-Lambert?' 'I think I can see five to six thousand men there; that is probably a detachment of Grouchy's.'

All the glasses of the general staff were fixed on this point. The weather was rather misty. Some maintained, as so often happens on such occasions, that they were not troops, but trees; others that they were columns in position; some others that they were troops on the march. In this uncertainty, without further deliberation, I sent for Lieutenant-General Daumont, and ordered him to go with his division of light cavalry and General Subervic's to reconnoitre the right, get into touch speedily with the troops that were arriving at Saint-Lambert, effect a junction with them if they belonged to Marshal Grouchy, hold them off if they belonged to the enemy. These 3,000 cavalrymen only had to do a right wheel in fours to get outside the lines of the army; they moved quickly and without confusion for three thousand *toises*, and there drew themselves up in battle array, as a cross-piece to the whole right of the army.

Quarter of an hour later, a chasseur officer brought in a Prussian Black Hussar who had just been taken prisoner by the despatch-riders of a flying column of three hundred chasseurs, who were out scouting between Wavres and Planchenoit. This hussar was the bearer of a letter. He was extremely intelligent and gave by word of mouth all the information that could be desired. The column which was to be seen at Saint-Lambert was the advance-guard of the Prussian General Bülow, who was arriving with 30,000 men; it was the Prussian IV Corps which had not been engaged at Ligny.

The letter was in fact the announcement of the arrival of this corps; the general was asking the Duke of Wellington for further orders. The hussar said that he had been at Wavres that morning, that the three other corps of the Prussian army were camped there, that they had spent the night of the 17th to 18th there, that there were no Frenchmen in front of them, that he presumed the French had marched on Planchenoit, that one patrol of his regiment had been as far as two leagues from Wavres during the night without encountering any French body. The Duke of Dalmatia [Soult] immediately sent the intercepted letter and the hussar's report to Marshal Grouchy, to whom he repeated the order to march, without halting, on Saint-Lambert, and to take General Bülow's corps in the rear.

It was eleven o'clock; the officer had at most only five leagues to cover, on good roads all the way, to reach Marshal Grouchy; he promised to be there at one o'clock. From the most recent news received of this marshal, it was known that he was to move, at daylight, on Wavres. Now, from Gembloux to Wavres is only three leagues whether or not he had received the orders sent from the imperial headquarters during the night, he must without doubt be engaged at that moment before Wavres. The glasses turned in that direction picked up nothing; no gunfire could be heard. Soon after, General Daumont sent word that some well-mounted despatch riders who were going ahead of him, had run into some enemy patrols in the direction of Saint-Lambert; that it could be taken as certain that the troops to be seen there were enemy troops; that he had sent out picked patrols in several directions to communicate with Marshal Grouchy, and take information and orders to him.

I immediately gave orders to Count de Lobau to cross the Charleroi road, by a change of direction to his right by divisions, and to go towards Saint-Lambert to support the light cavalry; to choose a good intermediate position where he could, with 10,000 men, hold up to 30,000, if that became necessary; to attack the Prussians vigorously, as soon as he should hear the first cannon shots from the troops which Marshal Grouchy had detached in their rear.

These dispositions were carried out at once. It was of the utmost importance that Count de Lobau's movement should take place without delay. Marshal Grouchy must have detached from Wavres 6,000 to 7,000 to search in the direction of Saint-Lambert, and these would find themselves compromised, since General Bülow's corps amounted to 30,000 men. In exactly the same way General Bülow's corps would be compromised and lost, if, at the moment when he was attacked in the rear by 6,000 to 7,000 men, he were attacked in front by a man of Count de Lobau's calibre.

Seventeen to eighteen thousand Frenchmen, disposed and commanded in this fashion, were worth a great deal more than 30,000 Prussians; but these events involved a change in my original plan. I found myself weakened on the battlefield by 10,000 men, whom I was obliged to send against General Bülow. I only had 59,000 men against 90,000; moreover, the enemy army, which I was to attack, had just been increased by 30,000 men, already on the battlefield. It was 120,000 strong against 69,000 – two to one.

'This morning we had ninety odds in our favour', I said to the Duke of Dalmatia. 'Bülow's arrival deprives us of three; but that still leaves us with six to four in our favour, and, if Grouchy retrieves the horrible blunder he made yesterday twiddling his thumbs at Gembloux, and sends his detachment with all speed, victory will be all the more decisive, because Bülow's corps will be entirely destroyed.'

No anxieties were felt as to Marshal Grouchy's safety. After dispensing with the detachment to Saint-Lambert, he still retained 27,000 to 28,000 men. Now the three corps which Marshal Blücher had at Wavres, and which, prior to Ligny, were 90,000 strong, were reduced to 40,000, not merely by the loss of 30,000, which he had suffered in the battle, but also by that of 20,000 who had fled in disorder and were ravaging the banks of the Meuse, and by that of some detachments, which the Marshal had been obliged to use to make good their loss, as well as by that of the baggage trains which were in the Namur and Liège areas. Now, 40,000 or 45,000 Prussians, beaten and disheartened, could not impose their will on 28,000 Frenchmen well placed and victorious.

It was noon, and the sharpshooters were engaged all along the line; but the battle had only really begun on the left, in the wood and around the château of Hougoumont. On the extreme right, General Bülow's troops were still stationary. They appeared to be forming up and to be waiting for their artillery to come through the defile.

I sent orders to Marshal Ney to open fire with his batteries, to get hold of the farm of La Haye Sainte and to put an infantry division in position there; also to get hold of the village of La Haye and turn the enemy out of it, in order to cut all communication between the Anglo-Dutch army and General Bülow's corps. Eighty pieces of artillery soon belched forth death upon the whole left of the English line; one of their divisions was entirely wiped out by the cannon balls and grapeshot.

While this attack was being unmasked, I watched closely to see what would be the movement of the enemy's general. He made none on his right; but I saw that on his left he was preparing for a big cavalry charge; I dashed there at the gallop. The charge had taken place; it had repulsed a column of infantry which was advancing on the plateau, had taken two eagles from it, and put seven guns out of action.

I ordered a brigade of General Milhaud's cuirassiers, of the second line, to charge this cavalry. It went off with shouts of '*Vive l'Empereur*!'; the English cavalry was broken, most of the men were left behind on the battlefield; the guns were re-taken; the infantry protected.

Various infantry and cavalry charges took place; the detailed narration of them belongs to the history of each regiment than to the general history of the battle, into which these accounts, if multiplied, would only bring confusion. It is enough to say that, after three hours fighting, the farm of La Haye Sainte, despite the resistance of the Scots regiments, was occupied by the French infantry; and the objective which I had set myself realised. The 6th and 7th English Divisions were destroyed, and General Picton was left dead on the battlefield.

During this engagement I went along the line of the infantry of I Corps, the cavalry of Milhaud's cuirassiers, and the guard in the third line, in the midst of the cannon balls, grapeshot and shells; they ricocheted between the lines. Brave General Devaux commanding the artillery of the Guard, who was beside me, was killed by a cannon ball. This loss was keenly felt, especially at that moment for he knew better than anyone the positions occupied by the artillery reserves of the Guard, ninety-six pieces strong. Brigadier-General Lallemand succeeded him, and was wounded soon afterwards.

Confusion reigned in the English army. The baggage trains, the transport, and the wounded, seeing the French approaching the Brussels highway and principal exit of the forest, scrambled *en masse* to effect their retreat. All the English, Belgian and German fugitives, who had received sabre wounds from the cavalry, rushed towards Brussels. It was four o'clock. Victory ought from then on to have been assured; but General Bülow's corps carried out its powerful diversion at this moment. From two o'clock in the afternoon onwards General Daumont had reported that General Bülow was debouching in three columns, and that the French chasseurs were keeping up their fire all the while they were retiring before the enemy, which seemed to him very numerous. He estimated them at more than 40,000 men. He said, moreover, that his despatch riders, well mounted, had gone several leagues in different directions and had not reported any news of Marshal Grouchy; and that, therefore, he could not be counted on.

At this very juncture, I received extremely annoying news from Gembloux. Marshal Grouchy, instead of leaving Gembloux at first light, as he had announced in his despatch of two in the morning, had still not left this camp at 10am. The officer attributed this fact to the horrible weather – a ridiculous reason. This inexcusable inertia, in circumstances of such delicacy, on the part of such a zealous officer, was inexplicable.

However, the exchange of artillery fire between General Bülow and Count de Lobau broke out with little delay. The Prussian army was marching in echelons, with the centre in front. Its line of battle was at right angles to the right flank of the army, parallel to the road from La Haye Sainte to Planchenoit. The centre echelon unmasked about thirty pieces of artillery. Our artillery opposed an equal number to it.

After an hour's cannonade, Count de Lobau, seeing that the first echelon was not supported, marched up to it, broke into it, and pushed it back a long way; but the two other lines, which appeared to have been delayed by the bad roads, rallied to the first echelon, and, without trying to breach the French line, sought to outflank it by a left wheel in battle. Count de Lobau, fearing that he might be turned, carried out his retreat, chequer wise, approaching the army. The fire of the Prussian batteries redoubled; up to sixty pieces of artillery could be counted. The cannon balls were falling on the roadway before and behind La Belle-Alliance, where I was with my Guard: it was the fighting zone of the army.

At the most critical moment the enemy got so close that his grape-shot raked this road. I thereupon ordered General Duhesme, commanding my Young Guard, to go to the right of VI Corps with his two infantry brigades and twenty-four pieces of artillery, belonging to the Guard. A quarter of an hour later, this formidable battery opened up; the French artillery did not take long to gain the advantage: it was better manned and placed. As soon as the Young Guard was in action, the movement of the Prussians seemed to be halted; one could see signs of wavering in their line; however, they still continued to extend to their left, outflanking the French right and reaching as far as the heights of Planchenoit.

Lieutenant-General Morand thereupon proceeded with four battalions of the Old Guard and sixteen guns to the right of the Young Guard. Two regiments of the Old Guard took up positions in front of Planchenoit. The Prussian line was outflanked, General Bülow was repulsed, his left moved backwards, closed in, and imperceptibly his whole line fell back. Count de Lobau, General Duhesme and Marshal [?] Morand marched forward; they soon occupied the positions which General Bülow's artillery had held. Not only had this general exhausted his attack, and brought into play all his reserves, but, held at first, he was now in retreat. The Prussian cannon balls not only fell short of the Charleroi road, but did not even reach the positions which Count de Lobau had occupied; it was 7pm.

It was two hours since Count d'Erlon had got possession of La Haye and outflanked the whole English left and General Bülow's right. The light cavalry of I Corps pursuing the enemy infantry on the plateau of La Haye had been brought back by a superior force of cavalry. Count Milhaud climbed upon the height with his cuirassiers, and warned General Lefebvre-Desnouëttes, who started at once at the trot, to back him up.

It was five o'clock, the moment when General Bülow's attack was at its worst, when, far from being held, he kept on throwing in new troops, which extended his line to the right. The English cavalry was repulsed by the bold cuirassiers and chasseurs of the Guard. The English abandoned all the battlefield between La Haye Sainte and Mont-Saint-Jean, which their left had occupied, and were brought to bay on their right. At the sight of these brilliant charges, shouts of victory were heard on the battlefield. I said 'it is an hour too soon; nevertheless what has been done must be followed up'.

I sent an order to Kellerman's cuirassiers, who were still in position on the left, to go at full trot to support the cavalry on the plateau. General Bülow was at this moment threatening the flank and rear of the army; it was important not to fall back at any point, and to hold their present position which the cavalry had taken, although it was premature. This move at the full trot by 3,000 cuirassiers who passed by with shouts of '*Vive l'Empereur!*', and under the gunfire of the Prussians, created a fortunate diversion at this critical moment. The cavalry were marching on as if to pursue the English army and General Bülow's army was still making progress on the flank and in the rear. To know whether we were victorious or in danger, the soldiers, even the officers, sought to divine the answer from the expression on my face; but it radiated only confidence. It was the fiftieth pitched battle that I had conducted in twenty years.

However, the heavy cavalry division of the Guard, under the orders of General Guyot, who was in second line behind Kellerman's cuirassiers, followed at a full trot and proceeded to the plateau. I noticed this, and sent Count Bertrand to recall it; it was my reserve. When this general got there, it was already committed and any movement of withdrawal would have been dangerous. From 5pm onwards, I was thus deprived of my cavalry reserve, of that reserve which, skilfully employed, had so often brought me victory.

However, these 12,000 picked cavalrymen performed miracles; they over whelmed all the more numerous enemy cavalry which sought to oppose them, drove in several infantry squares, broke them up, seized sixty pieces of artillery, and, in the middle of the squares, captured ten standards, which three chasseurs of the Guard and three cuirassiers presented to me in front of La Belle-Alliance. The enemy, for the second time that day, thought the battle lost, and saw with apprehension to what extent the bad battle-site which he had selected was going to add to his difficulties in his retreat. Ponsonby's brigade, charged by the Red Lancers of the Guard under General Colbert, was broken into. Its general was pierced by seven lance thrusts, and fell dead. The Prince of Orange, on the point of being seized, was severely wounded; but, not being backed up by a strong mass of infantry, which was still contained by General Bülow's attack, this gallant cavalry had to confine itself to holding the battlefield which it had conquered.

At length, at seven o'clock, when General Bülow's attack had been repulsed and the cavalry was still holding its own on the plateau which it had carried, the victory was won; 69,000 Frenchmen had beaten 120,000 men. Joy was visible on every face and hearts were lifted high. This feeling followed on the shock that had been experienced during the flank attack, launched by an entire army, which, for an hour, had even threatened to bring about the retreat of the army. At this juncture Marshal Grouchy's gunfire could be heard distinctly. It had passed beyond Wavres at the most distant point and at the nearest point; it was behind Saint-Lambert.

[*In the next few pages, Napoleon covers Grouchy's movements and the discussion of whether he should have marched to the sound of the guns. As this does not include action at Waterloo it is left out here.*]

As soon as General Bülow's attack had been repulsed, I gave orders to General Drouot, who was doing the duties of aide Major-General of the Guard, to rally his whole Guard in front of the farm of La Belle-Alliance, where I was with eight battalions drawn up in two lines; the other eight had marched on to support the Young Guard and defend Planchenoit. However, the cavalry, which continued to hold the position on the plateau from which it dominated the whole battlefield, saw General Bülow's move but, deriving confidence from the reserves of the Guard, which it saw there to hold them, did not feel any anxiety as a result, and gave vent to cries of victory when they saw this corps repulsed. They were only waiting for the arrival of the infantry of the Guard to decide the victory; but they were staggered when they perceived the arrival of the numerous columns of Marshal Blücher.

Some regiments were drawing back. I noticed this. It was of the highest importance to put the cavalry in countenance again; and, realising that I still needed another quarter of an hour to rally my whole Guard, I put myself at the head of four battalions and advanced to the left of La Haye Sainte, sending aides-de-camp along the line to announce the arrival of Marshal Grouchy and to say that, with a little determination, the victory was soon to be decided.

General Reille concentrated his whole corps on the left, in front of the château of Hougoumont and prepared his attack. It was important that the Guard should be in action all at once, but the eight other battalions were still in the rear. Being at the mercy of events and seeing the cavalry being put out of countenance, and realising that a reserve of infantry was needed to support it, I ordered General Friant to go with these four battalions of the Middle Guard to meet the enemy's attack; the cavalry pulled itself together again and marched forward with its accustomed dash. The four battalions of the Guard repulsed everybody they encountered; cavalry charges struck terror into the English ranks. Ten minutes later, the other battalions of the Guard arrived. I drew them up in brigades, two battalions in line and two columns on the right and the left; the 2nd Brigade in echelons, which combined the advantage of the two types of formation.

The sun had gone down; General Friant, who had been wounded and was passing by at this moment, said that everything was going well, that the enemy appeared to be forming up his rearguard to support his retreat, but that he would be completely broken, as soon as the rest of the Guard debouched. A quarter of an hour was needed!

It was at this moment that Marshal Blücher arrived at la Haie and overthrew the French unit defending it; this was the 4th Division of I Corps; it fell back, routed and only offered slight resistance. Although it was attacked by forces four times as strong, if only it had shown a little resolution, or had barricaded itself up in the houses, since night had already fallen, Marshal Blücher would not have had time to take the village. It is there that the cry of '*Sauve qui peut*' is said to have been heard.

The breach effected, the line having been broken owing to the lack of vigour of the troops at la Haie, the enemy cavalry swept over the battlefield. General Bülow marched forward; Count de Lobau put on a bold front. The rout became such that it was necessary to give orders to the Guard, which was formed up to go forward, to change direction. This move was carried out in good order; the Guard faced about, with its left on the side of La Haye Sainte and its right on the side of la Belle Alliance, confronting the Prussians and the attack on la Haie. Immediately afterwards, each battalion formed itself into square. The four squadrons detailed for action charged the Prussians. At this moment the English cavalry brigade, which arrived from Ohain, marched forward. These 2,000 horse got in between General Reille and the Guard.

The disorder became appalling over the whole battlefield; I only just had time to place myself under the protection of one of the squares of the Guard. If General Guyot's cavalry division of the reserve had not committed itself, without orders, to following up Kellerman's cuirassiers, it would have repulsed this charge, prevented the English cavalry from penetrating into the battlefield, and the foot Guard would then have been able to hold all the enemy's efforts. General Bülow marched on his left, still outflanking the whole battlefield.

Night added to the confusion and obstructed everything; if it had been daylight and the troops had been able to see, they would have rallied; nothing was possible in the darkness. The Guard began to retreat, the enemy's fire was already a hundred *toises* behind and the roads were cut. I remained for a long time, with my general staff, with the regiments of the Guard on a hillock. Four guns which were there, fired briskly into the plain; the last [dis]charge wounded Lord Paget, the English cavalry general. At last, there was not a moment to lose. I could only effect my retreat across country; cavalry, artillery, infantry, were all mingled pell-mell.

The general staff reached the little town of Gennapes; it hoped to be able to rally a rearguard corps there; but the disorder was appalling, all efforts were in vain. It was 11pm. Finding it impossible to organise a defence, I pinned all my hope on Girard's division, the 3rd of II Corps, which I had left on the battlefield of Ligny, and to which I had sent orders to move on to Quatre Bras to support the retreat.

Never had the French army fought better than on this day; it performed prodigies of valour; and the superiority of the French troops over the enemy was such that, but for the arrival of I and II Prussian Corps, victory would have been won, and would have been complete over the Anglo-Dutch army and General Bülow's corps, that is to say one against two (69,000 men against 120,000) ... The Imperial Guard upheld its former reputation; but it was engaged in unfortunate circumstances. It was outflanked on the right and left, swamped by fugitives and by the enemy, just when it was joining in the fray; for, if this guard had been able to fight, supported on the flanks, it would have repulsed the efforts of the two enemy armies combined. For more than four hours 12,000 French cavalrymen had been masters of a part of the enemy's side of the battlefield, had fought against the whole infantry and against 18,000 of the Anglo-Dutch cavalry, who were again and again repulsed in all their charges.

Chapter 3

Napoleon's Household

Jardin Aîné, Equerry to Napoleon

Griffiths, *With Napoleon at Waterloo and other Unpublished Documents of the Waterloo and Peninsular Campaigns* (London: Mackensie Macbride, 1911), pp. 183–5.

We know little of Jardin Aîné, who was Napoleon's equerry at Waterloo; he was responsible for the Emperor's horses. He is mentioned by Napoleon's valet Constant who left Napoleon's service in 1814, so he was surely employed close to Napoleon before that year. The story goes that on the day of Waterloo, Napoleon called for his horse, but Aîné being absent, a groom saddled a horse but put on the wrong bridle. The horse becoming restive, Napoleon was thrown heavily to the ground. As Aîné rushed up to him, Napoleon, in a rage and thinking Aîné responsible, struck him across the face with his whip. Aîné was insulted by this, but after Caulaincourt, the chief equerry, remonstrated with Napoleon, the emperor apologised and gave Aîné 3,000 francs. The following is the English translation of Aîné's journal that appears in the above publication.

Napoleon went into a kind of inn [in fact the farm of le Caillou] out of which the troops, who had installed themselves in it, were turned, and here he fixed his general headquarters, because he did not wish to go into the town of Genappes, which was only a league distant, saying that during the night he would here receive more readily reports from the army. At the same time everyone had found the best available quarters in which to pass the night. Generals Corbineau, La Bedoyere [*sic*], Flahaut, duty aides-de-camp on Napoleon's staff, spent the night in riding between the various army corps and returning to him to give an exact account of the movements that were taking place.

At half-past nine in the morning of the 18th, Napoleon, having left the bivouac on horseback, that is to say the village Caillou, came up to take his stand half a league in advance upon a hill where he could discern the movements of the British army. There he dismounted and with his field glass endeavoured to discover all the movements in the enemy's line. The chief-of-staff suggested that they should begin the attack; he replied that they must wait, but the enemy commenced his attack at eleven o'clock and the cannonading began on all sides; at two o'clock nothing was yet decided; the fighting was desperate. Napoleon rode through the lines and gave orders to make certain that every detail was executed with promptitude; he returned often to the spot where in the morning he had started, there he dismounted and, seating himself in a chair which was brought to him, he placed his head between his hands and rested his elbows on his knees. He remained thus absorbed sometimes for half an hour, and then rising up suddenly would peer through his glasses on all sides to see what was happening. At three o'clock an aide-de-camp from the right wing came to tell him that they were repulsed and that the artillery was insufficient. Napoleon immediately called General Drouet [Drouot?] in order to direct him to hasten to reinforce this army corps which was suffering so heavily, but one saw on Napoleon's face a look of disquietude instead of the joy which it had shown on the great day of Fleurus. The whole morning he showed extreme depression; however, everything was going on as well as could be expected with the French, in spite of the uncertainty of the battle, when at six o'clock in the evening an officer of the mounted chasseurs à cheval of the Guard came to Napoleon, raised his hand to his shako and said, 'Sire, I have the honour to announce to your majesty that the battle is won'.

'Let us go forward', Napoleon replied, 'We must do better still. *Courage mes braves*: Let us advance!' Having said this he rode off at a gallop close to the ranks encouraging the soldiers, who did not keep their position long, for a hail of artillery falling on their left [I suspect he must mean the right, intimating the arrival of the Prussians] ruined all. In addition to this, the strong line of British cavalry made a great onslaught on the squares of the Guard and put all to rout.

It was at this moment that the Duke of Wellington sent to summon the Guard to surrender. General Kembraune [Cambronne] replied that the Guard knew how to fight, to die, but not to surrender. Our right was crushed by the corps of Bülow who with his artillery had not appeared during the day but who now sought to cut off all retreat.

Napoleon towards eight o'clock in the evening, seeing that his army was almost beaten, commenced to despair of the success which two hours before he believed to be assured. He remained on the battlefield until half past nine when it was absolutely necessary to leave. Assured of a good guide, we passed to the right of Genappes and through the fields; we marched all the night without knowing too well where we were going until morning.

Louis Étienne Saint-Denis, otherwise known as Mameluke Ali

Souvenirs sur l'Empereur Napoléon, reprint presented by Christophe Bourachot (Paris: arléa, 2000), pp. 112–17.

Throughout the Waterloo campaign, Mameluke Ali filled the post of Napoleon's personal servant. It is probably well-known that he was not a Mameluke at all, but a Frenchman called Louis Étienne Saint-Denis, and, unlike the more famous Mameluke servant of Napoleon, Roustan, had not returned to France with Napoleon after the Egypt campaign of 1799. Ali was born in 1788 at Versailles and owed his entry into Napoleon's household in 1806 to his father's acquaintance with General de Caulaincourt. Saint-Denis followed Napoleon through the campaigns in Spain, Germany and Holland. In 1811 he became assistant to Roustan, as 'Second Mameluke' and Napoleon insisted on him taking the name Ali and adopting the distinctive Mameluke dress. Ali escorted Napoleon to Moscow and through the 1813 campaign. He often slept across the doorway to Napoleon's room when on campaign. On the retreat back into France he remained in Mayence until after the Allied entry into Paris, but rejoined Napoleon to share his exile on Elba after Roustan deserted the Emperor, not wanting to share his exile. Ali returned to France with Napoleon in 1815. It seems that on the day of Waterloo, Ali spent at least some time with Napoleon near the front line and met the officers of the Guard as they fell back after their failed attack. He left the battlefield with Napoleon and returned to Paris with him. He shared his exile on St Helena and only returned to France on Napoleon's death in 1821. He lived in Sens until his own death in 1856.

Ali inevitably gives us little detail on the battle, although he gives the impression that the arrival of the Prussians was a surprise. He gives an interesting account of the capture of Napoleon's carriages.

All the middle of the day [the 17th] the weather was very poor; it was only towards three or four o'clock that the rain ceased; but the weather remained stormy.

The emperor, arriving by a road which joined the main route from Brussels, then went a further quarter or half a league ahead and soon we found ourselves on elevated ground which dominated a large basin bordered to the north by the curtain of the Soignes forest. The horizon, being grey, did not permit us to see clearly with the naked eye; we only noticed, on our left, an English rearguard, followed by some French troops, where we saw from time to time a few cannon shots, of which we could see the smoke. We were at the end of the day. After the emperor had finished examining with his telescope an immense line of fires which shone in our eyes, suddenly there was the sound of cannon. It was the English artillery which showed the wide frontage of its army that was ranged for battle. There was only a single volley; from then we heard only a few shots fired to the left, by both our advance-guard and by the enemy rearguard which was retiring.

It was dark, or nearly so, when the emperor reached the Caillou farm; he fixed his headquarters there. As his room was not yet ready, they made a bivouac fire near the buildings (these were to the right of the road), and there, lying on a bundle of straw, he waited while his room was being put in order to receive him. When he had taken possession of the little hovel in which he was to pass the night he had his boots taken off, and we had trouble in doing it, as they had been wet all day, and after undressing he went to bed, where he dined. That night he slept little, being disturbed every minute by people coming and going; one came to report, another to receive orders, etc.

The next day, the 18th, the emperor got up very early. He breakfasted in company with the *grand-maréchal*, the Duke of Dalmatie [Marshal Soult] and some other people and he then mounted his horse, followed by the major-général, the Duke of Dalmatie, the *grand-maréchal*, General Fouler and all his suite. He moved to the advanced-posts to reconnoitre and examine the positions occupied by the enemy army and dictated the order of battle.

When all the corps had conducted their movements, he rode along the ranks where he was welcomed with enthusiasm; after which he came to establish himself on a height to the rear of Rossomme. The action started in the Hougoumont park. This place was distant and high up; we could see easily enough the attack and defence. It was only with much pain that we were able to dislodge the enemy. The other parts of the line of battle were a long way off or hidden by the lay of the ground; we could not easily see with the naked eye the various movements which took place. A good part of the day had passed and it was only very slowly that we had won some ground. In the afternoon, the Prussian corps of General Bülow, which at first had been taken for Marshal Grouchy, started to make some progress and to improve the enemy's chances of success. It was, I believe, three to four o'clock. At the time when the first Prussian cannonballs fell on our right, I was sent to Caillou farm to tell Pierron, *maître d'hotel*, to bring up a small canteen, the emperor and some of his suite having the need to take some nourishment. On the way, several cannonballs crossed the road, but on the return they were falling much faster.

A little further and to the rear of the place where the emperor was, there was a sunken road in which there were a large number of dead belonging to the English guard (Horse Guard); we recognised them by their tall stature and their large helmets decorated by a large black caterpillar.

Bülow repulsed, the emperor had the battalions of the Old Guard advance against the English. The cavalry had already been committed. As soon as the Guard struck the enemy, it sowed death there and everywhere they fell back. Our wounded, of which there was a great number, informed us of the fierce resistance of the English. Amongst the wounded, I saw General Friand [*sic*] who was still mounted; several moments later Colonel Mallet, who was escorted by his soldiers. This last recognised me and signalled to me to give him a drop of brandy. I satisfied him immediately; I carried the emperor's flask. The emperor, who half an hour before and perhaps more, had left most of his headquarters and his escort to direct the attack of the Guard infantry, came to join us half an hour later.

Darkness began to cover the battlefield in shadows when Marshal Blücher entered the line on our right and brought disorder into some French regiments and this disorder gradually communicated itself to others; in a short time this became general. It was necessary that the Guard made a change of front and then that it formed into squares, in one of which the emperor took refuge with his suite to escape the Prussian cavalry which flooded the battlefield. The storm past, the emperor gave the order to retreat. Bülow's corps, which had re-taken the offensive and which had already cut the main road, threatened to surround us completely.

The emperor's carriage and the vehicles of the household had remained at the Caillou farm. The emperor's carriage was captured in the evening. The driver Horn, who led it, not having the light to move the carts and other vehicles that obstructed the road, seeing the Prussian cavalry on the point of cutting him off and seeing besides the balls and bullets falling around him, unharnessed the horses whilst the first foot valet, Archambault, took from the carriage the wallet and the necessary. The vehicle remained there and was almost immediately taken by the Prussians who pillaged it, as well as that of Marchand, which contained the emperor's belongings.

In the emperor's carriage there was a sword which had been forgotten by Archambault; it was the same as the one carried by His Majesty, except that on this one was written, on the clearer side of the blade, these words in gold: 'Sword worn by the Emperor at the battle of Austerlitz'. I have not heard of this sword being taken in the vehicle. What became of it? It seems that it was read somewhere that it had fallen into the hands of the Duke of Wellington. It is more probable that some Prussian soldier took it, broke the blade and only kept the hand guard as having for him the true value. This hand guard was of gold as well as the trimming on the scabbard.

To return to Horn, this unfortunate, in the struggle, had his arm taken off by a ball. The next day, Blücher, passing over the battlefield with some of his officers, stopped in front of Horn, who was sitting on a stone and asked him who he was. The postilion replied in German that he was of the emperor's household and it was him who drove His Majesty's carriage. Blücher, who was a very violent man, very hot-tempered, and whose heart was full of hatred and vengeance against those who had been involved with the day of the 16th [the battle of Ligny], overwhelmed him with insults and had the malice, the barbarity, one might say, on the few words that Horn replied with, to shout at him. If the marshal had been a different man, would he not have had the wound bandaged of a poor devil of a servant and given him some money instead of mistreating him as insultingly as he did? Later, the vehicle having been bought by an Englishman, Horn became the guide to this vehicle which was shown to the curious.

In the long column of soldiers of all arms, of all corps, of all regiments which were retreating, marching mixed together, each looking out only for himself, the very small group which surrounded the emperor marched with everyone else, heading for Philippeville. The night was a night without a moon; we could see, but not distinguish things; here and there on the road were bivouac fires where men lay exhausted and dying of hunger. Slowly and quietly, we walked in the footsteps of the horses.

Count Louis-Joseph-Narcisse Marchand

Mémoires de Marchand, premier valet de chamber, exécuteur testamentaire de l'Empereur (Paris, Plon, 1952–1955), pp. 162–6.

During the Waterloo campaign Marchand served as premier valet de chambre *(senior personal servant) to Napoleon.*

Marchand was born in 1791 to a well-connected family, his mother was one of three nannies to the King of Rome and a friend of Madam de Montesquiou and later part of the household of the empress. It was thanks to this connection that Marchand became part of the imperial household in 1811 as a garçon d'appartement *when he was twenty. After accompanying Napoleon into exile on Elba, he filled the post of* premier valet de chambre *during the Waterloo campaign. After the battle he accompanied the emperor to St Helena and only returned to France after Napoleon's death in 1821. Napoleon nominated him as the executor of his will, leaving his former servant a total of 600,000 francs and writing, 'The services that he has rendered me are those of a friend'. Early in the battle he escorted Napoleon forward, but soon returned to le Caillou.*

Marchand tells a similar, though no less interesting, story to Ali. Once again, we see that an eyewitness appears to have been surprised by the appearance of the Prussians. Marchand clearly points the finger of blame for the defeat at Grouchy.

I arrived much later than the emperor at the general headquarters; my carriage had overturned in a torrent, it was several hours before I could get out; night had fallen, it was very dark, a heavy rain had rendered the roads difficult; we passed general headquarters and the postilion led me as far as the main guard where I stopped. I turned back and finally arrived at the farm of Caillou; the emperor had slept for the last hour according to Saint-Denis, astonished that I had not arrived earlier. I had hardly been there two hours when the emperor called me and asked me what the time was, I told him of the accident that had held me up, the poor state of the roads and the rain that had continued to fall.

At three o'clock his first *officier d'ordonnance*, Colonel Gourgaud, was called for, told to reconnoitre the state of the ground and determine if artillery would be able to manoeuvre; you could see that he was impatient to attack. The enemy had remained in position in front of the Soignes forest. It was believed the night before that he had only taken this position to give his convoys time to pass through the forest. The rations had not all come up, the weather had been terrible all night; several days of marching, a great battle and the other combats had tired the troops; they needed the dawn to bring the sun to revive them and heal the fatigues of the night. Drouot [General Drouot was the commander of the Imperial Guard and a close confidant of Napoleon] reported that the roads were so cut up and the ground so wet that he did not think that it was possible to manoeuvre artillery until they were a little drier. After this report the emperor continued to rest in his bed, but he got up early, and saw with pleasure that the weather was clearing . . . he walked backwards and forwards for a long time in his room, his hands behind his back. He took out a pair of scissors, and cut his nails, appearing to be more occupied with this part of his toilet than the battle that was soon to be engaged; he often went to the window and looked at the state of the sky; his shave complete, he dressed and dictated to General Gourgaud.

At nine o'clock, the emperor demanded his breakfast that he took with Prince Jérôme, General Reille, who commanded II Corps under the orders of the Prince, and several other generals that he had invited. 'Messieurs', the emperor said cheerfully, as he got up from the table, 'if my orders are well executed, we will sleep this evening in Brussels'. He told Saint-Denis to have the horses brought up and for him to mount up and follow the headquarters. The arrival of the emperor was saluted along the whole line by the shout repeated a thousand times, shouts of devotion, shouts of '*Vive l'Empereur*!' When the emperor considered the ground sufficiently dry to be able to manoeuvre, he gave the order to II Corps to attack the Hougoumont wood which was in front of the enemy's right. At midday, Prince Jérôme's division advanced to take it; it was repulsed and reformed for a new attack and this prince only managed to become master of it after a very dogged fight in which he was wounded. At the same time that this attack had taken place, I Corps established itself in the houses of Mont Saint-Jean, approaching the enemy's position. The English did not seem to me to be able to resist the united efforts of the divisions of the French army, whose emperor was awaiting the right moment. I returned to general headquarters with the assurance that a great battle had been won when towards five o'clock Noverraz came to tell me that a Prussian corps has joined the English, that General Lobau's division [corps] was opposed to it and that the battle continued. I was worried, despite myself, by the persistence of the enemy, and I became more so when Saint-Denis came in haste to find some things for the emperor and said to me quickly; 'Things are going badly, masses can be seen in the distance. At first it was thought that it was Marshal Grouchy, a cry of joy was heard, but it is a corps of Marshal Blücher, and there is no news of Marshal Grouchy. The emperor cannot understand why he did not arrive at the same time.' He departed at a gallop. It was then seven o'clock in the evening. I gave myself up to sad thoughts; General Bülow had already added his corps to the numerous English army. The emperor had not shown the slightest anxiety, since he had sent a courier to Paris announcing a victory. But the arrival of Marshal Blücher into line, adding to a numerous force against a tired army, and to turn round a day which was destined to add to the glory of the French army, into an unfortunate day if Marshal Grouchy did not arrive.

I told General Fouler, *écuyer* to the emperor, of my concerns, who told me that it was necessary to have everything ready to move, that it was against his advice that the equipages were so close to the battlefield, but that now they were there only an order from the emperor could allow them to withdraw. About an hour passed and the sound of artillery and musketry seemed to get distinctly closer. It was not so dark that you could not see the road covered in the artillery train and wounded soldiers supported by other men who were not hurt. This retrograde movement took on an alarming character. I provisionally put the emperor's bed into its cases, closed the *necessaire* and stood ready for any event. The emperor's carriage was on the battlefield; it made me very worried as it contained a large amount of gold, the necklace of Princess Pauline, and the diamonds put there by Prince Joseph, on the night of the departure from Paris. Thinking that it would always be out of the way, I had even congratulated myself on not having all these valuables with me, embarrassed enough by those that I had in gold amounting to 100,000 francs and 300,000 in bank notes that I kept locked in a large chest that was in my carriage. Soon we could hear the fusillade coming much closer, but someone came to order the officers and their men who provided the guard for the carriages, to move into the wood nearby and to delay those enemy who were approaching to give us time to get away.

Heaven came to decide against the favour of our arms. The best laid plan to win and destroy the hopes of the enemy, to lead to peace, were lost by the failure of execution of the emperor's orders to one of his lieutenants, Marshal Grouchy who, if he had pushed the enemy with his sword in their kidneys as he had been ordered, would have arrived with him on the battlefield to take part in the victory and not been responsible for the army's defeat. Fate saw to it that the Guard was engaged at the moment that Marshal Blücher's corps arrived; the service squadrons which were never engaged other than with the emperor's order were also, so that in the most critical moment, the emperor no longer had under his hand that reserve that he so often committed in a moment to seize a victory which may have escaped him. General Fouler [the acting Grand Equerry], hearing the firing in the wood approaching the carriages, took it upon himself to give the order to retreat. It was already quite late because of the obstacles already in the road. I had the emperor's bed put on a mule, the [money] chest in my carriage and some sturdy horses were harnessed. It was soon away from its resting place, but, arriving on the road it had to advance at the same speed as everyone else. Nevertheless, I thought it [his carriage] would escape until, arriving at Quatre Bras [he means Genappe], the obstructions were such that it could not pass. I wanted to see the cause of this hold-up; a howitzer obstructed the road and delayed everything that arrived; in an instant, a mass of vehicles were across the route and blocked the passage.

The enemy, stopping himself, began to pillage the rear vehicles and mine was to become his prey. I quickly opened the treasure chest and grabbed the 300,000 francs in banknotes which I stuffed down my chest and closing up my uniform I abandoned the rest. After many difficulties I managed to pass from one vehicle to the next and to escape the embarrassment in which I found myself. The Duke de Bassano and Baron Fain set off on foot, their vehicles remaining in the middle of this fray; like me they were without news of the emperor of whom some said he was dead, others said he wanted to sleep on the battlefield. How could they know of these things in the disorder in which they retired? Uncertain, I waited until the moment when I noticed the Guard, which followed this movement, but in better order. I asked several officers if they knew which route the emperor had been able to take, but none of them were able to tell me. I then travelled with them. The cannon had gone silent some time before. This Guard, so brilliant the day before, so full of enthusiasm that very morning, passed along the road sad and silent. Less anxious now, I marched with it all night and the next day. Passing through Beaumont and Charleroi, I arrived at Avesnes as night fell [the 19th]; the gates were closed. I learnt that Prince Jérôme, wounded, was in the town and that the emperor's horses were also there. I passed the night in the bivouac of some dragoons. I had approached one of their fires and luckily recognised an old comrade amongst the officers who offered to share a little bread that he was eating. I thanked him and we chatted about the misfortune and of our fears for our unfortunate that was again exposed to the ravages of foreigners.

Baron Pierre-Alexandre-Édouard Fleury de Chaboulon

Mémoires de Fleury de Chaboulon, ex-secrétaire de l'Empereur Napoléon et de son Cabinet, pour server à l'histoire de la vie privée, du retour et du règne de Napoléon en 1815 (Paris: Edouard Rouveyre, 1901), Vol II. pp. 135–52.

Fleury de Chaboulon served as Napoleon's secretary during the Waterloo campaign, but not as secretary to his cabinet as claimed in the title.

De Chaboulon was born in 1779 during the turmoil of the Revolution. It appears that at seventeen he fought with the Parisian national guard against the forces of the Convention. Ironically, the latter were commanded by Napoleon to whom he was later to attach his fortune. He embraced an administrative career and held a number of appointments until becoming the auditor of the Conseil d'État *and then* sous-préfect *in Château-Salins in 1811. In this latter appointment he came to prominence for his performance in his duties in the face of the Allied invasion at the end of 1813 and beginning of 1814. He joined Napoleon's staff at Montereau and was sent on a number of important missions to organise resistance and was nominated* sous-préfect *of Reims after its recapture by Napoleon in March 1814. After the First Restoration he avoided the new administration by travelling to Italy from where he returned on Napoleon's reassumption of power. He claims he was made second secretary to Napoleon's office, but it seems Napoleon himself declared that he was only fourth secretary! Following Waterloo he was forced into exile in England where he wrote and had published his memoirs of 1815 from which the following is taken. He eventually returned to France and was employed again after the 1830 July Revolution, even becoming a councillor of state. He died in 1835.*

De Chaboulon clearly follows Napoleon's accounts of the battle; he speaks of Napoleon's expectation that Wellington would have retired during the night, prior knowledge of the Prussian approach and suggests that Napoleon's whole plan was predicated on Grouchy's move against the Prussian rear. Like most French accounts, he falsely gives Wellington's army a numerical advantage over the French. The battle itself, to which he was not an eyewitness, follows Gourgaud's account almost exactly, including the claim that the British were defeated before the decisive intervention of the Prussians. Napoleon's accusations against Ney's commitment of the cavalry are repeated. It is only after the battle has ended does de Chaboulon return to some interesting personal experiences.

The night of the 17th to 18th was terrible and seemed to anticipate the misfortunes of the day. A violent and uninterrupted rain did not allow the army to savour a single moment of rest. As extra misfortune, the poor state of the roads delayed the arrival of rations and most of the soldiers had no food; however, they seemed unfazed by this double misfortune and at dawn they announced to Napoleon by many acclamations that they were ready to steal a new victory.

The emperor thought that Lord Wellington, isolated from the Prussians and sensing the march of Grouchy's corps, that would be able, by crossing the Dyle, to approach his flank or rear, would not dare to defend his position and would retire on Brussels. He was surprised when daylight revealed that the English army had not left its positions and appeared disposed to accept battle. He had their positions scouted by several generals and if I was to use the expressions of one of them, he thought they were defended 'by an army of cannons and by mountains of infantry'.

Napoleon immediately warned Marshal Grouchy that he was probably going to have a great battle with the English and ordered him to vigorously press the Prussians, approach the main army as quickly as possible and to direct his movements in a manner so as to link up with these operations.*

---

* I have heard it said that the officer who carried this order, instead of following the direct route, had thought he must make a long detour to avoid the enemy.

He called together his principal officers to give them his instructions.

Some, full of confidence and audacity, claimed that it was necessary to attack and take the enemy position by main force. Others, more wary, not less brave, protested that the rain had ruined the ground, that the troops and particularly the cavalry would not be able to manoeuvre without much difficulty and fatigue; whilst the English army had the immense advantage of awaiting us firmly in their entrenchments and that it was preferable to attempt to turn them. All rendered homage to the courage of their troops and promised that they would achieve prodigies; but they differed in their opinions on what resistance the English would offer. Their cavalry, said the generals that had fought in Spain, were not as good as our own; but their infantry were as good as could be imagined. Entrenched, it was dangerous due to its accurate fire; in the open, it held firm, and if it was broken, it rallied a hundred paces away, at most, and returned to the charge. They engaged in new discussions and remarkably, *it did not enter anyone's mind* [his emphasis], that the Prussians, despite numerous groups that had been seen towards Moustier, would be able to make a serious diversion on our right.

The emperor, after having listened and discussed all the advice, decided, taking into consideration all the collected viewpoints, to attack the front of the English. Confirmatory orders were sent to Marshal Grouchy, and Napoleon, to give him the time to carry out the movement prescribed to him, employed the whole morning in deploying his army.

The emperor personally made a new reconnaissance of the English army: its central position, based on the village of Mont-Saint-Jean, was supported on its right by the farm of Hougoumont; to the left, on that of La Haye Sainte. Its two wings extended to the end of the hamlet of Terre-la-Haie and Merkebraine [*sic*]; hedges, woods, ravines, an immense artillery and 85–90,000 men defended this formidable position.

The emperor deployed his army in the following order:

- II Corps, of which Prince Jérôme was still a part, was placed opposite the wood which surrounded Hougoumont.
- I Corps was opposite La Haye Sainte.
- VI Corps was sent to the extreme right in order to link up with Marshal Grouchy when he approached.
- The light cavalry and the cuirassiers were side by side in the second line, behind I and II Corps.
- The Guard and its cavalry remained in reserve on the heights of Planchenois [*sic*].
- The old division of General Girard was left at Fleurus.

The emperor and his headquarters established themselves on a small mound close to the farm of la Belle-Alliance, from where they dominated the plain and could easily direct the movements of the army and watch those of the English.

At 12.30pm, the emperor, persuaded that Marshal Grouchy would have started off, gave the signal to attack.

Prince Jérôme advanced with his division on Hougoumont. The approaches were defended by hedges and a wood, where the enemy had placed a numerous artillery. The attack, rendered so difficult by the lie of the ground, was launched with an extreme impetuosity; the wood was taken and then re-taken. Our troops and the English, most often separated just by a hedge, firing at point blank range and taking their fire without giving a pace; on both sides the artillery made terrible ravages. Success remained undecided when General Reille supported Prince Jérôme's attack with Foy's division and managed to force the enemy to abandon the wood and orchards that it had so valiantly defended and conserved until then.

It was 1pm: a few moments beforehand an intercepted despatch informed the emperor of the impending arrival of 30,000 Prussians, commanded by Bülow.

Napoleon thought that the strength of this corps, of which some scouts had appeared on the heights of Saint-Lambert, was exaggerated; and besides, he was convinced that Grouchy's army followed it and that it would find itself between two fires, so he was only slightly concerned. However, as a precaution rather than through fear, he ordered General Domont [sic] to move with his cavalry as well as that of General Suberwick [sic], to anticipate the Prussians and told off Count Lobau to take measures to support General Domont if required. Orderlies were sent at the same time to Marshal Grouchy to inform him of what was happening and to enjoin him again to hasten his march to pursue, attack and destroy Bülow.

Our army was thus reduced, by the detachment of Domont's and Suberwick's divisions and by the allocation of VI Corps to other tasks, to less than 57,000 men; but it displayed so much resolution that the emperor did not doubt that it was sufficient to beat the English.

II Corps (as I have already said) had succeeded in driving the English from the Hougoumont wood, but I Corps, despite the continuous fire of several batteries and the resolution of our infantry and the light cavalry of Generals Lefebvre-Desnouëttes and Guyot, had not forced La Haye Sainte nor Mont-Saint-Jean. The emperor ordered Marshal Ney to undertake a new attack and to have it supported by eighty guns. A terrible fire of musketry and artillery started from then along the whole front. The English, indifferent to danger, faced the charges of our infantry and cavalry with great firmness; the more resistance they displayed, the more our soldiers persisted in the fight. Finally, the English, pushed back from position to position, evacuated La Haye Sainte and Mont-Saint-Jean and our troops seized them to shouts of 'Vive l'Empereur!'

Count d'Erlon sent immediately the second brigade of General Allix to hold them. A body of English cavalry cut their route, put them into disorder and threw them back on our batteries, succeeding in upsetting several guns. General Milhaud's cuirassiers approached at the gallop to repulse the English cavalry. A new division of theirs threw themselves on our cuirassiers. Our lancers and chasseurs were sent to their assistance. A general charge began and the English, broken, thrown back and sabred, were forced to retire in disorder.

Until then, the French army, or more accurately the 40,000 men of Generals Reille and d'Erlon, had obtained and conserved a marked superiority. The enemy, put off, appeared uncertain of its movements. It was remarked of its dispositions that they seemed to announce an impending retreat. The emperor, satisfied, repeated with joy, 'They are mine, I have them!'; and Marshal Soult and all the generals regarded, like him, the victory assured.

The Guard had already received the order to move forward to occupy the ground that we had conquered and to finish off the enemy when General Domont warned the emperor that Bülow's corps was entering into line and was advancing rapidly on the rear of our right. This information changed Napoleon's resolution; instead of using his guard to support I and II Corps, he held it in reserve and ordered Marshal Ney to maintain himself in the Hougoumont wood, La Haye Sainte and at Mont-Saint-Jean, until the issue of the movement that Count Lobau was going to execute against the Prussians was known.

The English, informed of Bülow's arrival, retook the offensive and attempted to drive us from the positions we had taken from them. Our troops successfully repulsed them. Marshal Ney, carried away by his hot-headedness, forgot the emperor's orders. He charged the enemy at the head of Milhaud's cuirassiers and the light cavalry of the Guard and appeared, amidst the applause of the army, to establish himself on the heights of Mont-Saint-Jean, until then inaccessible.

This untimely and hazardous movement did not escape the notice of the Duke of Wellington. He advanced his infantry and launched on us all his cavalry.

The emperor immediately had General Kellerman and his cuirassiers hurried off to disengage our first line. The grenadiers à cheval and dragoons of the Guard, either by a misunderstanding by Marshal Ney, or spontaneously, set off and followed the cuirassiers without it being possible to stop them. A second mêlée, more murderous than the first, started at all points. Our troops, exposed to the uninterrupted fire of enemy infantry and batteries, remained engaged heroically for two hours of numerous and brilliant charges in which we had the glory to take six colours, overthrow several batteries and to cut to pieces four regiments; but in which we also lost the élite of our intrepid cuirassiers and the cavalry of the Guard.

The emperor, although put into despair by this unfortunate engagement, was not able to remedy things. Grouchy had not arrived; and already, to master the

Prussians, whose numbers and progress were always increasing, he had been forced to weaken his reserves by 4,000 men of the Young Guard.

However, our cavalry, exhausted by a considerable loss and unequal combats continuously renewed, started to become discouraged and to fall back. The outcome of the battle appeared to become doubtful. It was necessary to strike a great blow by a desperate attack.

The emperor did not hesitate.

The order was immediately given to Count Reille to assemble all his forces and to throw them impetuously on the enemy's right, while Napoleon in person went to attack the front with his reserves. The emperor had already deployed his Guard in attack columns, when it appeared that our cavalry had been forced to evacuate in part the heights of Mont-Saint-Jean. He immediately ordered Marshal Ney to take with him four battalions of the Middle Guard and to move off in all haste onto the fatal plateau, to support there the cuirassiers who still occupied it.

The fine bearing of the Guard and Napoleon's harangues enflamed the spirits; the cavalry and several battalions who had been moving to the rear, turned about to face the enemy to shouts of '*Vive l'Empereur!*'

At the same time, a fusillade was heard (one has learnt since that this was General Ziethen who, arriving into line, had taken the troops commanded by the Prince of Saxe-Weimar for the French, had forced them, after a heavy fire fight, to abandon a small village that they had been ordered to defend).

'*Voila* Grouchy!' shouted the emperor, 'Victory is ours!'

Labédoyère rushed to announce this happy news to the army; he penetrated, despite the enemy, to the heads of our columns: 'Marshal Grouchy has arrived, the Guard advances, courage! Courage! The English are lost.'

A last cry of hope left all the ranks; the wounded who were able to take a few more steps returned to the fight: thousands upon thousands of voices repeated, '*En avant! En avant!*'

The column commanded by the 'Bravest of the Brave' arriving before the enemy, is welcomed by discharges of artillery that caused terrible losses. Marshal Ney, tired of the fire, ordered the batteries to be taken at the point of the bayonet. The grenadiers rushed forwards with such impetuosity that they lost that admirable order that so much merited victory. Their chief, drunk with courage, did not notice their disorder. He and his soldiers approached the enemy in a tumult. A swarm of balls, canister, burst around their heads. Ney's horse was killed, Generals Michel and Friant fell dead or wounded, a crowd of men was knocked down. Wellington left our grenadiers no time to understand. He attacked them in the flank with his cavalry and forced them to retire in the greatest disorder. At the same moment, Ziethen's 30,000 Prussians, that had been taken for Grouchy's army, took by assault the village of la Haie and pushed us back before them. Our cavalry, our infantry, already shaken by the defeat of the Middle Guard, were afraid of being cut off and retired precipitously. The English cavalry skilfully profited by the confusion that this unexpected retreat caused, emerged through our ranks and finished off by spreading disorder and discouragement. The other troops on the right, who had already resisted with much pain the Prussian attacks and had been lacking ammunition for more than an hour, seeing some disordered squadrons and men of the Guard broken, fearing that all was lost, left their positions. This contagious movement communicated itself in an instant to the left and the whole army, having so valiantly taken the strongest enemy positions, abandoned them to him with as much haste that it had taken to conquer them.

The English army, that had advanced as we withdrew, the Prussians who had not ceased to pursue us, swooped down on our scattered battalions. Night augmented the confusion and terror and soon the entire army was no more than a confused mass that the English and Prussians knocked down without effort and massacred without pity.

The emperor, a witness to this terrible rout, could hardly believe his eyes. His aides-de-camp rushed to all sides to rally the troops. He threw himself into the middle of the crowd. But his appeals, his orders, his prayers, were not heard. How could the army manage to reform under the artillery fire and in the middle of continued charges of 80,000 English and 60,000 Prussians that had invaded the battlefield?

However, eight battalions that the emperor had previously concentrated, formed in square, blocked the main road to the Prussian and English armies. These braves, that were constant and courageous, were not able to resist for long against an enemy twenty times more numerous. Surrounded, attacked, struck down from every direction, the majority finally succumbed. Others sold their lives dearly; the others, exhausted from fatigue, of thirst and of hunger, no longer had the strength to fight and were cut down without being able to defend themselves. Two lone battalions that the enemy had not been able to break, retired disputing the ground until disorganised and carried away by the general movement, were themselves forced to follow the torrent.

A last battalion of reserve, the illustrious and unhappy remains of the column of granite of the fields of Marengo, remained unshaken in the middle of the tumultuous flood of the army. The emperor retired into the ranks of these braves still commanded by Cambronne! He put them in square and advanced at their head to meet the enemy; all the generals, Ney, Soult, Bertrand, Drouot, Corbineau, Flahaut, Labédoyère, Gourgaud etc., drew their swords and became soldiers. The old grenadiers, incapable of fearing for their own lives, were worried about the threat to that of the emperor. 'Retire!' one of them said to him, 'you can see that death does not want you!' The emperor refused and gave the order to fire. The officers who surrounded him took his horse and led him. Cambronne and his braves closed up around their remaining eagles and said an eternal farewell to Napoleon. The English, touched by their heroic resistance, called on them to surrender. 'No', said Cambronne, 'the Guard dies, but does not surrender!' At the same time they threw themselves on their enemies with cries of '*Vive l'Empereur!*'. . . Some, covered in wounds, fell to the ground drowning in their own blood. Others, more happily, were killed. Finally, those who had eluded death, shot themselves so as not to follow their companions in arms, nor to die at the hands of their enemies.

Wellington and Blücher, now untroubled occupiers of the battlefield, went over it as masters. But by how much blood was this unjust triumph bought? Never, no never, did the French strike their adversaries with more formidable and murderous blows. Full of blood and glory, contemptuous of danger and death, they rushed audaciously on the flaming batteries of the enemy and seemed to multiply to find, to attack and to pursue the enemy in their inaccessible entrenchments. 30,000 English and Prussians were sacrificed by their hands on this fatal day; and when one thought that this horrible carnage was the handiwork of 50,000 men*, dying of fatigue and hunger, and struggling on a marshy ground against an impregnable position, and a 130,000 combatants, one is seized by a sad admiration and we give to the victors the palm of victory.

At the moment when Bülow's corps broke our right, I was at headquarters at Caillou farm.

An aide-de-camp of the *grand maréchal* came to warn the Duc de Bassano that the Prussians were heading this way. The duke, having received the order from the emperor to remain here, did not want to leave and we resigned ourselves to await the event. Soon enemy dragoons captured the small wood that covered the farm and came to sabre our men. Our guard repulsed them with musket shots, but returning in greater numbers, they attacked us again and forced us, despite to stoicism of M. Bassano, to give the place to them. The imperial vehicles, with fresh horses, quickly got us away from the enemy pursuit. The duke was not so lucky; his vehicle, poorly drawn, suffered several volleys and he finished by being forced to save himself on foot and to come and take refuge in mine.

The end of the firing and the precipitate retreat of the debris of the army, confirmed to us the unfortunate result of the battle. We asked everyone for news of the emperor, but on one could appease our anxiety. Some assured us he had been taken prisoner and others that he had been killed. To put an end to the anxiety that overwhelmed us, I took the horse of the chief of our equipages and, followed by a first *piqueur* named Chauvin, who had returned from the island of Elba with the Emperor, I turned back towards Mont-Saint-Jean. After having vainly pestered

---

* I say 50,000 because more than 10,000 men of the Guard had so far taken no part in the action.

a multitude of officers with questions, I encountered a page, the young Gudin, who assured me that the emperor had left the battlefield. I pushed on further. Two cuirassiers, sabres raised, stopped me,

'Where are you going?'

'I am going to meet the emperor'.

'You are lying, you are a royalist, you are going to join the English!'

I do not know how this incident would have finished if a superior officer of the Guard, who came from the heavens, happily recognised me and delivered me from my situation. He assured me that the emperor had long been led off and was beyond me. I re-found the Duke of Bassano. The certitude that the emperor was safe and sound assuaged our concerns for a time. It soon returned with all its force. It would not be French to contemplate our terrible catastrophe with a dry eye. The army itself, returned to its first sentiments, forgetting the perils which threatened it again, to reflect sadly on the future; its march was despondent, its look appalled, no words, no complaint came to interrupt its sad contemplation; we said it was a funeral procession, that it was attending the funeral of its glory and of *la Patrie*.

The taking and pillage of the army's baggage had held up the enemy's pursuit for the moment. It caught us up again at Quatre Bras [he means Genappe] and fell on our equipages. At the front of the convoy was the treasury and then next was our carriage. Five other wagons which were immediately behind were attacked and sabred. Ours, by a miracle, was able to save itself. It was there that the emperor's clothing was taken; the superb diamond necklace which had been given to him by Princess Borghèse and his landau which had escaped the disasters of Moscow.

The Prussians, furious in our pursuit, treated with barbarity all those unfortunates that they encountered. With the exception of a few imperturbable old soldiers, most of the others had thrown away their arms and found themselves defenceless; they were mercilessly massacred just the same . . . A colonel, so as not to fall into their hands, blew out his own brains. Twenty other officers of all ranks followed his example. An officer of cuirassiers, seeing them arrive, said, 'They will have neither me nor my horse'. He killed his horse with one pistol and himself with the other. A thousand desperate acts no less heroic illustrated this fatal day.

Captain Jean-Roche Coignet

Les Cahiers du Capitaine Coignet (1799–1815) (Paris: Librairie Hachette, 1916), pp. 285–8.

Captain Jean-Roche Coignet served in the French army for sixteen years; from 1799 to 1816. He was present at forty-seven actions or battles, including Ulm, Austerlitz,

Jena, Eylau, Friedland, Essling, Wagram, Smolensk, la Moskowa, Lützen, Bautzen, Dresden, Hanau, Montmirail, Montereau, Ligny and Waterloo. He entered the Grenadiers of the Old Guard in 1800. He was commissioned from the ranks in 1812, and was made captain the following year.

Coignet served during the 1815 campaign as the wagon-master to Napoleon's headquarters. His participation in the Waterloo campaign was limited by his role; it is probable that he saw nothing of the battle and his account seems to be based on what he must have read in later years. His story of being sent on reconnaissance is likely to be included to give him some role in the action; it seems unlikely that the baggage master would be tasked with such an important task, even given his considerable experience. He speaks nothing of his key duties in the headquarters.

Coignet's account is very pro-Napoleon and therefore promotes the idea that Grouchy was expected to arrive on the battlefield during the day and his failure to do this was the reason for the defeat. His suggestion that the Allied artillery fired at him, a single horseman, is unlikely to say the least. Given that his post was with the headquarters at le Caillou, much of what he describes towards the end of the battle is almost certainly hearsay.

The emperor sent an officer of the engineers in order to reconnoitre their position on the height of Belle-Alliance [La Haye Sainte], and to see if they were fortified. On return, he said that he had seen nothing. Marshal Ney arrived, and was rebuked for not having pursued the English, for there were only some '*sans-culottes*' [literally, 'without trousers'; this refers to the Highlanders on account of their bare legs] at Quatre Bras. 'Go *Monsieur le maréchal*, and seize those heights; the enemy are standing close to the woods. When I have news of Grouchy, I will give you the order to attack.' The marshal left and the emperor went onto a height close to a château on the side of the road. From there he could see his left wing, the strongest part of the English army. He awaited news of Grouchy, but always in vain and he wore himself down; finally, he was found near a château by an officer who said to the emperor, 'We have lost precious time, I have not seen the Prussians on my route; they are not fighting'. He was anxious at this news; I was called for, given the order to go a little to the right of the road to Brussels, to make sure of the position of the left wing of the English which rested on the wood. I was forced, in descending, to skirt the road because of a broad and deep valley that I could not cross and a knoll where the artillery of the Guard was in battery. I must mention that we were drenched with rain, and the ground was water-logged; our artillery could not manoeuvre. I passed close to them and when I came to the edge of this valley, I saw columns of infantry closed up in mass in the bottom of it. I went across it, going a little to the right, and came upon an isolated shed, a little distance from the road. I stopped to look; on my right I saw some tall rye and the enemy's guns in battery, but no one moved. For a moment

I did a little swagger. I went near the tall rye and saw a body of cavalry behind it. I had seen enough.

It appeared that it did not suit them to see me approach so close to them; they saluted me with three rounds from a cannon. I went back to inform the emperor that on the right their cavalry was hidden behind the rye; their infantry hidden in the valley and that a battery had fired at me. The emperor gave the order to attack along the whole line; Marshal Ney performed prodigies of courage and bravery. In front of him, this intrepid marshal had a formidable position; he could not take it. Every moment he sent for reinforcements from the emperor to finish it off, as he said. At last, in the evening, he received some cavalry which routed the English, but without positive success. One more effort and they would have been thrown back into the forest. Our centre was making progress; they had passed the shed in spite of the grape-shot which fell in their ranks. We did not know the misfortunes which awaited us.

An officer arrived from our right wing. He told the emperor that our men were retreating. 'You are mistaken', he said, 'it is Grouchy arriving.' He immediately sent someone off in that direction to assure himself of the fact. The officer who had returned, confirmed the news that he had seen a column of Prussians was rapidly advancing upon us, and that our soldiers were retreating. The emperor immediately altered his dispositions. By a wheel of his army to the right, he came close to this column which was repulsed. But an army, commanded by Marshal Blücher, arrived, while Grouchy was looking out for it in the opposite direction. The centre of our army was weakened by this change of face; the English had time to breathe and reinforcements could not be sent to Ney, who, we were told by some officers, wanted to get himself killed. The Prussian army came into line; the junction was complete; we could count two or three of the enemy against each one of us; there was no means of holding on. The emperor, seeing himself outflanked, took his Guard and marched it forwards to the centre of his army in close columns, followed by his whole headquarters; he had the battalions formed into squares. This manoeuvre complete, he spurred his horse forward to enter the square commanded by Cambronne; but all his generals surrounded him. 'What are you doing?" they shouted, 'Is the victory not enough for them?' His plan was to get himself killed. Why did they not allow him to do this! They would have spared him much suffering, and at least we would have died at his side; but the great men who surrounded him had decided not to make such a sacrifice. However, I must say that we all surrounded him and forced him to retire.

We had the greatest difficulty to get away. We could not make our way through the crowd that was struck by fear. This was even worse when we arrived at Jemmapes [*sic*]. The emperor tried to re-establish a little order among the fugitives, but his efforts were in vain. Soldiers of all units and all arms marched without order, all mixed up, colliding with each other, crushed in the streets of this small town, fleeing before the Prussian cavalry, which hurrah'd behind them. Everyone thought only of getting to the other side of the bridge across the Dyle as quickly as possible. Everything was overthrown.

General Charles-Auguste-Joseph *Comte* Flahaut De La Billarderie

Letter from Flahaut to the *Moniteur*, dated 6 April 1857, published in *The First Napoleon, some unpublished documents from the Bowood papers* (London: Constable, 1925), pp. 129–31.

Flahaut was one of Napoleon's personal aides-de-camp during the Waterloo campaign.

Auguste Flahaut was the illegitimate son of Tallyrand and was born in 1785. He was brought up in England. Allowed to return to France in 1797, in 1800 he joined the Hussars of the Consular Guard, a unit formed from the families of reconciled emigrés. However, he soon transferred to the 5th Dragoons and fought at Marengo later that year. In 1801 he was commissioned sous-lieutenant. *Family influence secured him a post as one of Murat's aides, who was then governor of Paris. He distinguished himself during the campaign of Austerlitz during which he was wounded. He took part in the 1806 campaign against Prussia as captain and in Poland. Promoted* chef d'escadron *for the campaign in 1807, he served with the 13th Chasseurs à Cheval and was present at Eylau, but not engaged. Joining Junot's expedition to Portugal in 1807, he returned to France as aide-de-camp to Berthier. He went with Berthier to Spain, but returned with him for the campaign against Austria in 1809 during which he was present at all the major engagements. He was promoted colonel in May 1809. During most of this time he was probably best known for his affair with Murat's wife, and Napoleon's sister, Caroline. He started the Russian campaign attached to the Austrian corps, but was soon re-assigned as aide-de-camp to Prince Eugene. He fought throughout the main engagements of the campaign and retreat and was promoted* général de brigade *for his conduct at the Beresina. He remained with Eugene through the early part of 1813, but moved to Napoleon's staff when Eugene returned to Italy. In the Autumn Campaign he was present at Dresden, Leipzig and Hanau, after which he was promoted to* général de division *and made Imperial aide-de-camp. He served at Napoleon's side throughout the 1814 campaign. Placed on half pay after the First Restoration he rushed to join Napoleon on his return and returned to his former post. He was sent to Quatre Bras by Napoleon to keep an eye on Marshal Ney, but failed to quickly inform Napoleon of the outcome of the day. Present at Waterloo, he escorted Napoleon from the field and returned to Paris. After Napoleon's departure from Paris he took command of the 9th Cavalry Division and took part in the successful engagement with the Prussians at Rocquencourt before retiring with the army to the Loire. Although proscribed after the Second Restoration, no charges were brought against him (probably due to Tallyrand's intervention). He wandered Europe for some time before travelling to England, marrying and settling down there before returning to France in 1827. He was re-admitted to the army but spent the following years filling diplomatic posts and posts of honour in the government, including ambassador to Vienna. He filled similar posts under the Second Empire, but witnessed its slow decline, dying in 1870 on the day of Sedan.*

Flahaut was appointed as aide-de-camp to Napoleon on 20 March 1815, the day Napoleon entered the Tuileries, and served as such throughout the campaign. The following was written in response to Marshal Marmont's critical comments in volume seven of his memoirs. Marshal Marmont was widely accused of having betrayed Napoleon by surrendering his corps to the Allies in 1814, an act which precipitated Napoleon's first abdication. He was therefore hated by all of Napoleon's adherents and it is no surprise that he fled Paris with Louis XVIII when Napoleon returned in 1815 and was very critical of the emperor's handling of the campaign.

During the battle the emperor took up his stand on a hillock in the centre of the position. From this point he was able to take in the operations as a whole, and while there he saw the cavalry attack which Ney had ordered. He thought it indeed premature and ill-timed, and actually exclaimed, *'Voilà Ney qui d'une affaire sure en fait une affaire incertaine; mais maintenant, puisque le mouvement est commence, il n'y a plus autre chose à faire qu'à l'appuyer'*. ['Ney has turned what was a sure thing into an uncertain thing; but now, since the attack has begun, there is no option but to support it'.] He then bade me take his orders to all the cavalry, to support and to follow the squadrons that had already crossed the ravine between them and the enemy-and this was done. Unfortunately the moment had not yet come for an attack of this sort to meet with success, and of this the emperor had been perfectly aware. It was, however, impossible to either stop or to recall the troops that were already committed. In war there are sometimes mistakes that can only be repaired by persevering in the same line of action.

I will leave to Marshal Marmont all the credit (which I have no desire to share) of his endeavour to make comparisons between the commanders of the rival armies, and to apportion to each his due share of responsibility for the outcome of the battle. He is at pains to shower praises on the British general at the expense of the emperor, and to lay to the charge of the latter all the mistakes which, as he thinks, contributed to the disastrous result. It might, however, have occurred to him that the unexpected arrival on our flank of a body of 20,000 Prussians, whose artillery enfiladed and tore up with its missiles the whole of our ground, was the real cause of our losing the battle and of the disasters which ensued. The Duke of Wellington, in reporting to his own Government, was fair-minded enough to admit this.

As regards the panic which, as alleged by the marshal, overcame the emperor when the day was lost; this untruthful statement can best be refuted by an account of the events which took place before my own eyes, and no one is in a better position to give such an account than myself.

After taking part in the attacks of the cavalry and of the Guard I turned back, when the retreat had definitely set in, to find the emperor. Night had then fallen. I found him in an infantry square and from that moment I did not leave his side. He stayed there for a time, but the day being now irretrievably lost, he moved off in the direction of the Charleroi road. We made our way towards it, not at a gallop, as so infamously stated in these *Mémoires* [Marmont's], but at a foot's pace, nor would an enemy pursuit, had there been one, have inspired the fear to which the marshal [Marmont] in his hatred would have us believe the emperor was a prey. Of personal fear there was not the slightest trace, although the state of affairs was such as to cause him the greatest uneasiness. He was, however, so overcome by fatigue and the exertion of the preceding days, that several times he was unable to resist the sleepiness which overcame him and if I had not been there to uphold him, he would have fallen from his horse.

Colonel Gaspard Baron Gourgaud

Bataille de Waterloo, Relations d'un Officier Général Français, in the *Nouvelle Revue Rétrospective* Vol. 4 (Paris, 1896), pp. 370–7.

In 1815 Gourgaud served in Imperial Headquarters as colonel and senior officier d'ordonnance *(orderly officer) to Napoleon.*

Gourgaud was born in Versailles in 1783, son of a court musician. He attended the École Polytechnique in 1799 and then, as second lieutenant, the artillery school in 1801. He served for a short time in the 7th Foot Artillery Regiment, and then the 6th Horse Artillery Regiment in which he was promoted lieutenant in 1803. The following year he became aide-de-camp to General Foucher de Careil with whom he fought and was wounded at Austerlitz in 1805. He was promoted captain in 1808 after serving in the campaigns of Prussia and Poland, and served in this capacity with the 6th Horse Artillery Regiment in Austria in 1809. He became officier d'ordonnance *to Napoleon in 1811 and participated in the 1812 campaign in Russia where he was wounded at Smolensk. He distinguished himself at the Beresina where he twice swam the river (presumably on his horse) to carry out a reconnaissance of the far bank. He was promoted* chef d'escadron *and senior* officier d'ordonnance *in 1813. He took part in that campaign and in France in 1814 and famously shot dead a Cossack at Brienne who was on the point of attacking Napoleon himself. He was wounded at Montmirail and also fought at Laon and Reims. Promoted colonel shortly before Napoleon's abdication, he was confirmed in this rank by Louis XVIII and was posted to the artillery headquarters in the 1st Military Division. He returned to his place next to Napoleon on the latter's return and fought at Ligny and Waterloo. He was promoted to* maréchal de camp *on 21 June and accompanied Napoleon into exile on St Helena. He left the island in 1818 and returned to Europe, though he was not allowed back into France until 1821, but was not employed until after the 1830 revolution when he was confirmed in his rank as* maréchal de camp. *He filled a number of posts on the artillery staffs, was aide-de-camp to King Louis-Philippe and promoted to lieutenant general in 1835. He continued to serve on the artillery inspectorate and staffs, and was part of the commission that oversaw the return of Napoleon's remains to France. He retired in 1848 and died in 1852.*

We have already read Gourgaud's account of the campaign and battle in chapter two; it is widely accepted to either have been dictated by Napoleon, or a reflection of his views, opinions and thoughts on the battle that had long been discussed with Gourgaud during the emperor's exile on St Helena. In the following account, Gourgaud describes his own experiences during the battle which give it not only a more authentic feel, but also indirectly challenges some of what had appeared in his campaign overview. It is noticeable that, like Napoleon's initial account of the battle, he gets La Haye Sainte mixed up with Mont-Saint-Jean. It is also interesting that his account of the deployment and actions of the Guard differ substantially from his account of the campaign written after his return from St Helena; although lacking detail, as this is his personal recollection, it is likely to be a more accurate description than that put to him by Napoleon.

Although published under the anonymous title of 'A French General Officer' this account is undisputedly credited to Gourgaud. It is believed that it was written shortly after the battle and before Gourgaud was unduly influenced by Napoleon's own recollections and interpretation of the battle in The Campaign of 1815. . .

His Majesty lodged at the farm of Caillou, the rain fell in torrents; our bivouacs suffered much from the rain, hunger, fatigue, etc.

In the morning of the 18th, similar reports arrived. Various corps commanders wrote however, that the English army appeared to be concentrated with the intention of giving battle. His Majesty gave the order to Count d'Erlon to push forwards. Hardly had this order left than Ney, d'Erlon and Reille sent to inform His Majesty that the whole English army was in position and offering battle. His Majesty then mounted his horse and moved to our position. He went along the line and reconnoitred that of the enemy. All the troops, seeing the emperor, forgot the rain, the hunger, the fatigue, and sounded out from all parts, '*Vive l'Empereur!*'

His Majesty returned to place himself on a mound, close to the village of Caillou, asked for his maps, and called for the generals and marshals to give them his written instructions. After this conference, they returned to their corps at the gallop.

Our line was thus:

- To the right, the corps of d'Erlon, having in reserve behind him the corps of Lobau (VI) and Duhesme (Young Guard).
- In the centre was Reille (II Corps) with his right on the main road, where he supported d'Erlon's left.
- To our left was Kellerman's cavalry.
- The Imperial Guard was in front of the village of Caillou, behind the mound occupied by his majesty.

At eleven o'clock, General Reille attacked the village on which the enemy supported his right [he presumably means Hougoumont]. A lively cannonade was engaged at this point and, little by little, along the whole line as our troops came into range.

The English position was superb; they crowned the summit of a curtain of ground whose slope, facing us, singularly favoured the fire of their artillery. This position had, besides, the great advantage of forming a light semi-circle; their centre, on the main road, was supported by the village of Mont Saint-Jean [here he must mean La Haye Sainte], where they had established a 'poor traverse'.

The English masses were deployed to the rear of the summit of the position, in order to be less exposed to the fire of our artillery, so that we could only see the enemy skirmishers and batteries.

At midday, the emperor sent me to carry the order to Marshal Ney, who principally commanded the right, to attack the enemy with all force, having prepared the attack with much artillery. I put in battery, in front of d'Erlon's corps, sixty-four guns (of which thirty were twelve-pounders) and we engaged, from this point, a heavy barrage. The enemy suffered much; our skirmishers advanced, they were in Mont Saint-Jean. Marshal Ney advanced his whole line; the artillery left its good position to move forwards. Ney gave the order to four squadrons of cuirassiers to charge on the left of the road; I moved with them. Three or four hundred Brunswickers [this cavalry rode down a battalion of Hanoverians rather than Brunswickers], hidden in Mont Saint-Jean, were taken. Arriving on the height, we suffered much from the English musketry and artillery. During this movement, three or four hundred cavalry of the English guards charged our skirmishers on the main road; we deployed behind them from Mont Saint-Jean. The other squadrons of the division of cuirassiers (Milhaud) charged them from the front. The English guards [cavalry] were unable to advance or withdraw; I shouted to them to surrender, and suddenly, they jumped the ditches along the road and threw themselves in disorder into d'Erlon's infantry; we followed them. Quiot's brigade (infantry) was put into disorder, as well as the artillery, which was taking position. Happily, the English chose to save themselves rather than fight and order was re-established.

In this mêlée, I killed four English guards with my sabre and an officer with a pistol shot; my horse had its neck pierced by a sabre thrust by one of the English that I killed. I could have killed a greater number, but my scruples would not allow me to kill fugitives. An English guard that I had passed, threw down his sabre and asked for pardon. I made him dismount and march in front of me, leading his horse. I returned to join His Majesty. In passing between two battalions of infantry a sergeant left the ranks and knocked my prisoner out with blows of his butt and bayonet; it took some effort to save him from this barbarian.

His majesty sent me to tell Reille to advance. The cannonade on both sides continued with fury. A great part of the Guard artillery was engaged. General Devaux was killed at the moment that he came to give me a letter for his wife. Our cavalry moved onto the English heights, sabred the gunners and broke some squares, but other squares in *échiquier* caused us heavy losses. The English guns were not fixed to their limbers by a *prolonge*,[1] the gunners left their guns in place and retired with their horses behind their infantry. We passed the guns but were unable to carry them off. Despite the fusillade and the canister, our brave cavalry held their position there. The infantry delayed coming to their support.

I went to the farm of Mont Saint-Jean [La Haye Sainte], defended by the 72nd Regiment, which I encouraged. This farm and the whole village was full of bodies. I found the emperor in the middle of the fire. We could hear a vigorous attack on the right of d'Erlon; it was the Prussians who, after having left a corps in front of Grouchy, came to the support of the English.

His Majesty sent Mouton [Lobau] and Duhesme, two batteries of the Guard and a battalion of the Old Guard to the right. The Prussians were contained. It was seven o'clock; we showed to His Majesty the smoke of cannon on our right; it appeared to be in the Prussian rear. It was said that it was Grouchy deploying. Soult said that he had received the order. This sound got louder, some officers were sent to announce it on all sides. His Majesty thought the same and said, in joy, 'At last we shall have great results!' And, as he was impatient with the English resistance, and that he only awaited Grouchy's movement, he gave the order to his guard, infantry, cavalry, artillery, to march forwards, leaving in front of the village of Caillou only a single battalion of the Old Guard.

All started off; I marched with the two first battalions arriving on the plateau; the shock was terrible. We were welcomed by a terrible cannonade and volleys and we lost many men. Friant, Cambronne, Malet etc., fell. This attack of the Guard not having succeeded, I judged the battle lost and tried to get myself killed; I encountered *officier d'ordonnance* Amittet, who prevented me from throwing myself into the middle of my enemies.

Disorder was in our ranks; the shouts 'Save us, we are cut off!' were heard. The attack of the Prussians on our right had started again with renewed fury during our general movement against the English centre and Mouton and Duhesme were wiped out by numbers; finally, Blücher's army bombarded us on the road; all broke up, all fled.

The emperor, swept away by the fugitives, was only able to stop at the battalion of the Guard located at the mound close to the village of Caillou. The darkness did not allow him to see the troops and to put himself at their head and the rout becoming general, he wanted to die with this battalion and his faithful servants. At this moment, I lent a horse to Perrin to replace his own which had been killed. His Majesty told me to open up the battalion; I rushed there, but, at the moment of entry, the emperor was prevented by Soult, who took his horse by the bridle, saying to him, 'Ah! Sire, the enemy has already been happy enough!' Soult led him; we only walked, followed by enemy balls. We crossed the main road which was crowded with fugitives, marching to the left. The guide Lacotte [*sic*] was ordered to be tied to us to prevent him from leaving us. We passed Genappe in the middle of terrible disorder of fugitives, wounded, vehicles, over-turned caissons etc. At Quatre Bras, His Majesty stopped for a short time; previously, he had directed Soult to send orders to Grouchy and Rapp; we found the cavalry of Piré and set off again. His Majesty was so exhausted that I gave him my arm to support him on his horse. Close to Charleroi he dismounted to walk. Finally, at dawn, we arrived at this town.

Thus this battle was lost which, by its result, is so celebrated. One would think that if the attacks, instead of being made in isolation, had been carried out at the same time; that if Grouchy had more aggressively followed the Prussians, instead of remaining at Gembloux and Savenières on the 17th, and prevented them from throwing themselves on our right, one might think, say I, that this battle could have been won by us and, with it, peace, for the Prussian army, beaten on the 16th, that of the English on the 18th, the English government would have changed. The Russians and Austrians would have stopped, Belgium would have risen, the Saxons would have taken up arms and France would have been saved.

Chapter 4

Imperial Headquarters

Marshal Michel Ney, *duc d'Elchingen, prince de la Moskowa*

Letter from Marshal Ney to Fouché, Duke of Otranto, dated 26 June 1815 and quoted by George Jones in *The Battle of Waterloo with those of Ligny and Quatre Bras described by Eyewitnesses and by the series of Official Accounts published by Authority* (London: L. Booth, 1852).

During the 1815 campaign, Ney served as commander of the left wing until Waterloo, when he commanded I and II Army Corps and the III and IV Cavalry Reserve Corps under the overall command of Napoleon.

From humble origins Ney had enjoyed a meteoric rise through the ranks of the French army. Joining the 4th Hussars in 1790 aged twenty-one, he was a sergeant major just two years later and commissioned the same year. As a cavalry commander he quickly established himself as a leader of dash and courage. The future Marshal Bernadotte commented, 'Ney will go far if he doesn't kill himself first'. He fought under Moreau in these early stages and was no admirer of the young Buonaparte as the future emperor first started to establish his reputation. Ney was made général de brigade *at twenty-six, after only five years in the army, and* général de division *in 1799. By this time he had shown himself to be a leader of guile, in his capture of Wurzburg and Mannheim, and a determined and effective commander of an advance guard or rearguard. He had already been wounded a number of times.*

His achievements soon came to the notice of Napoleon and although his allegiance to Moreau, who some saw as Napoleon's rival for power, could have caused lasting damage to his career, the future emperor realised that this was a man he needed. In 1802 his growing reputation was enhanced by his invasion of Switzerland and from then on he took a leading role in most of Napoleon's campaigns, fighting against Austria in 1805, Prussia in 1806 and Russia in 1807. Throughout these campaigns he showed himself to be a brave and aggressive commander, but there were also occasions, most notably at Jena and during the winter of 1807, that he could be rash and prepared to ignore orders, even from the emperor himself. Sent to Spain in 1808, he performed well when under Napoleon's direct command, but once the emperor had returned to France, Ney became an unruly subordinate to both Soult and Massena. Happiest in action, he quickly gained a reputation for being thoroughly quarrelsome and uncooperative. Eventually relieved of his command in 1811 by an exasperated Massena, he was recalled to France to face the wrath of Napoleon.

As frustrated as Napoleon must have been by Ney's behaviour in Spain, the emperor was soon to have need of him. Once again under the supervision of Napoleon, Ney led a corps into Russia in 1812 and took a leading role at both Smolensk and at Borodino. Perhaps his crowning achievement was his command of the army's rearguard during the retreat. Cut off from the main body and presumed lost, he led it back to the army to the astonishment and approbation of all. His reputation amongst the rank and file was unrivalled except by Napoleon himself.

His command of the rearguard in Russia had shown that he was at his best with his back to the wall, fighting almost as an equal amongst his men with outstanding courage and resolve. But as the war continued into Germany his suitability for the highest levels of command came under scrutiny. Whilst the surprise of his corps at Lützen could hardly be blamed solely on him, he did not appear to fully comprehend his crucial role at Bautzen as the commander of the left wing and was humiliated as an independent army commander at Dennewitz. At the latter battle, he was accused of 'acting like a lieutenant in a general's cloak', showing no understanding of the wider strategic implications of the situation whilst becoming fixated by the lower-level tactical direction of the battle. He could not resist getting drawn into the fighting and this was a charge he faced many times in his career, perhaps confirming his unsuitability as an independent, high-level commander. After his defeat he was severely criticised by Napoleon and it is evident that this was deeply felt. These shortcomings were to be evident again in 1815.

After his failure at Dennewitz, Ney was drawn back under Napoleon's direct control and was present at the climactic battle of 1813 at Leipzig, where he commanded the northern sector of the battlefield. Another example of poor judgement resulted in him being overwhelmed by superior numbers and, in desperate fighting, he was shot in the shoulder and eventually evacuated from the battlefield.

It was January 1814 before Ney was fit to rejoin the army. Threatened by invasion, Napoleon welcomed him back and gave him command of two divisions of the Young Guard. Although he fought with his usual bravery operating directly under Napoleon's eye, at the battle of Craonne Ney once again showed his predilection to commit his troops too early in a rash attack and they paid a terrible price. The French historian Robert Margerit wrote of Ney in 1814, 'he re-entered France sick of fighting, sick of Napoleon, sick of a regime that was incompatible with peace'.[1] As the Allied armies bore down on Paris, Ney took a leading part in forcing Napoleon to abdicate. It was also he who delivered the abdication to Tsar Alexander.

*Ney was quick to be courted by the returning Louis XVIII and enjoyed the opportunity to relax with his family and bask in the glory of his military reputation and the honours he had earned (*Duc d'Elchingen *and* Prince de la Moskowa*). However, he quickly became disillusioned by the policies and behaviour of the émigrés who ignored his advice and treated him, and particularly his wife, with contempt at court. When Napoleon's* *escape from Elba was announced he found himself in a difficult position; apparently snubbed by the new regime yet horrified by the potential implications of Napoleon's return, he seemed to foresee the catastrophe that awaited France. Bound by his oath of loyalty he was one of the first of Napoleon's former marshals to offer his sword to the king, famously promising to bring Napoleon back to Paris in an iron cage. However, as he travelled south he reflected on the slights he had suffered under the Bourbons, the glory and rewards heaped upon him by Napoleon and saw for himself how the whole army and even much of the population rejoiced in Napoleon's return. He increasingly began to question his own loyalties and when he was finally approached by Napoleon's emissaries, he quickly transferred his allegiance back to the emperor he had been instrumental in deposing.*

After having promised Louis XVIII that he would bring Napoleon to Paris in an iron cage, Napoleon only called Marshal Ney to the army very late. He was to join Napoleon at Avesnes on 14 June; just two days before Ney fought the battle of Quatre Bras and with no time for the marshal to properly prepare for a campaign, let alone put together a complete and effective staff. In fact, Ney only met with Napoleon in Charleroi on the afternoon of the 15th when he was nominated as the commander of the left wing of the armée du Nord, *which consisted of I and II Army Corps and a division of cuirassiers. At Waterloo, Ney filled what appears to have been an unofficial role as the tactical commander of the battle and was allocated I and II Army Corps and the cavalry reserve; the other troops, VI Army Corps and the Imperial Guard, remaining under Napoleon's command. After Waterloo, Ney quickly left the army and returned to Paris. Addressing the Chamber of Peers, he did nothing to cover the disaster and almost exaggerated it; this destroyed any chance Napoleon had of clinging on to power. After the restoration, Ney was quickly brought to trial for treason and was shot on 7 December 1815 in the Luxembourg Gardens.*

What is significant about Ney's short account is that once again (a trend we shall see in many accounts) despite Napoleon declaring that he was aware of the Prussian presence and threat long before they actually appeared on the battlefield, one of his most senior commanders describes their appearance as a surprise. Ney actually beat Napoleon back to Paris, having deserted the army immediately after the battle, and it was his speech in the Chamber of Peers, describing it as a catastrophe from which there was no hope of further resistance, that went a long way in turning the chambers against Napoleon.

On the 18th, the battle began at one o'clock, and though the bulletin which details it makes no mention of me, it is not necessary to mention that I was engaged in it. Lieutenant-General Drouot has already spoken of that battle in the House of Peers. His narration is accurate, with the exception of some important facts which he has passed over in silence, or of which he was ignorant, and which it is now my duty to declare. About seven o'clock in the evening, after the most frightful carnage that I have ever witnessed, General Labedoyere came to me with a message from the emperor, that Marshal Grouchy had arrived on our right and attacked the left of the English and Prussians united. The general officer, in riding along the lines, spread this intelligence amongst the soldiers, whose courage and devotion remained unshaken, and who gave new proofs of them at that moment, in spite of the fatigue that they experienced. Immediately after, what was my astonishment, I should rather say indignation, when I learned, that far from Marshal Grouchy having arrived to support us, as the whole army had been assured, between 40 and 50,000 Prussians attacked our extreme right, and forced it to retire!

Whether the emperor was deceived with regard to the time when the marshal would support him, or whether the march of the marshal was retarded by the efforts of the enemy longer than was calculated upon, the fact is, that at the very moment when his arrival was announced to us, he was only at Wavre upon the Dyle, which to us was the same as if he had been a hundred leagues from the field of battle.

A short time afterwards, I saw four regiments of the Middle Guard advancing, led on by the emperor. With these troops he wished to renew the attack, and to penetrate the centre of the enemy. He ordered me to lead them on. Generals, officers, and soldiers, all displayed the greatest intrepidity; but this body of troops was too weak to long resist the forces opposed to it by the enemy, and we were soon compelled to renounce the hope which this attack had for a few moments inspired. General Friant was struck by a ball at my side, and I myself had my horse killed, and fell under it. The brave men who have survived this terrible battle, will, I trust, do me the justice to state, that they saw me on foot, with sword in hand, during the whole of the evening, and that I was one of the last who quitted the scene of carnage at the moment when retreat could no longer be prevented. At the same time the Prussians continued their offensive movements, and our right sensibly gave way. The English also advanced in their turn. There yet remained to us four squares of the Old Guard, to protect our retreat. These brave grenadiers, the flower of the army, forced successively to retire, yielded ground foot by foot, until finally overpowered by numbers, they were almost completely destroyed. From that moment, the retrograde movement was decided, and the army formed nothing but a confused mass. There was not, however, a total rout, nor the cry of '*sauve qui peut*', as has calumniously stated in the bulletin. As for myself, being constantly in the rearguard, which I followed on foot, having had all my horses killed, worn out with fatigue, covered with bruises, and having no longer the strength to walk, I owe my life to a corporal [Mauduit claims this was Corporal Poulet, of the 2nd Grenadiers], who supported me in the march, and did not abandon me in the retreat. At eleven at night, I met Lieutenant General Lefebvre-Desnoëttes; and one of his officers, Major Schmidt, had the generosity to give me the only horse that remained to him. In this manner I arrived at Marchiennes-au-Pont at four o'clock in the morning, alone, without any officers of my staff, ignorant of what had become of the emperor, who, before the end of the battle, had entirely disappeared, and who, I was allowed to believe, might be either killed or taken prisoner.

Colonel Pierre Agathe Heymès

Relation de la Campagne de 1815, dites de Waterloo, pour Servir à L'Histoire du Maréchal Ney, par M. Le Colonel Heymès, son Premier Aide-de-Camp, Témoin Oculaire (Paris, 20 July, 1829), pp. 18–28.

At Waterloo Colonel Heymès served as the senior aide-de-camp to Marshal Ney.

Heymès was born in December 1776, the son of a soldier in the French artillery. He entered the artillery as a soldier in April 1792 (aged just fifteen) and became sergeant in 1797, campaigning with the, armée du Nord, *and the* Moselle *and* Batavie *and was wounded in 1798. He took part in the expedition to Saint-Domingue in 1802–03 and was nominated to a commission in the latter year before being made prisoner by the British. However, he escaped from Jamaica and returned to France via New York. He served during the 1805 campaign before becoming aide-de-camp to General Séroux. In this capacity he served in Prussia and Poland in 1806 and 1807. He then served in Spain for a short time before returning to France to become captain in the 5th Regiment of Horse Artillery, serving with them in Russia in 1812. During this campaign he became aide-de-camp to Marshal Ney. He continued in this position as* chef d'escadron *and was wounded at Bautzen in 1813 and again in 1814 at Brienne. He was promoted colonel in February 1814. After Napoleon's abdication he served as a staff officer in the Royal army until Napoleon's return when he once more served as aide-de-camp to Marshal Ney during the Waterloo campaign. He was put on the inactive list in July 1815 and formally retired in 1823. He returned to duty as aide-de-camp to King Louis-Philippe in 1830 and was promoted to* maréchal de camp *and then lieutenant general in 1838. He then filled a number of staff and inspectorate posts before his death in 1842.*

Heymès did not write on his own adventures at the battle, but wrote with the emphasis on the participation of his chief on the campaign in an effort to counter the criticism that Napoleon and his adherents had raised against Ney. Like Napoleon, Heymès underplays both the scale of the disaster suffered by d'Erlon's corps and the effect of the British cavalry counter-attack. However, like many other French witnesses he appears to have been surprised by the appearance of the Prussians. He admits that Ney made a mistake in committing the cavalry, but says that Napoleon could have stopped them, but didn't. He is also one of only a few Frenchmen that describe the British use of rockets.

At six in the evening [of 17 June], the marshal arrived on the ground in front of the village of Planchenoit; he had the troops deployed for battle as they arrived, for the enemy had stopped on the heights that covered the forest of Soignes where he had established some batteries which caused us serious losses.

The emperor, arriving soon after, gave the order to advance, but the enemy were not shaken; one saw the enemy deployed and showing that he awaited a battle, with his back to the forest of Soignes; his right anchored on the wood and château of Hougoumont, the centre astride the main road, covered by a farm [La Haye Sainte], surrounded by thick hedges that he had strengthened; the left extended towards the village of Mont-Saint-Jean.

The emperor withdrew the troops, and took position for the night. The imperial general headquarters was established in the Caillou farm in the hamlet of Maison-le-Roi [*sic*]. The marshal was in a house close to the emperor with whom he dined and spent part of the evening.

Torrents of rain fell throughout the night.

On the 18th, towards 8am, appeared an order of the day signed by the Duke of Dalmatia, chief of staff which indicated that we were to prepare for the battle which would take place.

The weather was clear and the sun started to dry the ground out a little that had been flooded by rain during the night.

Towards 11am, II Corps took position; one division, its right anchored on the Brussels road, a second division, the left on the Hougoumont wood, each in two lines. The third division was in the rear in reserve, also in two lines. The light cavalry division scouted on the extreme left.

I Corps also took position; its right-hand division opposite the English left, supported on the village of Frischermont, the second division then coming to the third whose left was on the Brussels road, the fourth in the rear, in reserve: the light cavalry, under the orders of General Jacquinot, scouted the extreme right; the artillery was in front of each division.

A battery of sixty guns served by gunners of the Guard was established in range of the enemy with its left supported by the road.

VI Corps, commanded by Count Lobau, was in reserve to the rear of the second [corps], its right supported on the road.

All the cavalry reserves, including the regiments of the Guard, were closed up in mass, ahead of the village of Planchenoit, their left on the main road.

The infantry of the Guard was also in reserve, level with the cavalry reserves, astride the Brussels road. The emperor was on a mound which rose to the left of the road, from where he could see all the ground where the fight would decide the future of France. To the left of the road the ground dropped in a gentle slope to the foot of the position occupied by the enemy. To the contrary, to the right, it rose and formed like a large plateau, which was only at a cannon's range from the English, so that on the front of I Corps, the two armies were only separated by a valley without any obstacles.

Towards midday, a third aide-de-camp and the marshal's horses and equipages happily arrived.

At one o'clock the signal for the attack was given by the grand battery of the Guard; soon after, the action became general.

General d'Erlon directed the attack of the extreme right, the marshal commanding that of the centre under the fire of the grand battery; General Reille attacked the wood and château of Hougoumont.

Towards three o'clock, the enemy, despite the liveliest resistance, was forced to give in to the marshal's efforts and to vacate the centre of his position; but at the same time that he left the height to the left of the road, he executed to the right a cavalry charge which was thrown on a point of I Corps.

To support this charge, he advanced a battery of Congreve rockets, which launched on us more than three hundred rockets which astonished us at first, and then amused us without doing us the least harm.

It was not the same with the two regiments of English dragoons, which launched themselves and came together on one of the divisions of I Corps which having taken fright, became disordered and was soon mixed up in an unformed mass and beyond being capable of firing a shot; all went pell-mell, but we soon managed to make them re-take their order of battle. A battery of reserve artillery which, thinking itself protected by this division, was disorganised to the point that neither a single horse or gunner was to be seen, but these two regiments, wreaking havoc like a swarm of locusts were finally stopped in front of our cavalry reserves. Soon the scene changed; the victors were repulsed, broken, sabred or taken; not one of them was able to regain the English army.

It was a little later that the cannon were heard on our right flank in the rear of the village of Planchenoit; the emperor soon learnt that it was a Prussian corps which had escaped the pursuit of Marshal Grouchy, but he hid this disagreeable movement. This corps having identified the English left, had deployed on our extreme right and extended by its left in the direction of Charleroi.

Bülow, who commanded it, made progress and already his guns swept the road to the rear of the village where general headquarters was established, that the service battalion defended the best it could.

VI Corps, as well as some regiments of cavalry, were sent to oppose the Prussian march, who manoeuvred to cut our communications.

From then on, all the non-combatants, as well as our numerous wounded, retired, heading a little way off the road in the direction of Charleroi. Our batteries, who had only deployed with a first line scale of ammunition, having fired it all off, left the battlefield and took the same direction; all these formed a long column and already resembled a retreat.

It was at this time that the marshal judged the importance of occupying the centre of the position that had been abandoned by the enemy, and having no infantry available to him, demanded a brigade of cavalry. This troop executed its movement at the trot; but no one knows by what rush of blood to the head it was followed by all the reserves, not even forgetting those of the Guard, who as everybody knows, only followed the orders of its own officers or the orders of the emperor.

All this cavalry, totalling 15,000, were jammed together without order and got in each other's way; the first regiments on the summit of the position that was occupied by the enemy, the others on the slope of the plateau.

Several successful charges were executed, but the most advanced soon received fire from the front and flanks from the English infantry which were established in perfect order, along the edge of the Soignes forest in order to be sheltered from the murderous fire of our artillery.

It was later learnt that the spontaneous movement of our cavalry took place because the reserves, placed more than half a league from the battlefield, were not able to judge what was going on, had however seen the enemy abandon his position, thinking it was a retreat, this rumour moreover spread, and the advance of the brigade demanded by the marshal appeared to confirm it. There was danger and glory to be had in the pursuit, all wanted to take part. This false movement was blamed on the marshal, but it was executed under the eyes of the emperor; he could have stopped it, but he did nothing.

The enemy had made only a simple move to the rear to avoid our blows. The English infantry were indeed cornered in the Soignes forest and it was necessary to be on the high ground that it had abandoned to know and be able to judge the great order that it had conserved. The fortified farm which covered his centre resisted all our efforts [to take it]; more than 2,000 of our men had been killed attempting to take it. The attack on the left had not succeeded in making itself masters of the Hougoumont château and, however, all II Corps had been successively drawn there. The attack on the right had made no progress and Count d'Erlon had too much to do on his front and his right, mostly since the arrival of Bülow, to be able to give more troops to the marshal, or to move to support him.

General Durutte's division, of I Corps, had almost alone sustained the attack on the centre, which was the most important, and it maintained itself there with only the greatest efforts, when the marshal demanded the support of the cavalry to occupy the gap which was growing from one moment to the next, between I and II Corps.

The Prussian cannon, that could be heard on our rear, did not fail to worry us. In truth, to destroy this disagreeable impression, the emperor sent his aides-de-camp with the order to spread along the line that these cannon belonged to Marshal Grouchy.

It was six o'clock, the emperor gave the order to renew the attack in the centre that had drawn to a halt; but it needed fresh infantry to do this and the marshal had none available. Half of the soldiers that had been committed to it were dead

Napoleon wrote three accounts of the battle. Although followed by his closest supporters, they have been largely ridiculed by more serious historians.

Marshal Ney wrote nothing of the battle before his execution, but his verbal account to the Chambers that was recorded put a deliberately discouraging slant on the battle.

Along with Marshal Ney, Napoleon laid much of the blame for the failure of the campaign on Marshal Grouchy's failure to prevent the Prussians reaching the battlefield. History has judged him rather better.

Gourgaud was Napoleon's senior *officier d'ordonnance* (orderly officer). His published history of the campaign is widely credited to Napoleon, but he did write his own, more personal account of the campaign.

Flahaut was one of Napoleon's personal aides-de-camp. He does not give a full account of the battle, or his own part in it, but does give some interesting insights to Napoleon's actions during the day.

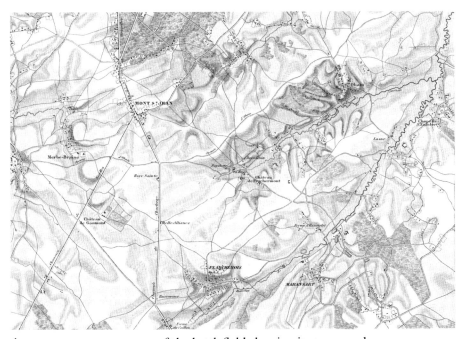

A near-contemporary map of the battlefield showing its topography.

Drouot served as the *Aide-Major-général* of the Imperial Guard and one of Napoleon's closest confidantes. Like Ney, he did not write of the battle but his account delivered to the Chambers was recorded.

D'Erlon commanded I Corps during the campaign. His account is not long but includes some interesting insights to the battle.

Captain Duthilt served as aide-de-camp to General Bourgeois, who commanded the 2nd Brigade of the 1st Division (Quiot vice Allix) in d'Erlon's corps. He gives a detailed and interesting account of the battle as it affected his brigade.

Durutte served as the commander of the 4th Infantry Division, part of I Army Corps. He gives a rather short, but interesting, account of his division's part in the battle.

Colonel Bro commanded the 4th Lancers which were part of the 2nd Brigade (Gobrecht) of the 1st Light Cavalry Division commanded by General Jacquinot. This division was part of I Army Corps and protected the right flank of the corps. He was heavily involved in the repulse of the Union Brigade and was wounded.

An artist's impression of one of d'Erlon's columns at Waterloo. Much criticised with the benefit of hindsight, early descriptions did not give them such a bad press. Neither d'Erlon, nor any of his commanders gave any explanation for their unusual formation.

Rather like the battle for Hougoumont, the fight for La Haye Sainte cost much French effort and blood. However, unlike Hougoumont, it did eventually fall to the French and offered Napoleon a springboard for an assault on the very centre of Wellington's line. Unfortunately, d'Erlon's corps had suffered so much in their main assault that they were unable to fully exploit the opportunity its fall offered.

or wounded, the other half, exhausted, lacked ammunition. The marshal sent his senior aide-de-camp to inform the emperor and to ask for new troops.

The emperor replied, 'Where do you want me to get them from? Do you want me to make them? . . . ' Prince Jérôme and General Drouot heard this reply; it was reported word for word to the marshal who could then see that the battle was far from being won.

However, a final effort finally put us in possession of the fortified farm which covered the enemy centre: it had cost us dear for the little time we were able to hold it.

Between seven and eight o'clock in the evening, the right of the Prussian corps joined the English left forcing our extreme right and pushing it back towards the centre, at the same time threatening the rear of VI Corps.

This audacious march decided the emperor to send four battalions of the Guard to Marshal Ney with which he held up for a short time the enemy's success. This troop paid with its life for the audacity of a defence which had become hopeless; other troops of the Guard also came successively to support the first battalions, but it was too late; everything was useless. The enemy, six times more numerous than us and encouraged by his success, soon marched without obstacle; night fell, disorder appeared in our ranks, all our troops were broken and swept away, even the Guard itself was unable to resist; it followed the torrent and the road was covered in fugitives.

The enemy retook the fortified farm and, having re-established batteries on the plateau that he had abandoned in the morning and let loose his cavalry, heightened our disaster. The emperor got mixed up in the terrible disorder; the rout was complete. Marshal Ney, who had had five horses killed under him on this fateful day, on foot, at the head of the remains of the four battalions of the Guard, was the last to leave the battlefield. An officer of chasseurs à cheval of the Guard gave him his own horse on which he was able to join the road and reach Marchiennes-au-Pont. There he found his vehicle and returned to Paris where the emperor had arrived twenty-four hours before him.

Such is the true account of the disastrous campaign of Waterloo, and what concerned Marshal Ney: can it destroy the false accusations that have spread against one of the bravest warriors of our century, who was at Waterloo what he had always been throughout his glorious career; that he had been at Hohenlinden, at Elchingen, at Guttstadt, at Friedland, in Portugal and during the memorable campaign of Russia where he showed all the energy and highest capacity? Courageous men who survived the misery and cold of that period owe him their lives, the joy of seeing their homeland again and returning to their homes! Can this piece, written after fourteen years by an impartial witness, prove to those who read it that sooner or later the truth will be revealed and do justice to the accusations with which ignorance or poor faith have attempted to denounce him.

Chef d'Escadron Octave Levavasseur

Levavasseur, *Souvenirs Militaires d'Octave Levavasseur, officier d'artillerie aide de camp du maréchal Ney (1802–1815)* (Paris: Plon, 1914), pp. 294–307.

At Waterloo, Levavasseur served as aide-de-camp to Marshal Ney.

Octave Levavasseur was commissioned into the artillery in 1803. He took part in the 1805 campaign against Austria and fought at Hollabrün and Austerlitz where he was wounded. He then entered Prussia in 1806 and fought at Jena and the taking of Magdeburg. He fought at the terrible battle of Eylau in1807 and later in that year was attached to Marshal Ney's headquarters before fighting at Friedland. After the peace of Tilsit he returned to France prior to spending two years in Spain with Marshal Ney, serving at a number of battles against the Spanish and in pursuit of Moore at Corunna and later Wellington after Talavera. On his return to France he resigned his commission and lived in Paris from 1809 to 1814 when he returned to service as an aide-de-camp of Marshal Ney. He took part in most of the key battles in this campaign including Brienne, la Rothière, Champaubert, Montmirail, Vauchamps, Montereau, Craonne and Arcis-sur-Aube. In 1815 he remained with Ney during this marshal's time near the king and his defection to Napoleon. He fought at Quatre Bras and Waterloo. He lost contact with Ney at the end of the battle and slowly made his own way back to Paris with the army where he once more met up with him. On Ney's departure from the capital, in July 1815 he became aide-de-camp to General Dessolle who was the commander of the Paris National Guard. In September of the same year he was admitted into the artillery of the Royal Guard. However, unwelcome in the Guard as an officer who had fought for Napoleon at Waterloo, he was sent home on half pay where he became an object of constant observation by the police. His souvenirs finish with the execution of Marshal Ney. At his own request he re-entered service in 1829, but moved from regiment to regiment without any real service. He finally retired in 1832 and died in 1866 aged eighty-five.

Levavasseur's account is largely self-serving but does include some interesting personal vignettes. He makes much of his own participation and contribution, although there is little to challenge in his narrative. His loyalty is clearly to Marshal Ney first and Napoleon second. What is of interest, and which contradicts many histories of the battle, is his claim that Marshal Ney used his senior aide-de-camp, Crabet (actually Crabbé), to command a composite force, composed of a squadron from each of the cuirassier regiments [probably of just Watier's division] to support the left flank of d'Erlon's assault. This was the force that was attacked and defeated by Somerset's Household Brigade. He too appears surprised by the intervention of the Prussians, apparently having been taken in by the deception that the firing from that flank was from Grouchy.

On 18 June, realising that the enemy had taken position in front of the Soignes forest and that the crest of Mont-Saint-Jean was bristling with cannons, the emperor judged that it was there that Wellington wanted to give battle; he had the army deploy into attack columns and disposed them in lines parallel to those of the English. Prince Jérôme commanded the left wing [actually it was Reille, who commanded II Corps of which Jérôme's division was a part]; Counts Reille and d'Erlon marched in the centre; Lobau and Duhesme on the right. Marshal Ney had the command of the infantry and cavalry. We were separated from the English army by a small valley in which was found the main road and the farm of La Haye Sainte, situated close to the enemy line. Whilst our troops took position, balls took off several files. But the order to attack was still not sent.

At daylight, the marshal gave me the mission of conducting a reconnaissance of the ground and the enemy's movements. I left on this mission on the extreme left; I had spoken to all the *vedettes* along the way, from which I learnt nothing. However, reaching the extreme left, the *vedette* pointed out detachments coming and going on this side; that single officers were sent off in this direction. I remained an hour on the ground and, after assuring myself of the truth of this observation, I re-joined the marshal, convinced that the enemy would manoeuvre on our right.

The marshal had moved close to the emperor; I hurried towards him and announced the result of my mission and my conclusions. Addressing himself to the emperor, he said, 'Sire, my aide-de-camp, who has just come back from a reconnaissance, has declared to me that the enemy seems to want to manoeuvre by our right'.

'It is well, that's fine', replied the emperor.

A little before midday, the emperor dictated the order that Soult wrote in his notebook, then the chief of staff tore off the page and gave it to Marshal Ney, who before he gave it to me to take to the commanding generals, wrote in the margin in pencil, 'Count d'Erlon is to understand that it is him that is to start the attack'.*

By ordering to push straight on Mont-Saint-Jean, Napoleon proposed not to turn the enemy's left, but to pierce straight through the centre of the English line.

---

* Note of the editor: The order dated 18 June, 11am, said that 'at a little after 1pm, when the emperor gives the order to Marshal Ney, the attack will start to seize the village of Mont-Saint-Jean'. An attack prepared by the artillery of I, II and VI Corps and directed by d'Erlon, 'advancing in the lead his left hand division and supporting it with the other divisions of I Corps'. On the copy of this order preserved in the Archives de la Guerre, it is mentioned that the original from the hand of Soult carried in the margin this note in pencil and signed by Ney, 'Count d'Erlon is to understand that it is by the left, instead of the right, that the attack is to start. Send this new disposition to General Reille'. This note, a little different from that of the memory of M. Levavasseur, seems to indicate that other instructions had been given to d'Erlon to attack with his right, that is to say on Papelotte and la Haye.

Towards 11.30am, the emperor ordered Reille to open the combat on the left (Prince Jerôme) against Hougoumont, to precede the principle attack with a demonstration. Then at 1.30pm, the order was sent to Ney in view of this last, who was to start immediately afterwards against La Haye Sainte and the crest of the plateau of Mont-Saint-Jean. At this same moment the approach of the Prussians was signalled far on the right, in the direction from which Napoleon awaited Grouchy! It was Bülow's corps, sent by Blücher as support to Wellington's 67,000 men. The Prussians deployed towards Planchenoit in front of VI Corps, setting off at 4.30, then a second attack against La Haye Sainte had been repulsed and Ney had launched at the charge the squadrons of Milhaud and Lefebvre-Desnouëttes. At the end of the day, two other Prussian corps followed successively onto the battlefield . . .

I departed by the left at the gallop and I first reached Prince Jérôme, whose troops occupied a valley in mass, in the rear of a small wood. I continued, but before arriving with General d'Erlon, my horse crashed down and the paper, falling onto the ground, became almost undecipherable, so that I was obliged to help his reading. Returning close to Marshal Ney, I found him behind La Haye Sainte. Count d'Erlon had already started his attacking movement; the battle was engaged. The marshal called together all the colonels of the cavalry and gave them the order for each regiment to send him a squadron. These squadrons being formed up behind him, he said to one of his most senior aides-de-camp, Crabet, a retired *générale de brigade*, who had returned to his service a few days before, to take command of this cavalry, and added, 'follow on the left and sweep aside all you find between the enemy artillery and his infantry on the ground behind la Haye Sainte'. During this time Count d'Erlon advanced in the middle of the canister shot on the slope of the plateau, but did not succeed in taking the position. Crabet set off and dropped into the valley; the marshal returned and addressing himself to me, said, 'Levavasseur, go with this charge'. I left and joined Crabet at the front. After having crossed the line of enemy artillery, Crabet formed them into column of squadrons and ordered the charge. We launched with shouts of '*Vive l'Empereur! En avant!*' Before us all the artillery horses rushed off, abandoning their guns. The infantry even appeared to conform with this movement and beat a retreat: not a shot was fired at us, even though we were in range. Clouet, who had deserted, later reported to me that this charge had routed the English army and that he was going to Gand [to join Louis XVIII] when the whole road was covered in fugitives that it had chased off. He then told me that his humiliation was at its height to see this stampede and the preparations for the departure of the king to Gand, where our movement had sounded the alarm.

However, deployed on the enemy's ground, having all his artillery unlimbered behind us, we remained in this situation for more than a quarter of an hour, in view of our entire army which remained motionless. Without doubt, the emperor did not want to leave his position to take that we had conquered before his was occupied by Grouchy's corps that he awaited.

But terrible shouts could be heard far to our right. I reached the sentries on this side and soon a considerable mass of cavalry appeared nearby, moving towards us at a gallop. At this perilous moment, I wanted to turn my horse round, which reared up; it was impossible to make it move. Happily, a cuirassier on sentry close to me took the bridle; I spurred it on and regained the rear of our cavalry which was already galloping back to our own lines. Crabet reached the road close to La Haye Sainte. At the same moment, a column of cavalry sent to our support, came down the road that we returned on, thus barring our passage. Suddenly, the head of the column stopped and the enemy cavalry fell on our rear; our troopers pressed up together in this enclosed space to such an extent that they could not defend themselves. I heard only the clashing of sabres that penetrated under the cuirasses of the cavalry; the enemy made a terrible slaughter. But General Colbert [this was General Louis de Colbert who commanded the 1st Brigade in Subervie's division, not to be confused with his elder brother Edouard de Colbert, commander of the Guard lancers], commanding the cavalry coming to meet us, took the squadrons that were not engaged in the defile, then, turning the knoll that held us, he fell unexpectedly on the enemy who, stuck also in the defile, cut to pieces the cavalry that had fallen on us. Thus we were able to break clear. I had been able, due to the speed of my horse, to regain the rear of Crabet's column, leaving behind me two hundred cuirassiers who were massacred; their horses formed a barrier which prevented the enemy from reaching us. An English officer having been killed in the mêlée four paces from me, I took his horse which served me though the rest of the battle.

During this charge, an artillery fire was maintained by both sides. A terrible fusillade was heard to our left, in the small wood in front of Prince Jérôme. The marshal sent me to see what was happening; I passed the prince at the gallop, who was still deployed in mass in the valley. Despite the balls that whistled past my ears, I approached the wood which held our infantry and I found all the men posted behind trees, pleading for support. The colonel asked me with authority to have more troops sent to disengage him. Jérôme had sent only two regiments to take this wood that was held by 6,000 men. These two regiments had crossed the open plain and had reached as far as the wood, but were not able to go further because the enemy were shooting them down. I returned as quickly as possible close to Prince Jérôme and told him heatedly that the wood could only be taken by force using his whole division and that by only sending two regiments he had got them massacred. This position, attacked again by Prince Jérôme and Count Reille, was taken and retaken several times during the day.

I galloped back close to Marshal Ney, who had then come to give General *** the order to take the farm of La Haye Sainte with about 3,000 men. These marched in close column towards the farm, but, arriving nearby, moved to the right and came under fire out in the open at close range of this building. The marshal, indignant at seeing the hesitation of this general, sent me to tell him to take the position with a charge. I went down towards the road where I found two companies of engineers lining a bank. The captain approached me and, handing me his card, said, 'Monsieur aide-de-camp. Take it, here is my name'. Then he had the charge beaten and his engineers ran towards the farm to shouts of '*En avant!*' and, whilst I moved off to the general to inform him of the marshal's order, the engineers had already seized the gardens and hedges and driven back the enemy towards their rear, all in view of the infantry, who marched forwards to support the attack. La Haye-Sainte was occupied by our troops, but the English, coming in superior strength, soon re-took it.

Whilst this was going on, the battle rumbled on all around, yet without our army making much progress. Our efforts to break the English line were fruitless. However, the enemy's resistance appeared to be weakening at several points.

At 6pm, General Dejean arrived close to Marshal Ney (one of Napoleon's aides-de-camp, as well as generals Drouot and Bertrand who were also sent out at this time to make the same announcement). '*Monsieur le maréchal*', he said, '*Vive l'Empereur!* Here is Grouchy!' The marshal immediately ordered me to ride along the whole line and announce Grouchy's arrival. Breaking into a gallop, raising my hat on the tip of my sabre and passing along the front of the line, '*Vive l'Empereur!*' I shouted to the soldiers, 'Here is Grouchy!' This sudden shout was repeated by a thousand voices; the excitement of the soldiers was indescribable; they all shouted '*En avant! En avant! Vive l'Empereur!*'

Hardly had I arrived at the extremity of our line, than cannon fire was heard in our rear. The greatest silence, astonishment, anxiety, followed the enthusiasm. The plain was covered with our wagons and a multitude of non-combatants who always followed the army; the cannonade continued and got closer. Officers and soldiers got muddled up, mixed with the non-combatants. I came, appalled, to the marshal who ordered me to go to find out the cause of this panic. I arrived with General *** who said to me, 'See! These are the Prussians!' I returned to find the marshal, but could not. Our army then only presented an unformed mass, with all the regiments mixed up. At this fatal moment, command had broken down, each remained taken aback in the presence of a danger they could not define. Drouot came shouting, 'Where is the Guard? Where is the Guard?' I showed it to him; he approached it calling 'Form square!' I then saw the emperor pass close by me, followed by his officers. Arriving close to the guard, which was in front of him on the other side of the road; 'Who will follow me?' he said, and he marched ahead along the road that was beaten by a hundred guns.

Then a hundred and fifty musicians went down at the head of the Guard, playing the triumphant marches of the Carrousel. Soon, the road was covered by this Guard that marched by pelotons behind the emperor; the balls and canister struck them down, leaving the road scattered with killed and wounded. Another few paces and Napoleon would have been alone in front. Without doubt his first resolution had been to take refuge in the square and to await death there; the second to perish in the advance.

However, in the middle of this carnage, behind the road, I saw a group of horsemen go past; I thought I recognised the emperor. I went towards this group; it was indeed Napoleon, who death had spared and who silently retraced his steps. He rode into the plain, to the right of the *chausée*. Our disorganised army, the head of which fled in disorder towards Genappe, blocked the route. I followed the emperor and his headquarters for some time; each maintained a sad silence. However, considering that I should re-join the marshal, I retraced my steps and searched in vain, for now the danger was at the rear. It was reported to me that the marshal, seeing this terrible rout, had dismounted and had stopped for an instant on a bank. There he doubtlessly considered the misfortunes that would again descend on France. He perhaps also thought what fate awaited him, for, since his proclamation, he no longer lived; he only desired death and did everything to find it.

It was night; desperate to find my marshal, I re-joined the column, which could hardly move and that the enemy did not pursue. What astonished me, on my arrival at Genappe, was to see this town full of vehicles, to the point that it was impossible to pass them on the roads. The soldiers were obliged to crawl under the equipages to effect a passage; the cavalry by-passed the town. Reaching beyond that place along the road, indignant at seeing no rallying, I placed myself across it and drawing my sabre, I shouted, 'From the emperor, no one is to pass!' A hussar officer, thinking that I had received the order to act thus, put himself at my side and the two of us blocked the passage. Then we heard all the officers and soldiers calling; 'Here the 25th, the 12th, the 18th etc. etc'. All tried to rally and the whole night passed to these calls. However, several general officers and others wanted to challenge the instructions that I had thought up: 'No one is to pass!' I said and they remained. I can name the aide-de-camp of the emperor, Forbin-Janson, who, despite saying he was wounded, was forced to stop by me like the others.

However, towards three o'clock, I thought that the emperor would have fixed the rallying point behind the Sambre and that when he was seen by the army it would reassemble there before day. Also, not having seen my marshal come by and thinking that he would have reached Charleroi, I persuaded the commander of the nearest regiment furthest from me to continue his retreat. Then, the whole column reassembled in order to raise the camp and to head for Charleroi. I went at the gallop and entered the town; a debacle worse still. The soldiers fled; terror was at its height: one could only see abandoned helmets, muskets, baggage.

The emperor had left without giving orders and everyone had fled as quickly as possible to Avesnes as if the enemy was after him.

Lieutenant-General *Comte* Antoine Drouot

Account of the Campaign in the Netherlands given by General Count Drouot, *Aide-Major-général* of the Imperial Guard on 18 June 1815 in the Chamber of Peers, 24 June 1815; translated from the *Moniteur*. Given by George Jones in *The Battle of Waterloo with those of Ligny and Quatre Bras described by Eyewitnesses and by the series of Official Accounts published by Authority* (London: L. Booth, 1852).

At Waterloo, Drouot served as the Aide-Major-général *of the Imperial Guard, effectively the overall commander of the Guard.*

    Drouot was the son of a baker, born in 1774. He was commissioned into the artillery in 1793 after graduating top in his class. He fought at the battles of Hondschoote, Wattignies and Fleurus and became captain in 1796. He then moved down to Italy where he was involved in the invasion and occupation of Naples before returning to France and then fighting at Hohenlinden. From 1804 he filled a number of administrative posts in the artillery and although these denied him active service, it exploited his identified organisational and training skills. It was only in 1808 that he got his big break when he was posted to the Imperial Guard to help organise its newly-formed artillery arm. He raised and organised the first four companies of the Guard artillery and then led them into Spain. However, he was recalled to face the Austrians in 1809 and his batteries made a significant contribution to the victory and where he received his only wound. Promoted colonel, he became the commander of the Guard artillery. In 1812 he left for Russia and fought at Smolensk and Borodino, then returned to Paris during the retreat when all his guns had been abandoned. Promoted to général de brigade, *he raised a new Guard artillery force for the 1813 campaign which fought with distinction at Lützen and Bautzen. He formed a grand battery which supported the attack of the Guard at Leipzig and fought again at Hanau. The Guard took a leading role in the 1814 campaign and Drouot fought at Brienne, la Rothiere, Montmirail, Craonne (where he fought as part of a gun crew), Laon and Arcis-sur-Aube. He accompanied Napoleon into exile on Elba and escorted him back to France in 1815, although he cautioned against it. At first he was appointed commander of the Guard artillery, but in April became* Aide-Major-général *of the whole of the Guard; in the absence of Marshal Mortier, this effectively gave him responsibility for the whole of the Guard. He fought at Ligny and Waterloo. In the latter battle he helped to organise the final attack of the Guard and after the defeat, he remained with the army as it retreated back to Paris. After Napoleon's abdication he was appointed commander of the Guard by the provisional government. He was prescribed by the Second Restoration, but refusing to flee, he was*

imprisoned in Paris. He defended himself in front of a Council of War and was acquitted.
Although recalled to the army in 1820 he refused any position and formally retired in
1825. He died in 1847.

This is a largely uncontroversial, even sterile, account which follows the generally
accepted phases of the battle.

[On the 17th] . . . The emperor followed the English with I, II and VI Corps,
and the Imperial Guard.

I Corps, which was in the van, attacked, and several times overthrew the
enemy's rear and followed it till night, when it took up a position on the plateau
behind the village of Mont-Saint-Jean; its right extending towards the village of
Braine, and its left stretching indefinitely in the direction of Wavre. The weather
was dreadful. Everybody was persuaded that the enemy was taking a position
merely to give time for his parks of artillery and baggage to traverse the forest
of Soignies, and that he would himself execute the same movement at daybreak.

At break of day the enemy was perceived in the same position. The weather
was horrible, which had so ruined the roads that it was impossible to manoeuvre
with the artillery in the field. Towards day, nine o'clock, the weather cleared up,
the wind dried the land a little, and the order of attack at noon was given by the
emperor.

Was it right to attack the enemy in this position, with troops fatigued by several
days' long marches, a great battle, and various actions; or should they have been
allowed time to recover from their fatigues, and the enemy permitted to retreat
quietly to Brussels?

If we had been fortunate, all military men would have declared that it would
have been an unpardonable fault not to pursue a retreating army, when it was but
a few leagues from its own capital, whither we were invited by numerous partisans.

Fortune has betrayed our efforts, and now it is considered as a great act of
imprudence to give battle. Posterity, more just, will decide.

II Corps began the attack at noon. The division commanded by Prince
Jérôme attacked the wood which was before the enemy's right. He advanced at first
and was repulsed, and did not remain wholly master of it till after an obstinate
combat of many hours.

I Corps, whose left leaned on the high road, attacked at the same time the
houses of Mont-Saint-Jean, established itself there, and advanced as far as the
enemy's position. Marshal Ney, who commanded the two corps, was himself on
the high road, to direct the movements according to circumstances.

The marshal told me, during the battle, that he was going to make a great effort
against the centre of the enemy, while the cavalry should pick up the cannon,
which did not seem to be much supported. He told me several times when I
brought him orders that we were going to gain a great victory.

Meantime, the Prussian corps, which had joined the left of the English, placed itself *en potence* [effectively at right angles to the main line of battle] upon our right flank, and began to attack about half-past five in the afternoon. VI Corps, which had taken no part in the battle of the 16th, was placed to oppose them, and was supported by a division of the Young Guard and some battalions of the [Old] Guard. Towards seven o'clock we perceived in the distance, towards our right, a fire of artillery and musketry. It was not doubted except that Marshal Grouchy had followed the movement of the Prussians, and was come to take part in the victory. Cries of joy were heard along our whole line. The troops, fatigued by eight combats [a note here suggests it meant eight hours of combats], recover their vigour and make new efforts. The emperor regards this moment as decisive. He brings forward all his guard; orders four battalions to pass near the village of Mont-Saint-Jean, to advance against the enemy's position, and to carry with the bayonet whatever should resist them. The cavalry of the Guard, and all the other cavalry that remained at hand, seconded this movement. The four battalions, when they arrived on the plateau, were received by the most terrible fire of musketry and grape. The great number of wounded who separate from the columns make it believed that the Guard is routed; a panic terror communicates itself to the neighbouring corps, which precipitously take flight. The enemy's cavalry, which perceives this disorder, is let loose into the plain; it is checked for some time by the twelve battalions of the Old Guard who had not yet charged: but even these troops were carried away by this inexplicable movement, and followed the steps of the fugitives but with more order.

All the carriages of the artillery hurry towards the great road; soon they are so thronged together that it is impossible to make them proceed; they are mostly abandoned in the road and unyoked by the soldiers, who carry away the horses. All hasten towards the bridge of Charleroi, and meet at Marchiennes, whence the wrecks were directed upon Avesnes and Philippeville.

Such is the account of this fateful day. It was to crown the glory of the French army, to destroy all the vain hopes of the enemy, and perhaps soon to give to France the peace so much desired; but Heaven has decided otherwise: it is thought fit, that after so many catastrophes our unhappy country should be once more exposed to the ravages of foreigners . . .

Chef d'Escadron Marie-Élie-Guilliame-Alzéar de Baudus

Études sur Napoléon, par le Lieutenant-Colonel de Baudus, Ancien Aide-de-Camp des Maréchaux Bessières et Soult (Paris: Debécourt, 1841), Vol. 1, pp. 224–30.

Baudus served at Waterloo as aide-de-camp to Marshal Soult, and was thus part of imperial headquarters. Whilst he does not give many personal anecdotes, his comments on the battle are incorporated into his two-volume study on Napoleonic warfare, he does include some interesting facts and insights. Baudus was wounded during the battle. We have little information on him prior to 1815; however, in the preface of his book he writes, 'Having made the ten last campaigns of the wars of the empire as aide-de-camp, first close to Marshal Bessières, from the battle of Eylau until his death [in 1813], and then close to Marshal Soult until the end of the war (July 1815), I was nearly always to be found at Napoleon's general headquarters.'

Baudus concentrates on the arrival of the Prussians and tells us that Soult had always been worried about their appearance, whilst Napoleon seemed unconvinced that they could have an impact on the battle. He is very critical of Napoleon's decision to inform the army that the Prussian arrival was actually that of Grouchy. Once more we have a credible witness undermining Napoleon's accounts that say that he was fully aware of the Prussian threat.

On the evening of the 17th, the headquarters was established in the farm of Caillou; all the reports received during the night confirmed that the English remained in their positions and therefore seemed disposed to accept battle. Besides, it was easy to judge by the fires which crowned all the heights; a spectacle that our army surely did not present to its adversaries, for parts of the units that composed it marched all night to arrive on the positions which had been designated for them, and occupied them so late that they hardly had time to light fires to dry themselves by.

The *major-général* [chief-of-staff; Soult], persisting in his opinion that Napoleon was at fault to give two complete infantry corps to Marshal Grouchy, believed he had to advise him [Napoleon] to immediately recall a large part for the action the next day, but his observation on this matter was not listened to in the evening any more than they had been in the morning.

Towards nine o'clock in the morning, the rain having ceased, a strong wind rose which quickly dried the ground which was elevated, the army deployed into its line of battle. The emperor placed himself to the left of the main road on ground which dominated the battlefield. He was brought a small table on which he spread his maps; he remained there for almost the whole time that the action lasted, in a kind of apathy very similar to that which he was accused of on the day of the battle of la Moscowa; he only closed up on his troops that were engaged at the moment that he had to direct the timely use of his reserve.

The chief-of-staff, always under the shadow of concern that the Prussians would arrive on our right during the action, observed this part of the battlefield with particular attention. I saw him, towards 1pm, approach Napoleon and warn him that he distinctly saw a numerous body of troops whose arms were glistening. A few moments later, a sergeant in the Prussian cavalry was led to him who had been captured and searched, and on whom was found a message written in crayon, addressed from General Bülow to the English general, announcing to him that he was in a position to support him. It was only then that the emperor decided to send an officer to Marshal Grouchy to order him to march, by Saint-Lambert, against General Bülow's corps; but it was too late and one could see by the report of this marshal that he would not be able to arrive close to him until 7pm. Thus it was nothing less than this discovery, made by the *major-général*, to convince the emperor that he ran the risk of seeing part of the Prussian army arrive on his right flank; until then he had refused to consider this regrettable possibility. Everyone judged that the adoption of Marshal Soult's advice on the evening of the 17th would have been advantageous to us, if one wanted to recall that Marshal Grouchy's infantry had almost sufficed to beat the Prussian army at Fleurus.

We will not enter into great details of the movements of the army during this unfortunate day, for there has been a relation made with accuracy for a long time. We will only observe that following the fine cavalry charge that Marshal Ney executed, for a moment we had in our hands sixty guns belonging to the English army, and that we were not able to carry them off because the limbers had been sent off, thanks to the speed with which they had been detached, as the teams had not been attached [to the *prolonge*].[2] Our artillery would do well to adopt this innovation in its new materiel; but a thing which I have never understood, is why we have not given to each regiment, to some men known for their daring, all that they need to be able to quickly spike, in such similar circumstances, the guns taken. We know well enough that sometimes there would not be time to achieve this, but in the affair of which we speak, after what I have heard from officers who were present, we had the opportunity to make these guns unusable before being forced to abandon them.

I cannot find the words to render the impression that I then suffered, returning from carrying orders to the right wing, where I had seen the balls and bullets of Bülow's corps falling around VI Corps, which had been deployed *en potence* parallel to the main road to oppose the attack of this part of the Prussian army. I heard Napoleon give the order to make it known along the whole line that it was the fire of Marshal Grouchy that could be heard on this flank. This significant lie, whose aim was to support by a last effort the attack by part of the Guard against the centre of the English army, produced its effect, but aggravated our situation; it animated not only the fit men, but to their credit, it animated even the wounded; for all those that were still able, dragged themselves up and advanced on the enemy to shouts of '*Vive l'Empereur!*' This enthusiasm, the hope for which was to regain the victory, burst through the army, only inspired more anger against the man who had abused those when he knew well to be able to flatter with success in the terrible situation in which we found ourselves. Besides, it had the immense inconvenience of almost completely disorganising the major part of this magnificent reserve of the Old Guard which, if it had remained complete, would have been able to protect the retreat and prevent in part, the enormous losses that we suffered as a result of the disorder in which we left the battlefield. The emperor, in giving the order to spread this fake information of Grouchy's arrival, made dupes even of his headquarters, for I heard a courtier say (he must be undoubtedly sincere to not forget his role in such a moment); 'It is a repeat of Marengo; the arrival of Marshal Grouchy today, is what in 1800, for the Army of Reserve, was the arrival of General Desaix's division.' This illusion did not last long. These veteran troops approached the enemy with all the vigour that one could have expected of them, but unfortunately, the game was too unequal; also they were decimated by canister and musketry fire from an enormous mass of enemy.

After the unfortunate result of this attack, there only remained a few regiments of the Old Guard that had not been committed; these troops formed in square to cover the retreat. It was into the middle of one of these squares that the Emperor placed himself; only a small number of officers were allowed in so it would not be overcrowded; for my part, I was not admitted.

I will not reproach Napoleon with not exposing himself to danger at this moment; there were certainly great dangers where he placed himself to supervise the execution of his last orders, since I was wounded by a shell splinter a few paces from him; but at the moment when he decided to attempt this desperate attack, I believe he needed to put himself at the head of his Guard and to have sought death if it did not succeed.

I examined him closely in this last act of his military life, and, in thinking of all the misfortune that this man had brought upon my country, for all the calamities this defeat had prepared for us, I suffered such a profound sorrow, that I was seized by such a lively indignation, that I still reproach myself today for all that caused me anxiety in the middle of the disorder of the retreat, the fear that he would fall into the hands of the enemy, if in this worry there had only been concern for his person. I would, I confess, considered as a good thing for my country if he had been killed, but I would have been sorry if he had remained a prisoner; this event would have appeared to me to be dishonourable for this army, which, on his return from the island of Elba, had thrown itself into his arms with such enthusiasm. Also, after having lost from view the square in the middle of which he had taken his place, I re-joined the debris of the cavalry of the Guard, which again maintained a perfect order. I shared my concerns with Generals Lefebvre-Desnouëttes and Lallemand, and I requested them to only retire slowly, in order to be able to offer him a point of refuge in case the infantry square which protected his retreat no longer offered him enough security.

Colonel Augustin Louis Petiet

Mémoires du Général Auguste Petiet, Hussard de l'Empire, Souvenirs Historiques, Militaires et Particuliers, 1784–1815 (Paris: S. P. M., 1996), pp. 441–7.

In 1815 Petiet served as adjutant-commandant *(staff colonel) attached to the* Grand-quartier général *(general headquarters) under the orders of Marshal Soult.*

Petiet was born in 1784 at Rennes; his father was a war commissary and he started his early military service in a similar role. However, in 1800 he was commissioned into the 10th Hussars in the Army of Italy. In 1803 he found himself working as a junior staff officer to the then General Soult and the following year, as lieutenant. In 1805 he became one of Soult's aides-de-camp. This did not stop him charging with a division of dragoons at Austerlitz. He took part in the campaigns of 1806 and 1807 before being promoted to captain in the 8th Hussars. After a short, but distinguished period of regimental duty, he returned as aide-de-camp to Marshal Soult. Promoted to chef d'escadron, *he served in Spain, taking part in a number of actions and being wounded twice. In January 1813 he became captain in the 2nd Regiment of Chevaux-Légers Lanciers of the Imperial Guard. He took part in the 1813 campaign in this regiment and became* adjutant-commandant *in November of that year; working in the headquarters of General Piré's cavalry division through the campaign of 1814. He fought at Brienne and was wounded twice at Nangis where he captured fourteen guns. He was retained in the army after the First Restoration and served in imperial headquarters during the 1815 campaign. Although promoted* maréchal de camp *in July 1815, on the Second Restoration this rank was not confirmed and he retired as* adjutant-commandant. *In 1818 he was recalled to service in Royal headquarters, but just a year later he moved on to a number of staff posts before finding himself in a divisional headquarters during the expedition to North Africa in 1830 at the end of which he was promoted to* maréchal de camp. *He continued to serve in various staff posts until his retirement in 1846. He died in Paris in 1858.*

As one of Soult's staff officers, it is unlikely that Petiet saw much of the battlefield, and yet offers us considerable detail on the battle. Despite his privileged position which must have given him a good understanding of the strategic situation and overview of the battle, there can be little doubt that much, if not all, of the detail must have come from hearsay and what he subsequently read. And all this despite the statement that he would not describe what he did not see for himself! He makes the claim that an order had been sent to Grouchy on the evening of the 17th informing him of the imminent battle; this is the same claim made by Napoleon in his memoirs, a claim that has been widely disputed. As we can see that Petiet wrote these lines after reading the accounts of others (see his reference to Heymès' account), it is likely that this claim is made on the basis of Napoleon's account rather than something he knew for himself. Despite all this, Petiet's is an interesting and well-written account.

It was six o'clock in the evening. Marshal Ney deployed his troops in line. The emperor, impatient to arrive in Brussels and who counted on the remaining two and a half hours of daylight, gave the order to advance. But the enemy deployed and showed that he was awaiting battle against the Soignes forest, the left extending towards the village of Mont-Saint-Jean and the right supported on the Houg[ou]-mont wood. His batteries had already caused us considerable casualties. Our army, tired out by a painful march on a muddy road, was not concentrated. Napoleon had the troops pulled back and we deployed ourselves to pass the night parallel to the enemy army in front of and behind the village of Planchenoit.

Imperial headquarters was located at the farm of Caillou on the road from Charleroi to Brussels, not far from that village. During the evening and entire night, the rain continued to fall in torrents, making the troops in their bivouacs suffer cruelly in the middle of the mud and destroying the wheat littered on the ground by the storm and this fatal deluge. The Anglo-Belgian army, arriving early at their position, had their rations assured. Our enemies were also able to dry their clothing and regain their strength. The French soldiers, without rations, were still on their marches and counter-marches to reach the areas fixed for their bivouacs. The obscurity, caused by this beating rain, extended its veil on us earlier than we would have expected in the month of June. The infantrymen, searching for their bivouacs and the isolated men their regiments, after a vain search found shelter in the houses and were the cause of some disorder.

I think it necessary to repeat here that I am not writing a history of the campaign of 1815, which is waiting to be done, but that I recount my souvenirs in a quick sketch. Consequently, most of the military events that did not pass before my eyes or of which I was imperfectly aware have been neglected in my narration. I would have liked, like my comrades, that this sad day of the 18th June took the name of Mont-Saint-Jean [rather than Waterloo], a small hamlet which is celebrated today, that we took from the English and which ended by costing us so dear!

Daylight having appeared, the French army took up its arms to the number of 65,000 combatants and not 120,000 as has been said too lightly. The enemy who had, including the arrival of the Prussians, a force equal to this latter number, found it better to confirm this version to guarantee their glory. One could see towards the centre and to the rear of Mont-Saint-Jean, strong masses of English infantry which crowned a vast plateau in front of which we thought we could distinguish redoubts, the ground appearing of a different colour to that of the soil. But general of engineers Haxo, who approached it and whose *coup d'oeil* was so sure, informed the emperor that he had seen no trace of fortifications. This plateau which stretched to both flanks along the edge of the forest, was covered in batteries.

The enemy made no movement; we were tempted to think that the day would pass in reconnaissances, the waterlogged roads not permitting either the artillery to move nor the cavalry to manoeuvre. But at nine o'clock in the morning, a strong wind dried the fields and roads a little. The orders of the chief of staff reached the various corps and made known that there would be an attack.

At eleven o'clock, the army, in several lines, had occupied the prescribed positions. The corps of General Reille was on our left, between the main road from

Nivelles and that from Charleroi. Jérôme's division, closer to the wood of Houg[ou]
mont, then that of General Foy and General Bachelu extended the troops to the
Charleroi road, close to the farm of la Belle-Alliance. Count Lobau's corps was
placed behind the second line of II Corps, along and to the left of the main road
from Charleroi. The light cavalry of General Jacquinot and Subervie's division were
to our extreme right to communicate with the troops of Marshal Grouchy, who
the emperor had ordered to direct his movements on Wavres in order to approach
our left [?; he must mean right] by Mont-Saint-Lambert, not neglecting to link
his communications with us. I Corps, commanded by Count d'Erlon, was astride
the main road and formed our centre. The cavalry were spread amongst various
points of the line. The Imperial Guard was in reserve on the heights in the centre.
Finally, eighty guns were deployed to beat the enemy positions.

The emperor passed through the lines of the army and was received, as always,
with acclamations. He dismounted and took up his position on a fairly high mound
just near La Belle Alliance, from which he could see the whole battlefield and the
two armies waiting to come to grips. Napoleon had spread a map on his small
table and whilst examining it, he appeared buried in deep strategic combinations.
From the foot of this mound where I found myself, I could not take my eyes off
this extraordinary man that victory had fulfilled his talents! His stoutness, his
dull white face, his heavy gait rendered him very different to General Bonaparte
that I had seen at the beginning of my career, during the campaign of the Year
VIII in Italy, in a state of thinness so frightening that no soldier of his army could
understand how a body so frail and an appearance so sickly could survive such
fatigues! Alas! his sufferings, his torments, had not yet come to an end. The martyr
of Sainte-Hélène had once more to exercise his courage.

The second letter from the army chief of staff addressed to the corps commanders, informed them that, towards 1pm, Marshal Ney would commence the
attack on the village of Mont-Saint-Jean, at the cross-roads, suggesting that the
emperor's project was to open up the Brussels road and to make a false attack on
the left, at the Houg[ou]mont farm, in order to draw English forces there con-
tinually and to separate the centre of the Anglo-Belgian army from its wings.
Napoleon, in separating the centre of the Russians from their left, had won the
battle of Austerlitz. The same plan would succeed against the English if the
cataracts of the sky, more fatal than Grouchy's movements, had allowed an attack
much earlier. Besides, on the 18th June, it was necessary to wait until nine o'clock
for it to get dark, which gave Bülow all the time he needed to become a new Desaix
in this new battle of Marengo, in making his junction before it was time to bivouac.

Prince Jérôme commenced the fire with an attack on the farm of Houg[ou]mont
on which rushed his brigade of light infantry (1st and 2nd *Légère*). This farm had
been loop-holed, the windows faced us, the entry of the house was on the far side
of the farm through a large barricaded carriage gate. Colonel Cubières, of the

1st *Légère*, had lost many men and was impatient of not being able to change the inequality of the fight. Nevertheless, thanks to the efforts of the soldiers, the first brigade had captured the small wood and the rest of the division, after a stubborn fight, took the gardens; the English threw themselves into the buildings of the farm from where they fired at our troops from under cover. General Piré approached the Houg[ou]mont position with his division of light cavalry and executed several successful charges on the English battalions which moved against our left flank.

Colonel Cubières formed an advanced guard and gave it to *sous-lieutenant* Bonnet[3] to command, an old soldier of the army of Spain, who had been made an officer by Marshal Suchet for being first into the breach at Lérida. This detachment turned the farm building, broke open the cart gate and entered the courtyard; the 1st *Légère* marched behind them. Bonnet struck with mighty blows the side opening at this entry, threw it down, penetrated into the courtyard, where he and his men were shot down at point-blank range from an elevated platform. All found death there. Cubières, arm in a sling, following his advance guard, his horse was felled by a shot. The colonel rose and continued ahead quickly, when he realised that the firing had ceased. He turned round and saw before their soldiers, English officers who covered him, admiring his courage. Cubières saluted and retired with the debris of his troops. This pause in the middle of a combat recalled the politeness of the English at Fontenoy who, removing their hats, shouted, '*Messieurs des Garde française*, you fire first'.

The farm and the garden were retaken by the English despite the determination of Jérôme's division which was all engaged and almost destroyed. The prince himself was wounded. The efforts of Foy's division, not being able to reach the enemy to flush him out, General Reille ordered this general to gather up a battery of howitzers and burn the farm. This means was successful and the English were forced to abandon their wounded in the middle of the flames.

Marshal Grouchy had made known to the emperor that, informed that the enemy was heading for Wavres, he left at dawn to press him in this direction. His letter was dated 2am, from Gembloux. He was given reason to believe that this marshal would be before Wavres at midday and that he would have received the first order by which, the previous evening, he had been warned of the battle. But, during the attacks on Houg[ou]mont, we saw, on the horizon, towards Saint-Lambert, the advance-guard of Bülow. An officer was sent to Marshal Grouchy to inform him of this important fact and giving him the order to approach us and destroy Bülow. Then, we immediately took measures to stop the Prussians whilst waiting for Marshal Grouchy to arrive on the rear of this corps. General Domon moved with his 3,000 cavalry to encounter Bülow and Count Lobau with his army corps, went to find a battle position behind the cavalry. Napoleon then directed Marshal Ney to attack La Haye Sainte which served as a support to the enemy's centre. It was about one o'clock in the afternoon.

For three hours, the efforts of the two armies were concentrated on the plateau of Mont-Saint-Jean. Beyond, the buildings of La Haye Sainte are taken and re-taken three times by Ney who had, in these various attacks, five horses killed under him. Eighty guns fired canister at the English who sought shelter in the Soignes forest. Our infantry had to be restrained as it rushed with ardour and enthusiasm in front of the enemy. However, a cavalry charge having brought some disorder in one of the columns of I Corps, the emperor mounted his horse and galloped over the ground. He gave orders to the brave Lieutenant General Desvaux, commander of the artillery of the army [he actually commanded the horse artillery of the Guard]; this illustrious general officer was struck by a ball. The emperor's headquarters was large and made an easy target. We were ordered to divide up this compact body into three or four different groups and placed apart, but close enough to be able to receive and send to the different corps the instructions of Napoleon or Marshal Soult.

However, we received no news of Marshal Grouchy's corps whilst the troops of Bülow arrived before our lines and outflanked the right of Count Lobau level with la Belle-Alliance. VI Corps was immediately reinforced with the division of the Young Guard commanded by Duhesme which Napoleon had followed by two batteries. Bülow attempted to destroy the French cavalry with his artillery because it had caused such damage in his columns. Lieutenant General Jacquinot displayed *sang-froid* and stoicism in the face of a situation that could have been so unfortunate for him. This general officer commanded two divisions of cavalry [he had received command of Subervie's cavalry division as well as his own that belonged to I Corps; his brother commanded the 1st Lancers of Subervie's division]. A cannon ball came in from the flank of the 1st Lancers and took off the head of *Chef d'escadron* Dumanoir, passed through the body of Colonel Jacquinot's horse and cut off two legs of *Chef d'escadron* Trentignant's horse. The three superior officers fell as one. Confusion spread through the ranks. General Jacquinot, sword in hand, reordered the line himself with a firm voice, and it was only after re-establishing order that he bent down to check if his brother was dead but who was happily unhurt.

The taking of the hamlet of la Haie stopped Bülow's movement which was attempting to turn our right. It was then that Marshal Ney launched himself on the plateau of La Haye Sainte with Milhaud's and Kellerman's 12,000 cuirassiers, followed by the cavalry reserve of the Imperial Guard. These braves broke the enemy lines and seized sixty guns that they could not recover because of a lack of horses. We watched this admirable charge with anxiety, for all our reserve of cavalry was engaged and the battle was far from being over! Here is how General Heymès explained this fact which seemed reckless and premature:

We then learnt that this spontaneous movement of our cavalry happened because the reserves, placed at most half a league from the battlefield, could not judge exactly what was going on, but had, however, seen the enemy abandon his position. They thought it was in retreat. This rumour spread and the forward movement of a cavalry brigade requested by the marshal seemed to confirm it. This troop executed its movement at the trot. But no one knows by what madness it was followed by all the reserves, including even that of the Guard who only ever obeyed their own officers or the direct orders of the Emperor who controlled them.

Wellington, desperate, had lost 10,000 men, the equipages of his army were fleeing towards Brussels. The general of the Anglo-Belgian army anxiously awaited the junction with the Prussians and thought all was lost if Blücher did not arrive.

The red lancers of the Guard, commanded by General Édouard Colbert, broke through Ponsonby's English brigade. This general, pierced by seven lance thrusts, was killed. The Prince of Orange, seriously wounded, was nearly captured. At this moment, the French thought they were victorious.

But the Prussians were gaining ground. It was then that Napoleon, who could no longer ignore that Blücher had slipped away from Grouchy, and had made his junction by crossing from Ohain to Wellington's left wing, wrongly spread along the whole line that the cannonballs that crossed over our heads with those of the English, came from Grouchy's army corps that placed the enemy between two fires. This news immediately produced an immeasurable effect in elevating the courage and vigour of our troops. But, later, in recalling it, the retreat became a rout, the soldier no longer believing the word, until then so venerated, of Napoleon!

Towards eight o'clock, the Prussians broke our right and threatened the rear of VI Corps. Four battalions of the Guard were sent by the emperor to Marshal Ney to stop the enemy. Guided by the brave Generals Friant, Michel, Cambrone [sic], Pelet and Petit, the success of the Prussians slowed down, although their numbers increased every moment. The veterans of our great wars died rather than retreat or surrender. Other troops of the Guard followed them and soon suffered the same fate as those that preceded them in this unequal struggle. Soon, surrounded by superior forces, disorder appeared in the ranks. There was a shout of 'treason', no one listened to the voices of their leaders. The whole Anglo-Belgian army advanced. Nearly all the generals were wounded. Among the dead were found Michel, Jamin and de Penne. Generals Lobau, Cambrone, Duhesme and Durrieu were also wounded, falling into the hands of the enemy. The French army left its positions and rushed off like a torrent. The troops of all arms were all mixed together and carried us along the road to Genappe where some soldiers were calling that the Prussian cavalry had already overtaken us. It was hoped that it would be possible to stop at this place and pass the night, but some enemy squadrons had shown up and the rout became complete. We marched at an unbelievable speed until daylight to cross the Sambre where we again wanted to stop and receive orders. But there was no longer any command. The generals, lost in the crowd, were dragged along by it and separated from their troops. It was said the emperor had been killed, that the chief of staff was a prisoner. Treason was spoken of, but not of where to rally . . .

Chapter 5

I Army Corps

Introduction

The French I Army Corps was commanded by Lieutenant General Jean Baptiste Drouet, Comte d'Erlon, generally referred to in French histories as d'Erlon. It was the strongest of the three French line army corps, consisting of four infantry divisions (1st [Quiot], 2nd [Donzelot], 3rd [Marcognet] and 4th [Durutte]) and a light cavalry division (the 1st Cavalry Division, commanded by Lieutenant General Baron Charles Claude Jacquinot). The 1st Infantry Division was to have been commanded by Lieutenant General Allix, but having been sent by Napoleon on a special task prior to the campaign, he had not arrived in time for the battle and the division was commanded by the senior brigade commander Quiot du Passage. The corps had famously marched backwards and forwards between the battlefields of Ligny and Quatre Bras on 16 June without fighting on either of them. At Waterloo the corps was therefore at full strength and determined to make up for the ignominy of that failure. It was no doubt for this reason that Napoleon chose them for the first major attack on the Allied line. The cohesion of the whole corps was smashed by their repulse and although individual brigades continued to fight bravely, it was unable to operate again as a cohesive whole. Jacquinot's cavalry division lost Marbot's 7th Hussars who were sent on a reconnaissance mission on the right flank which was apparently tasked with meeting up with Marshal Grouchy; the other three regiments (3rd Chasseurs à Cheval and the 3rd and 4th Lancers) launched a very effective counter-attack against the British heavy cavalry brigade which had discomfited d'Erlon's infantry.

Lieutenant General Jean Baptiste Drouet, *Comte* d'Erlon

Le Maréchal Drouet, comte d'Erlon. Vie militaire écrit par lui-même et dédiée à ses amis (Paris: Gustave Barba, 1844), pp. 96–8.

General Drouet d'Erlon commanded I Army Corps at Waterloo.
    Born in 1765, Drouet enlisted as a soldier in the Royal Army in 1782. After only five years' service he obtained an honourable discharge due to ill health. On the outbreak of the revolution he re-enlisted and was elected captain in 1793. In 1794

he became aide-de-camp to General Lefebvre with whom he served through several revolutionary campaigns and eventual promotion to adjutant général chef de brigade. *He commanded a brigade at Zurich in 1799 and then at Hohenlinden. After further success in the invasion of Hanover, he took part in the Austerlitz campaign as a divisional commander; his division took a distinguished part in that famous battle. During the Prussian campaign of 1806 he again commanded a division, although as part of Bernadotte's corps he missed both the major battles at Auerstadt and Jena. However, he took a leading and successful role in the pursuit of the Prussian army after these two battles and finished the campaign by sacking Lübeck. In the following campaign against the Russians in early 1807 he fought at Heilsberg and was seriously wounded by a musket ball to the chest at Friedland. His recovery took a year during which he was made Count d'Erlon. In 1809 General Lefebvre requested him as his chief-of-staff and he took part in the successful quelling of the Tyrol revolt and eventually took over command of the Bavarian corps from Lefebvre. In 1810 he became commander of IX Corps for operations in Spain, a corps made up of drafts for all the infantry regiments serving in that country. Although this was only supposed to be a provisional corps for the move into Spain, he was drawn into the battle of Fuentes d'Oñoro. In 1811 he received command of an operational corps; the V Corps of Soult's army. A re-organisation left him in command of a mere division, but in 1812 he became commander of the small Army of the Centre. In 1813, after being forced to withdraw from Madrid, he was at the disaster that was the battle of Vitoria, although his divisions fought well. After another re-organisation he commanded a corps under Marshal Soult and after initial success they were pulled back across the Pyrenees. He fought on the Nivelle and performed well on the Nive, although ultimately without success. In early 1814 he fought at Orthez and Toulouse before the war ended with Napoleon's abdication. He had collected considerable experience fighting the British. On news of Napoleon's return in 1815, he quickly rallied to the cause and conspired to rally the northern garrisons to Napoleon. This being a failure, he was imprisoned, but soon released as Napoleon took power. Early in April he was nominated to command I Corps of the* armée du Nord. *He famously missed the battles of both Ligny and Quatre Bras, and so, with a virtually intact corps took a major part in the battle of Waterloo. After his involvement in the conspiracy on Napoleon's return, he quickly fled the country on the emperor's abdication. He was sentenced to death in absentia in 1816 at the time he was running a successful inn in Bayreuth in Germany. Granted an amnesty on the coronation of Charles X, he returned to France. However, he remained unattached until his retirement in 1827. Re-instated by Louis Philippe, he resumed active command, although his time as governor-general in Algeria was not a success. He became Marshal of France in 1843 as a reward for his service, but died early the following year.*

D'Erlon's account of Waterloo is rather superficial and unsatisfying; it comes from the above pamphlet in which he says his aim is not to write his memoirs but merely to correct some mistakes of his biographers. Only 119 pages long, it briefly covers the outline of his career, but gives little detail. Disappointingly therefore, it does not touch on the more controversial aspects of the battle on which he might have enlightened us, not least the thinking behind his use of large divisional columns in his main attack on the Allied ridge.

The pursuit continued close to Planchenois [*sic*]. Arriving to the left of the road, on a small height, from where it was possible to see the position that the enemy wanted to occupy, the emperor placed himself there to observe their movements, and thinking that they would continue to retreat, he said to me, 'Continue to follow them'. It was already nearly dark. At that time, Milhaud's division of heavy cavalry arrived, which, as it formed into line in front of this position and to the right of the road, was heavily engaged by artillery. The emperor said to me, 'Have all the troops take position and we will see what tomorrow brings'.

The night was terrible; the rain fell in abundance and this had so waterlogged the ground as to much hamper the movements of artillery. The troops had passed the night without shelter, no musket would have been able to fire.

An officer, sent to the advance posts in the morning by the emperor, reported that the enemy was continuing his retreat; I received the order to set off and pursue him vigorously. Having judged the enemy's movements differently to the officer, I sent my chief-of-staff to the emperor, to tell him that I thought the enemy was disposed to accept battle.

The emperor immediately came to the advance posts. I accompanied him; having dismounted we approached the enemy's *vedettes*, and examined more closely the movements of the English army. He saw I was probably right, and, having been convinced that the army had taken position, he said to me, 'Order the troops to make their soup, to prepare their arms, and we will see what happens towards midday'.

Since dawn the two armies were already within cannon range; the first corps to the right of the main road to Brussels, the second corps to the left, and the Young Guard commanded by General Lobau [Lobau commanded VI Corps. Duhesme commanded the Young Guard.] in the second line with several regiments of infantry, forming 8,000 men at most; all the Old Guard were in reserve.

At precisely midday, the first cannon shots of the grand battery were heard; it was the signal to attack. All the troops engaged; the second corps attempted to seize the farm of Hougoumont and the first corps was to become masters of La Haye Sainte, located on the Brussels road. These two posts, which were at the foot of the English army, had been barricaded and crenulated, and were defended by a numerous body of infantry hidden behind the hedges. We suffered heavy loss at both places; several times we became masters of it, and several times we were forced to abandon it.

At this moment, a charge by English cavalry on a division of the first corps put it into disorder and caused casualties. The heavy cavalry of General Milhaud charged the English cavalry, but was thrown back. It was then that General Jacquinot, who commanded the light cavalry of my army corps, attacked the English cavalry again, on its left flank and entirely destroyed it. The enemy was forced to abandon the artillery of the division of the first corps which it had captured.

The combat having been renewed, La Haye Sainte was captured towards three o'clock; the battle appeared to be decided in our favour. At this moment, the Duke of Wellington would not have hesitated to order the retreat on Brussels, where great confusion was already reigned, if he had not learnt that the Prussian corps of Bülow, with a strength of 40,000 men, was going to deploy on our right. The Duke

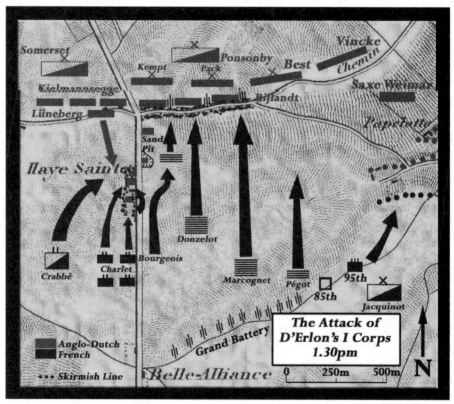

Diagram of d'Erlon's attack: This diagram shows the development of d'Erlon's attack. Only two of the four infantry divisions actually formed up in the dense divisional columns described elsewhere; it seems two brigades were tasked with attacks on la Haye-Sainte on the left and as flank protection covering Papelotte and la Haie on the right, leaving two of the columns consisting of only a single brigade.

of Wellington thus re-doubled the efforts to maintain his position; and, towards 4.30, the head of the Prussian columns deployed effectively.

The emperor directed General Count Lobau against them with the Young Guard, which stopped them for a long time; but soon noticing that he would not be able to resist such a considerable mass of troops, several plans of retreat were ordered, but then countermanded, to make a last effort against the English army before Bülow's corps was in line. However, General Lobau's troops, who had fought courageously, were forced back by numbers and outflanked completely. Then the English army advanced with all its forces to attack the front of the French army, which finding itself with its right flank turned, was forced to abandon the battlefield and to retire in disorder during the night after having suffered considerable losses. In this affair, two officers of my headquarters were killed and I had two horses killed beneath me.

1st Infantry Divison

Adjutant Dominique Fleuret

Description des Passages de Dominic Fleuret (Paris: Firmin-Didot, 1929), pp. 149–52.

At Waterloo, Fleuret was Adjutant of the 1st Battalion of the 55th de ligne, *which formed part of the 1st Brigade (Charlet) of the 1st Infantry Division (Quiot) in I Army Corps (d'Erlon).*

Fleuret was born in 1787 and was conscripted into the 55th de ligne *in 1807. In the following year he entered Spain as part of the 13th Provisional Regiment and found himself under fire for the first time that year in chasing a force of guerrillas. He fought his first battle at Medina del Rio-Seco. Through 1809 he fought the insurgents around Saragossa; he was made sergeant in March that year and fought at the French victory of Ocana. In 1811 he fought and was wounded at Albuera and then continued the fight against the guerrillas around Seville under Marshal Soult. He fought the British again at Vitoria and retreated into France. He took part in Soult's attempt to regain a foothold in Spain before their retreat back into France. At some time he was captured by the British and claims to have been questioned by Wellington himself. He credits his British escorts for stopping the Spanish from massacring all the prisoners he marched with. Sent back to England, he was imprisoned in Yorkshire before returning to France after the First Restoration. Having rejoined his regiment he found he had been passed over for promotion so took retirement. However, he hurried back to serve after Napoleon's return and served as adjutant in the 1st Battalion of the 55th. Having fought at Waterloo, he stayed with the regiment back to Paris, then south beyond the Loire after the capitulation. His memoirs end with the disbandment of his regiment.*

In most histories, Charlet's brigade (Charlet commanded the 54th de ligne, but had been promoted to command the brigade as the appointed brigade commander (Quiot) had been given command of the division because of the absence of its nominated commander, Allix, were responsible for the attack on the farm of La Haye Sainte. It is therefore odd that Fleuret does not mention this and describes that his battalion at least attacked the main Allied line. Also of interest is how the remains of his regiment were formed into a single battalion and moved to the right flank to fight with the Young Guard against the Prussians.

At 7am on the 18th, the whole army was in line and the bands of all the regiments were playing at their head. The signal was given. The first division of each corps attacked. We were the first division of I Corps on the right wing. We fought against the English skirmishers and fifteen guns that were in a battery which fired on us. In less than quarter of an hour the [enemy] infantry had been broken and the guns taken *à la baïonette* without firing a shot. Only our skirmishers had been firing.

After having taken the battery by assault, a mass of cavalry charged us and, as we had crossed some ditches, we did not have time to rally properly. Many were sabred and others made prisoner. The cavalry continued its charge and we were held by [enemy] infantry. But, as it found itself in a ravine, to our left, two regiments of French lancers came to our rescue and released us.

We crossed the ditches of the redoubt when a large number of English cavalry repulsed our lancers. We had still not re-joined our column and here we were, mixed up with the English dragoons. Finally, most of us threw ourselves to the ground in the corn. The English cavalry passed over us and it made the effort to push us in the back with their big boots like a vet testing the chickens to see if they were dead.

The cavalry passed and we dragged ourselves, face down, to re-join our squares which were firing on the English dragoons from each face. The regimental drums were beating the rally. We joined them. The regiment was reduced to four hundred men. These were formed into a single battalion and we were used as skirmishers with the Young Guard. We marched against the Prussians, who moved against our right to cut the army's retreat. We repulsed them twice, but the main body of the Prussian army arrived and forced us to retreat.

I remained with our light cavalry, hussars and chasseurs, with fifty men of my regiment to cover the retreat to Charleroi. The bridges were barricaded.

Captain Pierre Charles Duthilt

Mémoires du Capitaine Duthilt (Lille: J. Tallandier, 1909), pp. 300–7.

In the 1815 campaign, Captain Duthilt served as aide-de-camp to General Bourgeois, who commanded the 2nd Brigade of the 1st Division (Quiot vice Allix), of I Army Corps (d'Erlon).

Duthilt was born in February 1773. At the end of his memoirs, Duthilt wrote a resumé of his career, so in his case I thought it may be of interest for him to give his own summary of his military career; 'My services only date from the 27th September 1793, the time of the formation of the 1st Battalion of Requisition of Saint Omer; in line with the decree of the preceding 23rd August, which called to active service all unmarried young men aged between eighteen and twenty-five years, I entered the 8th Company of this battalion, elected to the rank of captain by my comrades of the company, conforming to this decree. With this battalion I was then incorporated, as a private soldier [!], to the Chasseurs of Mont-Cassel in December of the same year which, brigaded in Holland on the 22nd April 1795, formed the 14th Demi-Brigade of light infantry, which became the first of this arm and then the 1st régiment léger, with which I made the campaigns of the years 1793–94–95–96–97–98–99–1800, 1801–1802, 1803–1804–1805, 1806–1807 and 1808, then part of 1813–1814 and 1815, with the armies of the North, Sambre et Meuse, Holland, England, Mayence, Danube, Helvétie, the Rhine, Grisons, Italy, Naples, Calabria, Illyria and du Nord. After having filled all the non-commissioned ranks up to sergeant-major, and this in the course of my first six years service, I was promoted sous lieutenant on the 5th July 1799, lieutenant on the 15th December 1803 and captain on the 11th February 1808. Put on the inactive list on the 6th July 1814 because of the re-organisation of the army and the formation of the Régiment du Roi (light infantry), I was recalled by royal ordinance on the 9th March 1815 and attached during the Hundred Days, from March to June, to General Baron Bourgeois, commander of the 2nd brigade of the 1st Division of I Army Corps of the armée du Nord, as captain aide-de-camp, until the catastrophe of Waterloo, after which I was put on half pay after the disbandment of the Army of the Loire in 1815, then retired by a decision of the 20th April 1816.' Whilst Duthilt's service record is an impressive one, in fact he missed all the major battles of the Empire(!) and his service during this period was in theatres outside those of the major operations.

In contrast to Fleuret's account above, Duthilt appears to claim that it was his brigade, the 2nd, that was ordered to assault La Haye Sainte. However, the attack he describes clearly by-passes the farm and although he later says it was captured, he does not tell us who by!

After the combat of Quatre Bras, at 2pm the 2nd Division of I Corps was sent in pursuit of the enemy, whose rearguard had stopped at Genappe; half an hour later, the 1st Division of the same corps followed the 2nd and we met up with the emperor who, at the head of his numerous headquarters, travelled around the area watching the various regiments pass by.

He was noisily greeted by the troops who, seeing him for the first time, filled the air with their acclamations. All marching forwards, our advance guard heavily bombarded the enemy's rearguard and we passed through Genappe where the lancers made a resolute charge at full tilt which threw back the English.

We continued to march until the entrance to the plain at the village of Planchenoit, above which we took position on the crest of the heights to the left and right of, and perpendicular to, the Brussels road.

No road, after rain, is so disagreeable, so muddy, as those which are close to coalmines, or along which this fuel is transported: these are covered in a black mud mixed like ink, which made our cavalry unrecognisable. Their clothing, men, and horses were painted from head to foot in such a way as to present a black and muddy mass.

The unfortunate events of the 16th [when panic was spread amongst the baggage by the disordered retreat of Kellerman's cuirassiers after their charge at Quatre Bras] had reduced our resources; bread, rice and brandy destined for the soldiers, pillaged or spilled on the spot; not having enough to replace them sufficiently, it was necessary to cook hastily in the remote villages on the way; but this resource was insufficient, for these villages were deserted, the inhabitants having, for the most part, fled. Brandy and wine continued to be lacking. The English army, to the contrary, had all that was necessary in abundance; above all in drink of all kinds.

However, the battle was joined along the whole line; a numerous artillery struck down the attack columns from the enemy's right and his skirmishers began to withdraw. His left remained inactive and his centre appeared to hold the efforts of the French army.

The 2nd Brigade of the 1st Division of I Corps commanded by General Bourgeois was ordered to take the position of Mont-Saint-Jean, which had become the centre of operations and which held us up with far off masses of the enemy; this point taken, we would have become masters of the plain and then we could have reasonably counted on a prompt success.

Ahead of Mont-Saint-Jean, it was reported to us, was a farm [La Haye Sainte] whose courtyard was occupied by infantry; its approaches closed by wagons and ploughs and by the tops of trees with their branches sharpened and intertwined, thrown forwards as *chevaux de frises*, rendering the attack difficult; the surrounding hedges were also lined with Scottish skirmishers and several regiments were hidden there as well as a body of cavalry, protected by a formidable battery placed on a height and hidden, making this position exceedingly strong.

The 2nd Brigade, hidden in a fold in the ground, formed in attack column by battalion, set off at the *pas de charge*, preceded by skirmishers, and urged on by excited cries; but this haste and enthusiasm became deadly, because the soldier, who still had a long march before encountering the enemy, was soon tired out by the difficulty of crossing the greasy and waterlogged ground, in which he broke the straps of his gaiters and even lost his shoes, weighed down by the amount of dirt that attached itself to them and stuck to the soles and to the ground, and because commands could not be heard, lost in the thousands of repeated cries and drumming; there was soon a little confusion in the ranks, especially when the head of the column was in range of the enemy without it being noticed that it had a ravine between it and the enemy, with banks so steep that it could not be crossed.

Indeed, some yards above La Haye Sainte, the slope of the valley separating the two armies resembled an entrenchment; above, the level of the slope was broken by a large cutting parallel to the ravine and very steep-sided, cutting the Charleroi road and along the crest of the plateau, forming a ditch, and its escarpment, on the side of Mont-Saint-Jean was no less than seven to eight *poids* [roughly the same in feet] in height at the back of the farm of La Haye Sainte, a veritable advanced work; to its extreme right, by the château of Goumont, whose garden was protected by a hedge, very thick, very high, and separated from the slope by a large ditch, deep and full of water. It was to attack the bull by the horns. The column was forced to move to the left along this ravine until it levelled out, a distance of several hundred metres; but the command had not been well heard throughout the column, some battalions moved to the left whilst others moved to the right which caused confusion and loss of time.

During this mix-up, the enemy made use of all his means: a terrible fire exploded onto our column; balls, bullets, caseshot killed a third of the men of this brigade in an instant; the cavalry rapidly crossed the road we wanted to take and moving to the left it arrived inopportunely on the column, penetrated the intervals and sabred all those that the balls, caseshot and bullets had spared. The brigade was thrown into retreat, broken up, penetrated everywhere by this cavalry, and the ground scattered with dead and wounded. It was then that two regiments of lancers commanded by General Gobrecht, came to counter this charge and to free several thousand prisoners and a battery of six guns that we had limbered up and attached to the column.

When the ground became clear, the 1st Brigade of the same division commanded by General Quiot, marched ahead, took the same route, made the same mistake and encountered the same obstacle; but it was not as disrupted as the 2nd Brigade. However, it was able to overcome the difficulties it encountered with the aid of fresh troops sent to the same point.

These troops were all those that remained of I Corps which, in mass, came in support and to decide the movement to which the two brigades of the 1st Division had been so entirely and unhappily sacrificed.

It took more than an hour to recover from the first check and to reform the attack columns.

All of I Corps were exhausted through tiredness and hunger; its four divisions had been cruelly tested from nearly seven hours of fighting without respite, but badly commanded and directed.

The farms of Papelotte and la Haye had been taken, and the extreme left of the English position was thus threatened as well as he whole of the Mont-Saint-Jean plateau from the rear. Everyone was exhausted, regiment, by regiment, the courage of despair was not able to make up for their shortage of numbers.

Derlon [*sic*] lost 10,000 men in this unhappy battle. The strength of I Corps, commanded by Count d'Erlon was, at the beginning of the campaign, 20,000 men present in line, forming thirty battalions, composing four infantry divisions. He had fixed his left on la Belle Alliance, on the Charleroi to Brussels road, and his right facing the farms of Papelotte and la Haye, where the enemy's left rested; each division in two lines having their artillery in the intervals between the brigades.

The 28th and 105th Line Regiments, forming the 2nd Brigade of the 1st Division, were entirely torn to pieces and lost.

The account of the English general Alison is full of exaggeration in favour of the heroism of the English, without giving the least justice to the insurmountable resolution displayed by D'Erlon's men. But he confuses the two attacks made by I Corps into just one: the first was made by Jérôme's division, the 2nd of I Corps [Jérôme's division was in Reille's II Corps!] onto the wood and farm of Hougoumont, a position that was taken by the 1st *Léger*, and then occupied by Reille, and that remained in our possession until the end of the battle [the French never took Hougoumont]. The second by the 2nd Brigade of the 1st Division of I Corps, was directed more to the right on the farm of La Haye Sainte, but he does not say that it was a ravine that forced us to present our right flank for several hundred paces to find firm ground across which came the English cavalry, until then covered by a hedge, but this cavalry did not have to cross the hedge, nor did it leap it to fall on us, the road was clear and we were lacking it; and taken without warning, we did not have time to form square; there were only the dead and wounded who fell to the ground, and as for the 2,000 prisoners and the battery that were taken, the assertion is not true; the column was effectively broken through, the battery overtaken, but the brigade of lancers who made an immediate counter-attack forced the English to retire and return to their lines pursued with a lance in their backs, leaving on the ground all those who they had overtaken. This charge was made by General Gobrecht.

Anyway, at this fatal moment, the emperor, seeing I Corps advancing, had their old position occupied by the Guard, in the middle of the plain.

In the attack, I was knocked from my horse, wounded by a sabre blow to my head, made prisoner, and taken away, but happily retaken by the 4th Lancers who charged with General Gobrecht.

The charge made by General Gobrecht incited several other cavalry regiments to depart spontaneously to take part, then those who were in reserve and finally the whole of the French cavalry.

Thus the part of VI Corps who were destined to hold against the Prussians found themselves deprived of cavalry and Wellington had held back all his reserve intact, whilst ours were occupied for the battle in the centre.

Nevertheless, everywhere the battle appeared to be even, but our forces were completely exhausted; independently of the dispersion of the two brigades of the 1st Division of I Corps and the absence of the cavalry reserve, each wounded took with him from two to four healthy men, who left the ranks to take them to the ambulances, or to accompany them there. These men, not being watched, did not return to their units under the pretext that they did not know where to find them; with the result that the road to Charleroi was soon covered with these kind of fugitives who carried ahead the consternation and confusion amongst the equipages in the rear, whose drivers, who perhaps were seeing fire for the first time, were ready to flee and to renew the sad scenes of the 16th.

Freed from Bülow's Prussians, the emperor ordered a great effort in the centre; the English army hesitated, it seemed victory was ours, but then the arrival of the whole Prussian army; our troops rushed back in disorder; Wellington noticed this and had all his troops advance.

Apart from the Old Guard, everyone ran off at once through the caissons, the broken guns and baggage of all kinds. Carried along, numb, they passed over the heaps of dead and trampled the wounded under their feet without hearing their groans and cries of pain; these sad victims of the war were crushed without pity; they died under the wheels of the caissons and guns. The soldiers of all arms fled mixed together and without leaders, and the desperate leaders fled without soldiers; the last pushing the first and the guns, wagons and caissons closed up against each other, without teams, obstructed the road, were delivered up to the greed of the pillagers and blocked the route. Despite the terrible state in which I found myself, on foot, covered in blood and alone, because my general and his second aide de camp were also seriously wounded, I only left the battlefield when all hope was lost. Pulled along by the disorganised and fleeing mass, I marched throughout the night of the 18th/19th without rest or nourishment. Those who had already bypassed Charleroi, whose gates were closed, did not believe that they were any more secure at Marchiennes-au-pont. Never had anything so upsetting struck the imagination of the old soldiers of the republic, even those who had been witnesses of the retreat from Russia; despair was in the heart of these old warriors and fury was painted in their looks. It was only at Beaumont that I was able to rest a little at the table where I took a poor meal. It was in vain that several leaders tried again to rally the fugitives in the plain of Beaumont, on the limit of the soil of *la patrie* that they had left in glory and which they saw again with shame. The disordered march continued.

Private Louis Canler

Mémoires de Canler, ancient chef du service de sureté (Paris, Mercure de France, 1968), pp. 24–30.

During the Waterloo campaign Canler was a private in the 28th de ligne. This regiment was part of the 2nd Brigade (Bourgeois) of the 1st Infantry Division (General Quiot vice Allix), part of I Army Corps (d'Erlon).

   Canler was born in 1797 and his comprehensive memoirs (first published in 1862, the account below comes from the 1882 edition) are overwhelmingly concerned with his service in the police in which he served from 1820, and life and crime in Paris during the early nineteenth century. We can only presume that he had retired some time before his memoirs were published. He was the son of a soldier; his father had served throughout the campaigns of the Republic until 1796. When Napoleon visited Namur where he lived in 1805, his father requested he be admitted into the army as an enfant de troupe and drummer (aged twelve); this was agreed. At first he was attached to the 3rd Hussars, but in December 1811, he enrolled in the 28th de ligne as a drummer. In 1813 he 'gave up my drumsticks for a musket' and served in garrison in Antwerp. He served during the siege that was vigorously and successfully defended by Carnot. He returned to France after Napoleon's abdication and records that the regiment maintained its enthusiasm for the emperor and prayed for his return. Organised into two war battalions his regiment reached Valenciennes on 13 June where their royalist-leaning colonel (Saint-Hilaire) left to join Louis in Gand. Their new colonel was Saint-Michel. As part of I Army Corps he explains the regiment's exasperation after marching backwards and forwards between the two battles of the 16th. Having fought at Waterloo, he retreated to Paris. After Napoleon's abdication he was enrolled into his departmental legion and married in 1817. He left the army on 31 December 1818 before making his successful career in the police. He died in 1865.

   Canler's account is full of interest, mainly because he gives a clear and atmospheric description of what it was like to be in the midst of one of d'Erlon's huge columns and restricts himself solely to what he saw and experienced for himself. According to Duthilt's account (above), Canler's regiment, as part of the same brigade, was to have attacked La Haye Sainte, but Canler does not mention this. Canler's adventures after the repulse of d'Erlon's attack are also of great interest.

I will not recall all the acts of heroism accomplished by the French army, and, without speaking hereof those men who crushed their crosses [of the *légion d'honneur*] between their teeth, who ripped their colours into small pieces that they kept to ensure these emblems did not fall into the hands of the enemy, but I must recount one of the peculiarities of this memorable day.

   Occupying our new bivouac [late in the night of the 16th/17th], we noticed on the edge of the road a young soldier, or rather part of a man, for the unfortunate had had both legs taken off by a cannon ball! His wounds had not been treated, someone had only tried to stop the bleeding by wrapping the wounds with a shirt. This poor man also had signs of recent wounds to the face and chest. He must have had extraordinary strength to have survived his wounds and the loss of blood that had resulted. Seeing us passing close by, he raised himself on his hands excitedly and shouted in a loud voice, '*Vive l'empereur*! I have lost both my legs, I am finished! Victory is ours! *Vive l'empereur!*'

The face, the words of this brave man who, without doubt, died unaware of what happened, have remained engraved in my memory, and, as I write these lines, I still cannot master my emotions at the memory of the sentiments of patriotism so courageously expressed.

The division to which I belonged was composed of my regiment and the 54th, 55th and 105th *de ligne*, under the orders of Generals Bourgeois, commanding the first brigade, and Allix, the division. Arriving at our destination we took off our packs and stacked our arms; then some bands of men left marauding. I took four men with me and we went off on an adventure, leaving our muskets in the care of our friends. There is an old proverb that says it is very difficult to comb a devil that has no hair; *ma foi*, I think that it was even more difficult to find something to eat, for every house, every barn that we visited had already been visited by others. Finally, I noticed, in the middle of a wood, a kind of barn that was in ruins; we went there and I entered the dilapidated building through a hole that the weather had made in one of the corners. The night was very dark and it took me a few minutes to distinguish the objects that surrounded me. Finally, in the opposite corner, I noticed something white; it was certainly not the moment to be thinking of phantoms or apparitions. I went over to this object and I recognised to my great satisfaction, that this was a sack of flour! We resolved to take it. To ease the burden, each filled with flour our pockets, handkerchief, shako, then the rest was left in the sack, that each took their turn with it on their shoulders.

By these continuous changes of position, these successive loading and unloading, the cursed sack had so covered us that in arriving in the camp it was difficult for others to recognise us, and officers and soldiers received us with happy laughter. We resembled not only millers, but also those worthy imitators of Debureau [actually Deburau, a character in a French play], attending our masked balls.

At 1pm on the 17th, a cannon shot was fired from the height where the Brussels *chausée* made a bend; it was the signal to start our advance; we pursued the enemy with 'a sword in his kidneys' until seven o'clock in the evening. Then we took position close to the village of Sainte-Alliance and the heights of Rossomme, then each began his preparations to dine and some left marauding. This time, we only returned with some wood and a small live sheep; but as, from all appearances, the next day would be rough, we conserved our sheep for our next dinner and passed the night around a fire. This was not, to be honest, a point of luxury, for throughout the night the rain did not cease to fall. Finally, at daybreak, each company disassembled their muskets to grease them, change the priming and to dry their greatcoats; then, these preparations complete, we considered eating. The marmite [cooking pot] was put over the fire; one of our corporals, a sometime apprentice butcher, killed, skinned and cut up our poor little sheep, which we cooked with some of the flour that I had found on the 16th. After an hour of cooking, the captain and the second lieutenant of the company came to take their share of our meal, which, I hate to say, had a terrible taste, for, instead of salt, which we were absolutely lacking, our cook decided to replace it by putting a handful of powder in the marmite.

The sun having come over the horizon, we formed up and took our battle positions. The emperor then passed along the front of all the corps, and by a spontaneous movement that resembled an electric shock, helmets, shakos, fur caps, were put onto sabres or bayonets to frenetic shouts of '*Vive l'empereur!*'

Towards midday, we went to take position on the plateau of la Sainte-Alliance, where a battery had been established of eighty guns, then we descended into the valley which had the same name and where we were sheltered from a formidable battery that the English had established during the night facing ours and which kept up a continuous fire.

Soon there was a terrible duo executed by the two batteries composed of nearly two hundred cannons; the bullets, bombs, shells, passed whistling over our heads. After half an hour of waiting, Marshal Ney gave the order to attack and to capture by assault the English battery; three beats of the drumstick on the drum sufficed to have the corps ready to march; we were formed in close columns by battalion; I noticed that the adjutant-major Hubaut, responsible for forming the divisions, an old soldier having made all the campaigns of the Empire, was pre-occupied and extremely pale. Finally, the columns were formed, General Drouet d'Erlon put himself in the middle of his army corps and with a powerful and stressful voice pronounced these few words: 'Today it is necessary to vanquish or die!'

The shout of '*Vive l'Empereur!*' left every mouth in response to this short address, and, with shouldered arms, to the sound of the drums beating the charge, the columns shook themselves out and headed towards the enemy batteries without firing a single shot. Then the enemy batteries, which until then had only fired balls and shells, decimated our columns with caseshot. Hardly had we gone a hundred paces when the commander of our second battalion, M. Marins, was mortally wounded; the captain of my company, M. Duzer, was struck by two balls; adjutant Hubaut and the man carrying the colour, *porte-drapeau* Crosse, were killed.

In the middle of all this, the calm and serious voices of our chiefs called the single command: '*Serrez les rangs!*' [Close up!]

At the second discharge of the English battery, the drummer of grenadiers Lecointre had his right arm taken off by caseshot, but this courageous man continued to march at our head beating the charge with his left, until he lost consciousness through loss of blood.

The third discharge from the English battery reduced the frontage of the battalion to that of a company; the terrible cry of '*Serrez les rangs!*' was heard again. This cry, far from causing fear or despair in our hearts, produced a completely contrary effect. It inspired us with courage and not only with the determination to overcome, but also to avenge our unhappy brothers in arms who died before our eyes.

After a journey of twenty minutes, we arrived close to the fortification where the English cannons were emplaced and we started to climb it. The rain that had fallen all night had thinned out the ground, normally heavy, so that in the course of my ascent, the strap of my right gaiter broke and the heel came off my shoe. I quickly bent down to sort this out; but at the same moment, I felt a violent shock that threw my shako back, it would probably have fallen without the chinstrap that held it on my head. It was a ball that had struck it, and which, on the '28' on my shako plate, made a zero and exited through the back, shaving my head.

Still with shouldered arms, we thus mounted as far as the guns which vomited waves of canister against us. Hardly had we reached the summit of the plateau than we were received by the Queen's Dragoons [*sic*] who fell on us with savage cries. The first division did not have time to form square, could not meet this charge, and were broken. Then started a veritable carnage; each found himself separated from his comrades and fought only for himself. The sabre, the bayonet, opened a passage in the thrilling flesh, for one was too close to others to use a firearm.

But the position was not tenable for infantrymen fighting alone surrounded by cavalry; I thus found myself a disarmed prisoner. Suddenly, the command, '*Au trot!*' could be heard; these were French lancers and cuirassiers which came to our rescue. The English dragoons, to meet this charge, were obliged to abandon me. Then I profited from this moment of freedom to throw myself into a field of corn that was to one side. The French cavalry furiously attacked the English dragoons, sabring and playing the lance wildly, in such a way that the latter were forced to retreat, leaving a good number of their men on the battlefield. This allowed me to cross it and attempt to rejoin my unit. When making a detour to the left, I found myself close to an English dragoon officer who had been killed in the melee. A sabre blow had split open his head and the brain had burst out of the skull.

His fob pocket held a superb gold chain: despite the speed of my flight, I stopped a moment to grab this chain and a beautiful watch that was also gold. The English having stripped off my pack and arms, I applied the law of an eye for an eye, a few paces on, I found a ration bag under the cover of which was engraved on a leather label; 'Labigne, second lieutenant of the 55th Line'.

I quickly inspected my second find, which consisted of a writing case and some linen, which was very valuable, possessing then only that which I actually had on my body. A little after, I met up with my colonel, accompanied by some officers, who ran round like a madman to right and left, as fast as his horse would go, shouting out, 'On me 28th! On me!' and these cries, that were marked by the most profound despair, spoke highly of how the disaster experienced by his regiment had struck his sense of honour. I went to join him when some lamentable cries could be heard to my right; I went over to this side and noticed, lying on the ground, a young soldier of the 105th *de ligne*.

This unfortunate, who had had his right tibia broken by a ball, was suffering horribly from his wound which had not been treated or even bandaged.

'Comrade', he shouted to me, 'I pray in all grace that you will not abandon me here! I cannot drag myself as far as the ambulance, and if the cavalry comes past here I will certainly be trampled under the hooves of the horses.' And in saying these words he extended his hands towards me in a suppliant way; I could not resist this appeal and hurried towards him.

Immediately dropping to my knees, I took a shirt from the satchel that I had found, I bandaged his wound, then I took him on my back and carried him like this, with much trouble and fatigue across the battlefield as far as the first ambulance, where I managed to place him, though not without difficulty. I then went to reunite myself with some of my comrades, and, wandering around a little, we were seen by a general who called us and asked where we were going; at our response that we were trying to rejoin our unit; 'It is useless', he told us, 'your regiment has broken up. Come with me, I will put you in position.'

He put us on the road, with instructions to only allow the wounded to pass and to turn back all the soldiers capable of carrying arms. Three lancers were already there with the same mission; in less than an hour we had stopped more than 400 fugitives (I had taken the musket from a wounded man to whom it was of no further use).

We did not leave this position until the whole army began its retreat towards Charleroi, with the caissons, baggage and wagons full of unfortunate wounded with broken arms or legs, and for the most part having had no medical attention.

One can imagine the desolation that was presented by this scene, rendered even worse by the confusion that was occasioned by the darkness of the night.

Because of the disastrous crowding on the road, we each marched on our own, each searching to clear a path on one side of the road or the other across the fields.

At 5am, I arrived at Charleroi, which I only passed through; from there I headed towards Beaumont, where I found a considerable number of soldiers of all arms, who had come like me in the hope of rejoining their regiments and to march again against the enemy.

When we had set off on campaign, the regiment counted fourteen hundred men, hardly two hundred were found at Laon. In this campaign of four days, the emperor had fought the two great battles of Fleurus and Waterloo.

On the 23rd or 24th June, Marshal Soult, *major-général* of the army, passed in review the troops that were at Laon. Arriving before me, my colonel stopped him and pointing to me said,

'Marshal, here is the youngest soldier of my regiment; he is an *infant de troupe* aged eighteen, he made his first campaign at sixteen. After having fought bravely at Waterloo, he carried from the battlefield on his back, a dangerously wounded French soldier.'

I was dumbstruck by this accolade, for I did not know that my colonel knew of the action I had taken.

'Well!' the marshal replied to him, 'you will wear the "cross."'

And he moved on.

But the circumstances were very serious then for promises of this kind to be carried out, and the events that followed, in changing the face of France, put an end to the legitimate hopes that other soldiers held, as well as me.

3rd Infantry Division

Maréchal de Camp Antoine Noguès

Mémoires du général Noguès (1777–1853) sur les guerres de l'Empire (Paris: A. Lemerre, 1922), pp. 270–5. (His memoirs were written in 1840.)

During the Waterloo campaign, Noguès commanded the 2nd Brigade of the 3rd Infantry Division (Marcognet) in I Army Corps (d'Erlon).

Noguès was born in 1777 and volunteered for service in 1792. He was sergeant less than a year later and before the end of 1793 he was commissioned sous-lieutenant. *He served in the Pyrenees campaign and was wounded there as* adjutant-général. *He became aide-de-camp to Marshal Lannes as captain and campaigned with him in Italy. He became aide-de-camp to his brother in the West Indies on the 5th Messidor, Year X, and was nominated* chef de bataillon. *He was captured on Saint-Lucia by the British and sent back to be imprisoned in England. On his return to France on the 6th Pluviôse Year XIII, he was attached to the 81st de ligne. A year later he was appointed aide-de-camp to Marshal Augereau and served in the campaigns of 1805 and 1806, but took no part in any of the major battles. In the latter year he transferred his service to the Kingdom of Holland with whom he became colonel and then* brigadier des armées, *serving in the campaign in Germany in 1808. Returning to French service as* adjutant-commandant *(staff colonel) in 1810, he entered Spain the following year, serving in Catalonia where he became chief-of-staff to General Lamarque. He was promoted* général de brigade *in 1813, but continued his service in Spain until 1814 when, after Napoleon's first abdication, he was put on the inactive list until the emperor's return. Wounded at Waterloo, he was again listed as inactive, but back on the active list he commanded a sub-division of the 20th Military Division. After similar appointments, he again commanded an infantry brigade in 1833, but was put into reserve in 1834 and retired in 1848. He died in 1853.*

Noguès' account tells us of Napoleon's wish to attack the Allied army on the evening of the 17th and makes the unusual and unsubstantiated claim that d'Erlon's attack went in with no skirmishers in front.

[On arrival on the heights opposite Mont-Saint-Jean on the evening of the 17th] the emperor joined the advance-guard of which I was a part. He immediately gave orders to attack. A hundred guns of the Guard, protected by several bodies of cavalry, opened fire. Then, several generals who surrounded the emperor, amongst whom was Donezelot, said, 'Sire, our soldiers are exhausted and dying of hunger; allow them to make their soup'. 'No', replied Napoleon, 'forwards, forwards, it is a good opportunity!' However, pressing their point, the generals achieved their aim that soup should be made. *Soup, a disastrous time to stop; the cause of our disaster the next day* [his italics].

Indeed, the English army had then all its reserves in and behind Brussels. It would have been cut up in less than two hours!

General Subervie, with his light cavalry division, passed before my brigade; we were only able to salute each other with our swords; we had not seen each other for more than ten years. Colonel Marbot, today lieutenant general, was in his division. I had not met him since 1806.

During the whole night, a beating rain did not cease. At daybreak on the 18th, each dried his arms and soon the general attack began. It was Ney who, misled by the enemy, engaged the cavalry of the Guard against the squares of English infantry, deployed deliberately to draw us on, but supported by hidden reserves of artillery and cavalry. Some squares, it is true, were broken and colours taken, but the élite of our cavalry was destroyed. The first act of this great drama went to the English.

At midday, the corps of General d'Erlon, on the extreme right, shook itself out against the enemy left, towards La Haye Sainte. We were formed by battalions in echelon. No squares served us as a point of support in case of retreat. General Marcaguet [Marcognet] in starting his advance, proposed to General d'Erlon that he form his brigades in square, to wait in the corn, rye and wooded valley that we were crossing. 'Keep going', d'Erlon replied, 'do not fear'.

Thus we went forwards, while answering, in the middle of bullets, shells, the fire of Congreve rockets and balls, without fear! We reached the point of the English line with shouldered arms, not having sent out a single skirmisher from our ranks nor replied to a single shot from the enemy, when a body of cavalry, in full flight, fell on us, passed before us, the generals, without threatening us, and outflanked the battalions to the rear, one after another. These battalions, without firing a shot, turned, raising their bayonets above their heads to parry the sabre blows. Thus this cavalry, after having broken up the troops which fell under their first blows, continued to do the same as far as the rear of our column. There it fought on our left flank. The cuirassiers of Lefebvre-Desnouëttes [this general commanded the Guard light cavalry, not cuirassiers] sabred and annihilated this English cavalry.

I was wounded by a ball to my left hand, being on my horse: I rallied in the rear the debris of my brigade in the area from which we had started our advance. There I was bandaged, but absolutely refused to have my hand amputated.

At three o'clock in the afternoon, we saw on our right and a little behind us, the Prussians who had escaped from Marshal Grouchy. Count de Lobau, with his reserve, marched against them, but, inferior in strength, was forced to retreat. We followed this movement towards five o'clock. Then, and after the last efforts attempted by the emperor against the centre, the whole army retired by Genappe, Quatre-Bras towards Charleroi.

My wound gave me a fever. I lay down in a field on the main road, not far from Genape [*sic*]. Dupuy was watching and had to warn me when the last body of troops passed close to me, so that I could follow them on foot or mounted. An officer of the Grenadiers of the Guard proposed that I should be put on a stretcher. I somehow remounted my horse. In our retreat, an hour later, by a coincidence I found myself side by side with Marshals Soult and Ney. All the corps, all arms, were mixed up in a procession on the main road and either side of it. At daybreak we found Charleroi and the thirty-six guns taken from the Prussians on the 16th.

The emperor was on the other side of the Sambre, in a plain. I did not meet him. From then, I never saw him again.

The two colonels of my brigade were wounded. Their regiments were the 23rd and 63rd *de ligne* [this statement is very odd; the two regiments of his brigade were the 21st and 46th!!].

Lieutenant Jacques-François Martin

Letter (*Waterloo. Lettre d'un officier genevois du 45e*) addressed to his mother and dated Arras, 1 August 1815; published in *Carnet de la Sabretache* (1895), pp. 500–7.

During the Waterloo campaign, Jacques-François Martin served as a lieutenant in the 45th de ligne; part of the 2nd Brigade (Grenier), 3rd Infantry Division (Marcognet), part of I Army Corps (d'Erlon).

Jacques Martin was born on 12 August 1794 in Geneva, Switzerland. Becoming a French 'fellow citizen' in 1798, he entered the 154th Line as a second lieutenant in 1813 after attending the École *Militaire. He joined his regiment close to Magdeburg in April 1813. He did not fight at Lützen, but saw action at Weissig, just prior to Bautzen, where his regiment lost heavily. He also fought at Löwenberg and Goldberg, before taking part in the disaster that was the Katzbach. Over these four battles, his regiment of four battalions had forty-eight officers killed or wounded. During the retreat, the engagements that followed and the battle of Leipzig, they lost another thirty-two. During the retreat from that battle towards France, Martin was left as part of the garrison of the small fortified town of Juliers. After a three-month siege they handed the town over to the Allies in line with the Treaty of Paris that had been signed to end the war. The regiment went into garrison in Avesnes. In the re-organisation of the army, the 154th was amalgamated with the 42nd and 45th to become the new 42nd de ligne. Quickly disillusioned with Royalist rule and with little wish to serve in peacetime, Martin planned to leave the army, but the return of Napoleon re-ignited his enthusiasm. His regiment was re-numbered the 45th and in this regiment he fought at Waterloo. Finding himself in Cambrai during the retreat he lodged with a royalist family with whom he had stayed in 1814. He stayed with this family until the end of the war. He was offered a place in the* Garde de Corps, *but soon realising that he was not welcomed by those already in it he determined to return to Switzerland, which he reached in October 1815.*

Martin's account below is particularly useful because of how soon after the battle it was written. We can therefore be confident that both the more mundane and dramatic events that he describes were still fresh in his memory and that there were few pressures on him to tell anything other than the exact truth. Rather like Canler's account, this is written solely from the point of view of what he experienced and saw for himself and, also like Canler's, paints a vivid picture of his experiences in one of d'Erlon's massive columns. He was later to publish a book covering his interesting, if relatively short, military career (Souvenirs d'un Ex-Officier (1812–1815) *[Paris: Librairie Cherbuliez, 1867]). As can be seen, the book was published much later and contains many details on Waterloo that he could not have known at the time, thus exposing a natural tendency to add detail that must have been read later. It is also interesting as it is the first account from a junior rank that accuses some of treason; perhaps an understandable reaction to the defeat and an attempt to find an explanation for the inexplicable.*

Night came [on the 17th] which prevented us from continuing our march; we were forced to stop half a league from Mont-Saint-Jean, otherwise called the farm of la Belle Alliance [these were actually separate places], at Waterloo, a position very famous, where many thousands of brave men were to perish the next day who were without a doubt the day before. Indeed, we basically knew that Wellington still had a large part of his army around Brussels, but we did not expect a general action for several days, that we knew were necessary for him to fully concentrate.

Besides, the chase that he had received from us, in our minds, assured us of at least the possession of Brussels, which was only two leagues from there. Who knows? Perhaps, it is true, other reasons than the darkness of the night had forced us to stop; but, perhaps also, if we had marched an hour longer, if we had put this unfortunate position behind us, perhaps . . .

As to the rest, it is not for me to judge, the soldier only obeys and fights, except for that which he sees for himself, is perhaps the man the least instructed in operations of war where, however, he puts so much of himself. Anyway, it is there that we stopped. We wished them goodnight with some cannon shots until towards nine o'clock when our compliments finished and we thought to camp, which was not an easy thing.

The whole army was united as if by magic on this plain. The villages were not big enough for the generals, their servants, their horses, the commissaries, butchers etc., everyone who hardly bivouacked because of the weather. The houses were full of these leeches. They were overflowing, and I think, in truth, that even the emperor himself was not able to find anywhere, for we saw him erect his tent and sit by a fire.

It was therefore impossible to find wood or straw; the honest men who occupied the village, and who were in the lap of luxury, they would rather choke than leave anything for the soldiers. It is their commendable custom; it is of little importance to them whether their defenders eat or not, sleep or not, as long as they had more than enough of everything and, to ensure that no one took anything from them by the use of violence, they shouted until they were hoarse, 'It is the lodging of General such and such, it is that of his aide-de-camp. It is *M. le maréchal*, it is *M. le Prince*, etc.', and this strategy nearly always succeeded for them. Meanwhile, we were soaked to the bones, we spread out in all ways, manoeuvring in the mud up to our knees in order to be in an advantageous position to cover these 'sirs'.

What a night! It seemed that the sky was wrapped in complete darkness, had opened all its sluices. The water fell in torrents without a break. By additional luck, the regiment found itself in ploughed ground which was completely flooded. It was there that we had to rest our exhausted limbs; it was there that we had to enjoy some gentle rest. No wood, no straw; nothing for any and no means of procuring anything. What a sad state! What, however, we had the least to complain of, was sleep. On the contrary, it was not hard. Immediately that one lay down, one felt oneself sink softly down to mid-body and with the single precaution of putting a shako under the head by way of a pillow, the finest duvet was not softer. One was a little cooler, it is true, but there was another advantage; when one turned over, to be washed by the rain on the side that had got dirty when it was underneath. Despite all these conveniences, many men still moaned, cursing, sending to the devil everyone who had got them into this situation; then, having had their grumble, they all fell asleep; a remedy for all ills.

It is hard to believe, but ask a man who is on campaign what it is that he wishes to sleep on when he is excited on forced marches, by the fatigues of the march, by all kinds of fatigues that are common in war, and he will tell you that in this case one would sleep on bayonets [because they were so tired].

Early the next day, we jumped out of bed and, after our toilet, the soldiers raced off in all directions to find wood and other things they needed. Having collected enough, fires were lit in spite of the rain which had not stopped; several chops from a cow were grilled which were truly delicious, and a lot was drunk as brandy was not lacking. After this meal we patiently awaited the order to depart, which we imagined would soon come. But we were mistaken. The whole morning passed by with only a change in position.

We were the furthest forward, it is true; seeing us, the other army corps pass by in front of us; some to the right, some to the left, finally taking all the usual dispositions for a general engagement.

We realised that the moment had come when, as soldiers say, one is going to give your hair a good combing. Everyone prepared themselves; cleaned their arms, urged everyone to do well and finish the campaign with a single blow. Alas! No one knew how true this would be.

Finally, we departed. The weather was clear; the sun, in all its brilliance, shone on this imposing sight. The army deployed with magnificence before the enemy position. All contributed to render more majestic the terrible act that it prepared for.

We advanced on a hill, which disclosed to us a magnificent view in all directions. We deployed by brigade 'en masse' [closed up without intervals] and we stopped at the foot of a small height which again hid us from our enemy.

Then the artillery barrage began and it was terrible from the very start, for once we came into view from behind the height, the distance between the two armies became extremely small. We were in column by battalions and *en masse* at the moment the order arrived to climb the position and to seize, *à la bayonette*, the English batteries and anything else that offered resistance. The mountain bristled with their cannons, covered with their troops; it appeared impregnable. No matter, the order arrived, the charge beat, the shout of '*Vive l'Empereur!*' came from every mouth and we marched ahead, in closed ranks, aligned as if on a parade.

I can attest to the fact: at this critical moment, I did not see a single cowardly thought painted on the face of our soldiers. The same ardour, the same gaiety shone there as before. However, the shot had already killed many, and this foresaw that the carnage would be terrible when we arrived on their guns.

Death crept up on us from every side; entire ranks disappeared under the caseshot, but nothing could stop our march; it continued with the same order as before, with the same precision. The dead were immediately replaced by those who followed; the ranks, although becoming fewer, remained in good order. Finally, we arrived on the height. We could reap the reward of such bravery; already the English began to give way; already their guns retired at the gallop. A hollow road, lined with hedges, was the only obstacle which still separated us from them. Our soldiers did not wait for the order to cross it; they rushed over it, jumped over the hedges and broke ranks to run on against the enemy. Fatal carelessness! We were forced to get them back into order. We held them back in order to rally them . . . At the moment that I succeeded in pushing one of them back into the ranks, I saw him fall at my feet from a sabre blow; I turned around quickly. The English cavalry had charged us from every direction and we were cut to pieces. I only had time to force myself into the crowd to avoid the same fate. The noise, the smoke, the confusion, inseparable at such moments, had prevented us from noticing that, on our right, several squadrons of English dragoons had approached a sort of hollow, had deployed, formed in our rear and charged us from behind.

It is extremely difficult with even the best possible cavalry to break soldiers formed in square and who defend themselves with courage and *sang-froid*. When infantry is in disorder, it is nothing more than a massacre, almost without danger to the cavalryman, however brave the troops that are attacked. So it was here, a general massacre. The cavalry penetrated into the middle of us; our batteries, seeing we were lost and fearing that they would be taken in their turn, fired into the mêlée and killed many of us. For ourselves, in the constant flood of a confused and agitated crowd, our musket shots aimed at our enemies were as likely to hit our own men. Even courage is of little use. After prodigies of valour, our eagle, taken and re-taken, finally remained in the hands of the enemy; in vain did our soldiers, who were still on their feet, stretch their weapons to reach and stab with their bayonets the mounted cavalrymen on their lively and high horses. Useless courage; their hands and their muskets fell to the ground together and left them defenceless to a fierce enemy who sabred without pity even the children who served as drummers and fifers in the regiment who pleaded for mercy in vain.

It is there that I saw death at close quarters; my best friends fell at my side, I realised the same fate awaited me, but I had no distinct thoughts; I fought like a machine and awaited the fatal blow. I do not know how fate or rather perhaps Providence ensured the blows fell to each side of me which were perhaps destined for me and that until this moment I did not suffer a severe wound.

It was at this time that, seeing we were offering no more resistance, the English split into two groups, of which one collected the prisoners and led to the rear what remained of the division, the others crossed to our side [of the valley] to attempt to take our guns. An instant before I had been knocked over by a dragoon who passed close by me at speed; I remained on the ground amongst several dead, others who were wounded, and still others that were in the same position as me; that is to say, knocked over by a horse. Those who were leading the prisoners only forced away those who were still on their feet, without bothering themselves with searching amongst the dead for those who were still alive; they left me thus on the battlefield, where it seemed I would have to remain until the battle was decided, for, at that moment, I was only able to either surrender as a prisoner or to try to save myself by moving towards our batteries. Yet this was the path that I took. Love of freedom, almost as great as a love of life, made me determined and I succeeded after having escaped the dangers to which many others had succumbed. Indeed, I did not know if others apart from me had been saved in the same manner. One thing I did know, was that I was not in a state to take charge. Drunk with fatigue, of grief, unable to breathe, I wanted to run, but found myself in one of those dreams where, wanting to flee from danger, you move your legs without being able to advance a single step. I thus marched with luck in the middle of the cavalry which had come up from all sides of our guns. I looked around me and could only see enemies and, without hope, I marched on. This inconceivable apathy was what saved me, whilst it should have lost me a thousand times. Indeed, if I escaped the fire of our artillery, which fired on me as on them, since we climbed together, how could I hope to escape them? Three or four times I saw them find themselves very close to us make a move to turn bridle to ride over me. I don't know what stopped them, if they disregarded such a weak enemy or, which is more probable, if the balls and canister which flew around us drew their attention onto something more important. Whatever it was, we arrived together at our batteries and while they skirmished with sabre blows against the gunners, I passed through them and reached the foot of a dip some three or four hundred paces in the rear. Arriving there I threw myself to the ground to regain my breath. Whilst the danger had been pressing, my strength had been supernatural; but once I was safe it abandoned me and I could not move.

The fatigue that this march had caused me through the beaten-down corn and thick mud, from the light wounds that I began to feel, the astonishment of an almost miraculous deliverance, above all, loaded as I was, for I had my pack and my greatcoat rolled around me over my shoulder which had saved me from many sabre blows; all this, I say, caused me more fear of the danger I had just escaped than I had when I was there. I finally recovered and turned towards the flank of a unit of the Imperial Guard which was still fighting stubbornly on my left.

During this time, the cavalry that had been left half a league behind us, came up. I passed the 3rd Lancers who were preparing to charge and I was a witness to the discomfiture that they caused to the dragoons who had fixed us up. I have read since in the gazettes that there only remained thirty men from the regiment called Royal George, and I can well believe it. Our lancers worked them over so well that all who watched them, envied them; they pursued them across the battlefield where they brought back a great number of our wounded who would not otherwise have got back, and released a lot of prisoners.

The rest of the army corps were concentrated, about a few hundred men, and we were ordered to secure the edge of a wood where the enemy skirmishers had wanted to enter.

However, the battle continued with fury. The whole army achieved prodigies of valour, but the Old Guard were incredible; its squares, almost formed under canister fire, could not be broken. Three times they climbed the fatal hill, three times innumerable numbers pushed them back rather than destroy them. What rage! Mutilated soldiers, almost lifeless, found the strength to fire a last shot and avenge themselves in death. You could say that anger animated them more, even when life had already left them. But it is impossible to relate all in a combat where the rest of the army competed with the guard for courage, and above all the gun crews and the cuirassiers who were also almost destroyed. This massacre, which is perhaps unequalled in history, lasted until dark. Part of the army were strewn across the battlefield that the sad remains still defended.

Who could now explain the precipitous flight which followed so closely such heroic courage? It is not me, I am still to understand it. I know that the retreat had become indispensable, but what prevented it being conducted in order? Was it treason? Was it a terror-struck panic as some have wanted it heard? I do not know. As to the rest, this is what happened.

Night covered us with its shadows, the cannon could no longer be heard, a sad silence had succeeded the tumultuous horrors of the day, each searched for a disturbed rest interrupted painfully by the wailing of the wounded.

Suddenly, a dull sound spreads through the ranks; 'Move! Move!' We look and indeed, in the darkness we see armed men reach the Charleroi road. We fear being abandoned, we no longer hear our leaders, we rush onto the road where the greatest disorder already reigns. Artillery, cavalrymen, infantrymen, all march pell-mell, all mixed up and, from this moment, it becomes impossible to rally the army. Thus we march throughout the night, dying of hunger, exhausted, each moment risking being crushed under the wheels as happens to the unfortunate wounded who, lacking the strength to stand in the crowd, were knocked under the vehicles.

4th Infantry Division

Lieutenant General Pierre François Joseph Baron Durutte

'Movements of the 4th Division of the 1st Army Corps from the 15th to the evening of the 18th', published in the *Sentinelle de l'Armée*, No. 134, of 8 March 1838.

Reproduced in Bernard Coppens and Patrice Courcelle, *Les Carnets de la Campagne* No. 4, *La Papelotte* (Brussels: Editions de la Belle Alliance, 2000.), pp. 44–6.

During the Waterloo campaign, Durutte served as the commander of the 4th Infantry Division, part of I Army Corps (d'Erlon).

Durutte was born in 1767 and volunteered for service in 1792 with the 3rd Battalion, Volunteers du Nord, seeing immediate service in Belgium. He was commissioned as sous-lieutenant *the same year and joined Dumouriez's staff with whom he distinguished himself at Jemappes, earning promotion to lieutenant. Having been wounded the following year he missed the purges of Dumouriez's staff that followed his defection. His promotion to captain came in the 19th Dragoons and his meteoric rise continued; being promoted to* adjutant-général chef de brigade *in September 1793. He worked in various staff appointments through the revolutionary campaigns from 1795 until 1801 including the battles of Hochstadt and Hohenlinden. He was promoted to* général de division *in 1803 in the brief period of peace around that time. Durutte had become a good friend of Moreau's and consequently was very suspicious of First Consul Bonaparte's ambitions, finding himself drawn into the Moreau affair and posted by Napoleon to a dead-end job in Toulouse and then as the governor of Elba. This apparent exile ended with the war with Austria in 1809 when Durutte was re-called to active duty with Eugene's Army of Italy. He was given a divisional command and played a major role in the successes in northern Italy, ending with the victory at Raab. He was then present at Wagram and his rehabilitation was complete; Napoleon made him* baron de l'Empire. *He started the campaign of 1812 as governor of Berlin, but soon moved to divisional command under Augereau. However, he did not advance deep into Russia and did not fight in the major battles of the campaign. He missed the battles of Lützen and Bautzen, and although part of Ney's defeats at Gross Beeren and Dennewitz, his division fought well and he only enhanced his reputation. He fought at Leipzig and became military governor of Metz in 1814 which he held against overwhelming odds until breaking out to try and join Napoleon's army, but was disrupted by the Allied march on Paris. In 1815, his lukewarm support of Napoleon, at least in his earlier days, put him above royalist suspicion and he waited until Louis was out of the country before committing himself to the emperor. Even then, some of Napoleon's closest advisers were against employing him, but Davout knew his worth on the battlefield and supported his employment as a divisional commander. Left by d'Erlon on the Prussian flank at Ligny he was criticised for his caution when a bold attack may well have had important consequences for the outcome of the battle, he re-joined I Corps in time to fight at Waterloo where he was seriously wounded. Nursed back to health in Paris he retired as a result of his wounds and emigrated to Belgium where he lived quietly until his death in 1827.*

Durutte's account tells us that the battle had already started as his division took its position in line. He is clearly critical of the handling of d'Erlon's corps, though he seems to make clear that his column was not broken by the counter-attack of the British heavy cavalry. It is also interesting to note his comments on the French use of the lance. Although he talks of deploying skirmishers and then two battalions towards Frischermont, this was to counter a threat from this direction, leaving one to wonder which French troops actually attacked La Haie and Pappelotte as described by the Allied forces posted there. By the end of the battle, Durutte tells us that his whole division had been sent to the centre despite the growing pressure from the Prussians on the French right. He writes in the third person until the last paragraph.

During the night, General Durutte received the order to move on the morning of the 17th to Villers Perwin. He arrived at this village early. After several hours rest, he received the order to try to re-join I Corps that was marching on Genappe. Following the Brussels road, General Durutte marched until evening to be able to join this corps; he only stopped when night fell, half a league from Genappe. The troops were assailed in the bivouac by torrential rain which lasted until daybreak. They then started their march and re-joined the other divisions of I Corps on the Brussels road in the area of the Hougoumont wood: they took position on the height which overlooked this wood. It was on this height that the English had constructed a high framework in order to establish a telegraph. [This was in fact what became known as the 'observatory'; a wooden frame that had been erected the previous year by Dutch engineers for trigonometry.]

After about two hours rest, the 4th Division of I Corps received the order to move to the right of the main Brussels road. This important order arrived very late with the divisional commander because the officer from headquarters that had been ordered to carry it was disorientated, not knowing where he was and having rushed everywhere trying to find him. Also, when the division entered into line, the artillery were already busy firing along the whole length of the line of battle. It was immediately ordered that all divisions were to form in column by battalion, and that the enemy were to be attacked *de vive force* [by main force] in this order, in echelon, with the left leading.

General Durutte noticed that his right was exposed and that a village [probably Fischermont or Papelotte], that was at the extremity of our line, was occupied by enemy troops, observed that it was appropriate that he should cover these troops and that consequently, he would form *en potence* to the line. But he was told that there should be no change to the emperor's dispositions, and he carried out the order received when he saw the divisions to the left in motion.

The artillery of the Guard placed on the heights to the rear of this division, fired briskly at the enemy who replied with about the same number of guns. Several regiments of cavalry were also nearby. As he set off, General Durutte urged this cavalry to deploy to his right and support his movement, but it did nothing. The persistence of the emperor in separating the different arms and not subordinating the cavalry to the generals who commanded the infantry divisions, often had fatal results and such happened on this day. The 4th Division had Donzelot's 3rd Division to its left, but it could not see it; it was probably in a dip.

Arriving on a height, General Durutte saw that a column of enemy cavalry was advancing on the 2nd Division, commanded by General Marcognet; this cavalry charged this division with vigour and broke it entirely. General Durutte advanced his division quickly towards this column, but was soon forced to stop to receive this cavalry that started towards him. When it was within musket range, a volley from the first battalion stopped it and it is believed that several officers of this column were wounded; a hundred and fifty drunken cavalrymen, who were unable to hold back their horses, reached our positions.

General Durutte had ordered the divisional artillery to deploy on a height in front of that of the Guard; whilst it executed this movement, these cavalrymen reached it, sabred several gunners and the others took flight as well as the drivers who cut the traces of their horses, so that the divisional artillery remained on the battlefield without horses.

Some French lancers, about a squadron, approached in skirmish order close to the division; they killed all the cavalry that had come from the English column. On no occasion was the superiority of the lance over the sabre more clearly seen.

After this event, General Durutte formed his division into two columns by brigade; one commanded by General Pégot and the other by General Brue. General Marcognet's division was obliged to rally behind our line.

The corps commanded by General Lobau that was deployed behind General Durutte's division that was obliged to weaken itself by sending out some skirmishers and to face those of the enemy which threatened its right. It was soon forced to send one or two battalions towards Frischermont.

The cannonade continued for some time, always in the same direction; but in the distance on the right was seen a body of cavalry. Sometime after, a cannonade was heard on this side and no one doubted that it was the Prussians who were approaching our rear right. All the cavalry that was close to Durutte's division, as well as the guard artillery, received the order to march on this flank.

Marshal Ney continued to attack the enemy along the main road towards Mont-Saint-Jean, with the troops of the first division. It appeared that he used them successively, by regiment, in a way that just destroyed them one after another. He then did the same with Donzelot's division, so that by evening there was only the 4th Division that was left holding its position before the enemy. It was without artillery; General d'Erlon finally procured four twelve-pounder guns for it.

The corps of General Lobau had changed front to the right, to face the Prussian troops. This position was maintained for some time; a big engagement was seen towards the left, on the side of Braine La Leude. On this side our troops were weakened and to our right, the Prussian army was still approaching, although it had established a lively cannonade. The numbers of our troops had reduced to such an extent in the centre, close to the main road, that General Durutte was forced to send a brigade to the left of this road, and a regiment on the main road to support the troops that had taken position at la Maison-Carrée. Towards 7pm, one could see that our two wings were weak. It was then that the emperor decided to make an effort in the centre with part of his guard, that had been kept in reserve until now.

He was seen to advance at the head of a column of grenadiers along the main road on the left, heading towards a height where the enemy had a large quantity of artillery. The undulating ground did not allow General Durutte to get a good view of what happened at this point. He was pre-occupied by watching a column of cavalry that was approaching his right.

He sent several officers of the headquarters to warn the emperor to put some cavalry at his disposal, in order to oppose this column which continued to advance and which appeared to be strong. Suddenly, he noticed on the road, a large number of French soldiers that were retiring. Some of them approached the four twelve-pounders that General d'Erlon had put at his disposal; it communicated the terror that had seized it to the drivers and gunners.

He saw this battery flee at the gallop; the efforts of officers from the head-quarters could not stop it. Then he marched rapidly with Brue's brigade towards the main road to attempt to stop the fugitives and to rally them behind this brigade which was in good order and calm. Their efforts were useless. The left of the army was rapidly withdrawing. As General Durutte found himself in the most advanced position, he was threatened with being outflanked by the enemy if he did not move back. He executed this move with the intention of crossing the road to attempt to rally General Pégot's brigade to him who was on the far side, and to which, at the instigation of the emperor, had been ordered to follow the movement of the Guard.

At this moment he met General d'Erlon, who was accompanied by only a few of his headquarters and General Garbé [the commander of the Corps' engineers].

General d'Erlon decided to remain close to General Durutte and to march with the brigade that, probably, was the only body of troops of his army corps that maintained its order at this moment: everybody was retiring in confusion and moving too quickly for the infantry to keep up.

General Durutte soon lost sight of General d'Erlon; the light was fading. Always attempting to approach the main road, he was stopped by a ravine. Fearing that his men would disperse if he tried to cross it, he tried to cross himself, not having any officers of the headquarters near him.

On returning, he was very surprised not to find the brigade where he had left it. An officer shouted to him from the other side of the ravine, that Marshal Ney had taken it and had ordered it to march to the rear. In attempting to locate the main road, he saw a mass of men who were withdrawing in disorder. They were followed by English skirmishers who were causing them casualties as no one was facing up to them.

General Durutte noticed a platoon of about fifty French chasseurs à cheval a short distance away. He rushed to them and urged them to charge the English skirmishers; they did not hear. A sort of stupor had seized their spirits.

[*There is a break here and the account that follows becomes the first person; there is no explanation for this. It is likely that this was added by Durutte after the completion of the original narrative.*]

I remained behind several times to observe the enemy. Hearing some noise behind me, I turned and found myself in the middle of a body of enemy cavalry who sabred me. I received a sabre blow in the face and another on the wrist of my right hand. The blood of my wound to the cheek having spurted into my eyes blinded me for some time. I remained in the middle of the enemy in the belief that they would finish me off, but my hat had fallen off and the horse I was mounted on had only a simple saddle, because several hours earlier having had my horse wounded, I had had to mount that of my servant; what's more, having a greatcoat over my uniform, the enemy did not take me for a general officer, they left me and occupied themselves by retiring from the crowd in which they found themselves and where they feared they would suddenly be attacked by a unit of cavalry stronger than themselves.

Captain M. Chapuis

Waterloo, Notice sur le 85e de Ligne pendant la Campagne de 1815 (Annonay, Librairie P. Ranchon, 1863), pp. 44–50.

During the Waterloo campaign Chapuis commanded a grenadier company in the 85th de ligne (Colonel Masson). This regiment was part of the 2nd Brigade (Brue), 4th Infantry Division (Durutte), part of I Army Corps (d'Erlon).

The above pamphlet, published in 1863, brought together a number of letters that Captain Chapuis had written to the editor of the Sentinelle de l'Armée, *written in response to the publication of a volume on Waterloo which was published as a part of a multi-volume history of the wars of the Empire by Thiers. It was written to highlight many errors that Chapuis had identified and which he wanted to correct. One of the letters, dated Paris, 1st February 1838, included an account of the actions of the 85th de ligne at Waterloo from which the account of the battle is reproduced below. At Waterloo, Chapuis was wounded seven times; four of the wounds were serious and he only escaped from the battlefield thanks to the Duke de Bassano, who, touched by*

the poor state he was in, had him put on his carriage and taken as far as Charleroi
where the vehicle had to be abandoned. Chapuis was then aided by an army commissary.
He later became colonel of the 4th Legion of the National Guard.

Chapuis gives us a detailed and interesting account of the battle from his regiment's
perspective and how it was left out of d'Erlon's attack in order to protect the artillery.
He speaks disparagingly of his divisional commander, Durutte, who he could not forgive
for not taking a more active role at Ligny on the 16th and wondered if Durutte was
implicated in the desertion of his chief-of-staff and aide-de-camp on the same day.
He does not mention a movement to support the centre as Durutte claims; perhaps the
85th were left behind as they had been during d'Erlon's attack.

The 85th Regiment of the Line was part, with the 95th Line, the second brigade
(General Brue) of the 4th Division (General Durutte) of I Army Corps (General
Drouet d'Erlon) . . . This regiment was composed of only two battalions,
forming together a total of little more than 900 men; but it must not be ignored
that these same men were commanded by the brave Colonel Masson, who had
come from the 3rd Tirailleurs of the Guard a few days before the start of the
campaign, were experienced and resolute soldiers who would fight to the end.
Most of them came from the English prison ships at the peace of 1814, in which
a long and diabolical agony had been their lot; they looked forward to the
time that they would find themselves face to face with their torturers.

If at Waterloo, they would be able to take a just revenge for the cruel agonies
that they had had to endure, it was the only destiny they wished for; for, during
the struggle, their conduct was admirable: they nearly all fell, but, in falling, their
last words indicated that they understood that the battle was a fight to the death.
At no other time, in no other place, did the soldiers of the 85th display greater courage.

Why was it necessary that fate was to paralyse such great efforts and such
noble devotion?

. . . On the 17th, the 4th Division left Wagnelé to re-join the other three divisions
of I Corps, which had been directed towards Quatre Bras on the evening of the
16th. This reunion was not effected; the 4th Division having received the
order to stop behind the emperor's general headquarters.

Held up in our march by the rain, the mud and the numerous columns that
were all advancing towards the same point, we arrived so late at the position that
had been designated to us, that it was impossible for the soldiers to shelter from
the poor weather.

Beaten by continuous rain, without any fires, the night was very cruel; all of
us saw the arrival of day with satisfaction; but the muster that brought us together
under arms, showed us, by the dismal silence that reigned in our ranks, that we
had lost our energy and that several hours of rest were necessary to properly
prepare us to appear before the enemy.

A halt having been ordered, we took the position that you have indicated in your narration.

All that you say on the subject, *Monsieur le directeur*, is perfectly accurate; I would only add that on leaving the location of the telegraph to re-join the other three divisions of I Corps, the officers of the 85th found it very difficult to prevent the soldiers from shouting '*Vive l'Empereur!*' when they passed him. In order not to indicate to the enemy the point that we approached, the place that he occupied, the order had been given to keep completely silent as we went by; also, our soldiers deeply regretted that they were prevented from showing the feelings that they had experienced, for it was the first time that most of the 85th had been able to see the great captain for whom they had so much admiration and devotion.

As you indicate, I Corps took a very poor deployment to march on the enemy, but you have been misled when you say that it was to remedy this and to have a reserve that General Durutte ordered the 85th to maintain its position.

Such a contingency did not exist; one had not wanted to rectify a position that no one thought was as bad as it became. In admitting the opposite, this was not a weak reserve that in a few minutes found itself far from the division of which it was a part, that one would have to wait for assistance, which no one sensed the vital necessity, because it did not occur to anyone that the offensive movement of I Corps would be, from the start, completely paralysed.

It was to support a battery of twelve guns, placed on the left flank of the 4th Division, that the 85th did not follow; so it found itself then in a position to defend itself vigorously, it is to its chief alone, and to no other, that this happened.

The corps advanced, Colonel Masson understood that his isolated position would be dangerous. He had the 85th formed into a single square in two ranks; its numerical weakness did not allow it to form in three. Full of self-confidence, our worthy chief knew how to communicate with his subordinates and it was in this appropriate deployment (so much is it true that good colonels make good regiments) that we encountered the English dragoons that had passed through the divisions of I Corps.

Following their success, they arrived at the front face of the square, but a lively fire, properly aimed, paralysed the élan of this cavalry which nothing seemed capable of stopping, such was their impetuosity, so great was it.

The ground was strewn with red jackets and grey horses; and our shouts of '*Vive l'Empereur!*' proved to them that we would not be easy to beat. It whirled around us, and everything that our fire spared was soon destroyed by a regiment of lancers and a regiment of chasseurs à cheval that were a short distance behind the 85th.

These two regiments profited admirably from the situation. They gave us the spectacle of one of those clashes, where the individual courage of our soldiers was displayed so brilliantly.

At the 'port arms', whilst the cavalry fought bravely man to man, the fire of the 85th had ceased as if executing it at training.

The rolling of the drums, the blows of the drumsticks to send the officers to their battle positions, demonstrated clearly the merit of our colonel and how we would have been able to count on him. With a less experienced colonel, instead of a steady resistance, we would have been wiped out, for it was necessary to recall that the divisions of I Corps were thrown back in the greatest disorder and that our soldiers had to cross bayonets to prevent all these demoralised men destroying the surviving elements of our force, which had been lost in the other regiments because of the faults that had been committed. This instant, where an army corps sought safety in a precipitous retreat, whilst a handful of soldiers faced with success the dangers which surrounded them, was, for the 85th, one of the best moments that made them from then on an invincible regiment and placed them highly in the opinion of the army, that all envied its fortune and tried to imitate it.

This great moment we owed to two great chiefs; Colonel Masson and our *général de brigade* Brue. The latter had followed with the 95th, the second regiment of our brigade, the offensive movement of the 4th Division. At the retrograde movement, he entered our square at the time that we came to open fire, and he strongly contributed by his energy to the great success that we obtained.

With two men of the calibre of those I have named, with a high number of soldiers that had formerly come from the English pontoons, one knew that there was the courage, the dedication and means of resistance in a numerically weak square, but as solid as the living 'redoubt' of Marengo.

As you say in your narration, 'the debris of the 4th Division rallied behind the 85th', but you are in error when you add several lines later, 'that the emperor, to repair the disorganisation of Pégot's brigade, sent several batteries that were guarded by Brue's brigade'.

As I have already said, the battery, and not the batteries, was established before the offensive movement. Forced to pull back into the rear at the time of the charge of the English dragoons, it re-entered the line when they had been thrown back.

Opposed to an English battery, it was supported by the 85th alone, and by no other regiment, for without the lively opposition of General Brue, the 85th would have left its position from where it had offered such a spirited resistance, in order to join the rest of the 4th Division, which had stopped several hundred metres behind this position.

Our brigade commander knew that in the critical state that I Corps was in, there was an absolute necessity not to make a retrograde move by the only regiment that remained intact, that he haughtily refused, on two different occasions, to obey General Durutte's orders to re-join the division.

Established close to the battery with ordered arms, for several hours the 85th suffered considerable casualties so that the grenadier company alone had twenty-two killed or wounded.

Seeing these men fall horribly mutilated by cannonballs, one would have thought that the morale of those who remained standing would have been shaken; but not one weakened.

Admirably commanded, our soldiers always remained full of courage of which our colonel gave us such a good example. Also, in these difficult hours, there were acts of such firmness that it was hard to believe in such heroism and self-sacrifice. The following event offers the proof. The first grenadier of one of our two companies, a man remarkable for his impressive physique, his moral force and his great height (close to six feet), was killed by a ball. As he fell, he uttered these words, 'Here goes the most handsome man in the regiment!'

These words are forever engraved in my memory; they indicate to you, *monsieur le directeur*, what our soldiers were made of and what part could be drawn from men that died with such courage. As I have already said to you, and as I must repeat again, at no time, in no place, had the 85th displayed more bravery or more devotion.

The English skirmishers, and then the Prussian skirmishers, had advanced close enough to worry us, so the companies of our regiment were sent against them one after the other. The turn of the grenadier company that I commanded had arrived; we marched to half range of the enemy. There we employed all the willingness and energy to worthily fulfil the mission that had been confided in us. I believe that we were not lacking, and that if success did not crown our efforts it was because of a lack of something other than courage, since we did everything that it was humanly possible to do, and that the grenadier company performed as well as skirmishers as it had been remarkable under artillery fire.

Charged at the end of the day by enemy cavalry, it died almost entirely and everything that cannonball and musket ball had spared was sabred and trampled under the hooves of the horses.

Wounded myself, successively by seven blows, of which four were very serious (the first struck me at the beginning of the struggle and the last at the end), I owed my survival only to the lively fusillade of a battalion of the Imperial Guard which stopped the charge in the centre in which I found myself. This murderous fire allowed me to escape the situation in which French musket balls would no more spare me than the enemy cavalry that they killed and wounded around me . . .

Chef de Bataillon Joseph-Marcelin Rullière

Letter written in January 1856 and sent to Colonel Charras who was writing an account of the 1815 campaign. In Jean-Marc Largeaud, *Napoléon et Waterloo: la Défaite glorieuse de 1815 à nos jours* (Paris: La Boutique de l'histoire, 2006), pp. 374–7.

During the battle of Waterloo, Rullière commanded the 2nd Battalion of the 95th de ligne. *This regiment was part of the 2nd Brigade (Brue) of the 4th Infantry Division (Durutte), part of I Army Corps (d'Erlon).*

Rullière was born in 1787. He accumulated forty-three years of service and made twenty-two campaigns. Vélite in the Guard in 1807, lieutenant in 1811, captain in 1812, chef de bataillon *in 1813 and in 1815. His personal file carries the following specifics: 'This superior officer saved at Waterloo, at seven thirty in the evening, the eagle of the 95th Regiment at the moment when Brue's brigade of Durutte's division was thrown into the middle of the English army by Marshal Ney who had put himself at the head of this brigade when the whole army was beginning its retreat'. [S.H.A.T. Dossier Rullière, G.D. 2nd Série 1135.] He went on to become a* général de division *and then a politician, though the latter only for a short time. The* coup d'état *of 2 December 1851 put an end to his career. He died in 1863.*

Rullière's account is of particular interest, not least because I am unaware of its use, or any part of it, in any other English language book on Waterloo. I have therefore taken the liberty of presenting it in full and not restricting myself just to the day of the 18th, in the hope that this will be of interest to readers. Rullière's account is the only one that seems to describe in detail the formation of d'Erlon's corps for its attack on the allied left centre and he also speaks of its weaknesses. Like Chapuis, he makes no mention of his regiment moving to the French centre late in the battle.

Before 20 March 1815, the regiment had three battalions and only a cadre of officers for the 4th Battalion. These last, were almost all on leave. Each battalion had about 400 men, which made the regiment about 1,200 men. The youngest soldiers had two years' service and the others three to twelve. 120 to 150 old soldiers had come from the English pontoons; they had been made prisoners before Cadiz.

As a result of the decree of 29 March, promulgated on 11 April, the regiment received 250 to 300 experienced soldiers. We soon formed two war battalions of around 550 men each; these battalions were well organised, ready for war and animated by a good spirit.

Going on manoeuvres, or en route through the towns and villages, the non-commissioned officers and soldiers often by the spirit of teasing the inhabitants of northern France who they thought were hostile to the emperor, often shouted '*Vive l'Empereur!*' These shouts were deafening and even contrary to good discipline, to good order, for they announced to the enemy the presence of our columns, when the ground did not otherwise allow them to be seen; however, I defended them many times and the emperor himself recognised the necessity of condoning them at Ligny and at Waterloo.

In the first days of May, we formed the division and the army corps. The regiment was part of the 4th Division of I Corps: it was composed of four regiments, two battalions per regiment (8th, 29th, 85th and 95th). The 85th had 800 bayonets at most. The other regiments were stronger. We estimated the strength of the army corps at about 19,000 infantry, not including artillery. A light cavalry brigade was attached, of about 800 sabres.

During the First Restoration, the regiment received the uniforms and equipment that it required and even the necessary linen and shoes; it was probably the same across the army. It is thus an error that General Gourgaud wrote somewhere that the soldiers were naked.

I Corps was commanded by General Count d'Erlon; he first had his headquarters at Lille, then at Valenciennes. The troops were lodged in the barracks, the houses of the local inhabitants and in the villages around this place. They manoeuvred three times each week by regiment. The Division, of which the regiment was a part, was commanded by *Général de Division* Count Durutte who had been distinguished in all the campaigns in Germany and some of those in Italy; he had an understanding of the great war.

Late in the morning of 13 June, General in Chief d'Erlon concentrated his army corps on the glacis of Valenciennes and ordered the troops to be prepared to go on campaign. There, the regiments received their eagles that the colonels had carried from Paris, where they had received them from the hands of the emperor. Immediately after this solemn parade, which lasted hardly two hours, I Corps set off on its march towards the frontier; and on 15 June it crossed the Sambre at Marchiennes au Pont and bivouacked astride the road to Brussels, a league and a half in front of the junction of the road to Charleroi. II Corps bivouacked in front of I Corps, also on the road.

On 16 June, we waited to march forwards at a very early hour. General Kellerman's cavalry corps marched along the road towards 8am and deployed, I cannot say the hour, a little to the right of the road, behind a wood: it was in the first line of II Army Corps, commanded by General Count Reille. This corps was in contact with the English who were established at Quatre Bras. I cannot say the hour when it arrived at this position.

Finally, towards ten or eleven o'clock in the morning, I Corps left its bivouacs and stopped a little to the right of Kellerman's cavalry behind the wood. A division of light cavalry of the Imperial Guard had joined General Kellerman.

The 4th Division, because of the seniority of General Durutte, marched at the head of the army corps; and from the position where we halted, we could see the extreme right of the Prussian army supported by a unit of cavalry; it was about 12.30pm.

Soon, it would have been 1.30pm, General d'Erlon set I Corps off on a march to turn and fall on the right of the Prussians. Everyone had high hopes for this movement, we said the Prussians would not be able to hold there without exposing themselves to a flank attack which would seriously compromise them, while the corps under the direction of the Emperor attacked the front of the Prussian army. We had already made three-quarters of a league when an aide de camp from Marshal Ney came to stop I Corps and to order it to return to its previous position behind the small wood close to Kellerman's cavalry. General d'Erlon obeyed, but in the whole army corps numerous murmurs were heard against this false movement; it was said that II Corps was engaged, we heard the cannon, but this was not the sound of a serious engagement. It was at this moment that we learnt that I and II Infantry Corps and Kellerman's cavalry had been placed under the orders of Marshal Ney.

Hardly had the corps arrived close to Kellerman's cavalry than a superior officer sent by the emperor, carried the order to I Corps to march, immediately, on the right flank of the Prussian army; it was around 3pm. For a second time General d'Erlon started his march against the Prussians to the joy of all I Corps. But it was of short duration. Indeed, half a league from our position, a second counter-order from Marshal Ney recalled I Corps to its first position behind the wood, making General d'Erlon responsible for its execution. The discontent in the whole of I Corps was very lively. Thus, for the second time, we turned, to our great regret, our backs to the Prussians. Arriving close to the wood, we heard a very lively cannonade at Quatre Bras. II Corps were fighting and in second line it had part of General Kellerman's cavalry; it was almost 6 o'clock. The troops had only been halted there half an hour when an officer, sent by the emperor, arrived with the imperative order for General d'Erlon to make a very rapid movement without delay against the Prussian right. The cannonade and musketry were very heavy at Quatre Bras*. General d'Erlon did not think it his duty to conform to such a precise order, but General Durutte then observed to him that an order coming directly from the Emperor, overall commander of the two armies, it was necessary to execute it. General d'Erlon did not want to. Then General Durutte proposed to the general in chief that his own division should make this important movement and the light cavalry brigade. General d'Erlon agreed and General Durutte immediately set off. When the voltigeurs of General Durutte's division opened fire on the Prussian scouts it was about eight o'clock; we soon noticed a retrograde movement in the right wing of this [the Prussian] army. It perfectly

---

* The text in the margin about the cannonade said: 'It was even livelier at Ligny!' Perhaps this was written by Charras

demonstrated to us that if I Corps, at 2pm, had vigorously engaged the Prussians, their army could not have held with the resistance it was able to deploy in front of Ligny.

The simultaneous attack of the corps that the emperor directed in person and of the four divisions of d'Erlon, would certainly have forced the Prussians to retreat, and this retreat would have caused them considerable losses and we would not have had to regret, at Ligny, the thousands of brave men that we left there in killed and wounded. The Prussian army, whose advanced sentries were at half musket range from ours, operated its retreat during the night without being pursued.

Thus, we had, on 16 June, the very lively regret to see the 20,000 men of I Corps march from left to right and right to left, with shouldered arms, without firing a single cannon shot at Quatre Bras against the English, or to our right against the Prussian army.

It is without doubt that the English would not have held at Quatre Bras if they had learnt during the day of the 16th of the retreat of the Prussian army; and neither would they have stopped at the Soignes forest the next day; and on the 18th there would have been no battle of Waterloo. All this would certainly have changed the state of affairs, we would not have allowed ourselves to have committed the enormous faults, of such a general in chief; we still do not know how the general orders were given.

In all I Corps, we did not think that the battle of Ligny was decisive; I Corps not having been engaged, all the important successes that we could have gained at Ligny, did not happen. In the evening we took all the positions of the Prussian army; but we lost there many men and the Prussian army was not wiped out as it should have been with the timely assistance of I Corps.

We knew that until two o'clock in the afternoon, the English hardly had more than 10 to 12,000 men at Quatre Bras and that from 3 to 8 o'clock in the evening their forces increased to about 25 to 30,000 men, but from one o'clock in the afternoon Marshal Ney had under his hand I and II Corps, the cavalry of General Kellerman and of the Imperial Guard; about 50,000 infantry and 8,000 sabres [actually an exaggeration]. We could even have brought them together several hours earlier by making them leave their bivouacs earlier. These 60,000 men launched with impetuosity, with the vigour that Marshal Ney knew so well how to transmit to the troops on a field of battle, would certainly have wiped out the English who had not been able to take position in the evening of the next day, in the Soignes forest, either to accept battle on the 18th or to receive the support of the Prussians.

We are forced to think that if the 60,000 men of our left had simultaneously attacked the English, it would have been an affair of an hour and a half. I Corps would then have had the time, then, to throw itself onto the Prussian right at an opportune and decisive moment.

The emperor, by his strategic movements that one has to admire, would have been able, unknown to Wellington and Blücher, to throw the different corps of his army into the middle of the cantonments of the Prussian and English armies. The faults of the day of the 16th meant he lost the fruits, the immense advantages, that he could have expected.

In the night of the 15th/16th, Colonel Gordon, chief-of-staff of the 4th Division, and *chef d'escadron* Gaugler, General Durutte's aide-de-camp, passed to the enemy.

On the 17th, Durutte's division re-joined, towards 9am, I Corps in the area of Quatre Bras, where II Corps and Kellerman's cavalry had bivouacked.

The English army had operated its retreat during the night.

The emperor, followed behind by his guard, VI Infantry Corps and the Artillery Reserve, arrived at Quatre Bras towards 10am and appeared very unhappy that all the corps of the left wing were still in position; he immediately had them set off in march in the direction of Brussels along the main road.

They were followed by the troops that the emperor had led to Quatre Bras.

The hold-ups of the morning of the 17th, were all the more prejudicial to the French army, that the rain having started at 2pm had soon soaked the ground and forced the army to march on the main road in a single column; the general movement was considerably held up. It was almost night when I Corps, formed in column along the road, a short distance to the rear of La Belle Alliance, where the emperor's general headquarters had been established. It rained a lot and the soldiers had mud up to their knees; impossible to light a fire, even for their soup. Thus the night was very poor for the French army. There, we learnt that the English army had taken position a short distance ahead, backed onto the Soignes forest where it was sheltered by the trees of the forest and could make fires.

Towards 4am on the 18th, the rain stopped; but on our side, it had so soaked the ground that it was impossible for artillery, cavalry and even the infantry to manoeuvre immediately; it only really became practicable towards 11am.

At 6am, Durutte's division received the order to go and establish itself on a height to the left of the main road, where the English had established some time before a telegraph. We arrived there towards 8am and immediately started to make soup and light fires to dry ourselves. From this height, which dominated all the surrounding area, we were able to distinguish the English and French lines. I will not describe the ground as it is well enough known. The English had covered their front with a numerous artillery. Their principal forces of infantry and cavalry were a little to the right of their centre in front of the forest, but hidden by the elevation of the ground. They strongly occupied the château of Goumont, the gardens and a wood. Their left extended as far as Papelotte in front of the forest.

Towards 10.30 am II Corps took position a short distance from a small wood and the gardens of the château of Goumont; their right supported on the main road and their left at the foot of the telegraph height, called Mont Plaisir, I think. The cavalry of our army and that of the Imperial guard (about 10 to 11,000 sabres) formed in mass in second line to II Corps. The artillery reserves were a little to the rear. The infantry divisions of the Imperial Guard were astride the road and level with the small elevation where the Emperor had already established himself and from where he did not move until towards 6 or 7.30pm when he moved forwards.

I Corps took position to the right, level with II Corps. Its left was on the main road and its right opposite the English left. The 4th Division moved down from the telegraph height and came to form on the right, on the same line as the other divisions of this Corps; it was thus charged with attacking the extreme left of the English. We were in such a hurry that General Durutte was forced to order the marmites to be turned over; the meat was not yet cooked. The soldiers thus only had a small piece of bread to eat before fighting.

We have already said that the four divisions of I Corps each had four regiments, or eight battalions. General d'Erlon ordered the forming of a single column by each division. The 1st Battalion deployed [in line] and the seven others also deployed and closed up on the 1st with only five paces distance from one guide to the other – this appeared extremely defective to everyone, as it deprived the *chefs de bataillon* [battalion commanders] of the freedom of action to deploy their battalions as necessary. The 1st Battalion was able to use all its firepower to the front, but the others were not able to, since they were masked by those who marched in front of them. The two flanks were only able to fire thirty or forty shots and would be unable to offer any resistance to cavalry charges. The *chefs de bataillon*, colonels, generals, were able to march well enough, on horseback, on the flanks of the column, but they could not be in [their correct] place in the centre of the columns.

Only that [the commander] of the eighth [rear] battalion had the possibility of manoeuvring: he thus formed his battalion in square in the rear of the 1st Division from where he noticed the English cavalry fall on the divisions of I Corps which were to the left of Durutte's division. But this general, whilst approving the reason which had influenced the *chef de bataillon*, directed him to again deploy his battalion like the other battalions of the division.

II Corps had already started its attack on Goumont, or Hougoumont, when I Corps started its advance. The left-hand division of I Corps, with its left on the road, marched on La Haye Sainte and the other divisions of the army corps on the English troops that were in front of them. The divisions maintained a distance of 4 to 500 paces between each other – we were separated from the English by small undulations of the ground. Despite a strong cannonade and a lively skirmish

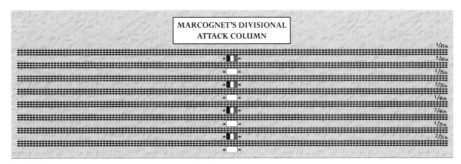

Diagram of one of d'Erlon's columns: For his attack on the Allied centre left, d'Erlon deployed his corps with each division in a type of column unseen on any other battlefield of the Napoleonic wars; with each battalion deployed in a line of three ranks and each formed one behind the other with only a short interval between each battalion. No French eyewitnesses, including d'Erlon, explain this unique formation, but many condemned it retrospectively after its spectacular overthrow by the British heavy cavalry. However, d'Erlon and some of his senior commanders, having been consistently bettered by the British in Spain, may have felt that such a formation offered the firepower of line and the momentum and power of column.

fire, I Corps arrived, with shouldered arms, to within half musket range of the English line. But several regiments of English dragoons charged the left flank of our divisions at this moment who were unable, because of their poor formation, to offer any resistance!

These divisions, successively broken, were thrown into each other and thus arrived on Durutte's division which suffered the same fate. I Corps was thus disorganised and lost many men killed, wounded and prisoner, without counting the fugitives who went to sow alarm in the rear of the army.

For a few instants I Corps was thus mixed up with the English dragoons; we fought with bayonet blows and musket butts. Happily, a division of cuirassiers and lancers, who had been temporarily attached to I Corps, arrived at the gallop and charged the English dragoons vigorously, who were nearly all killed there.

I Corps concentrated and reformed. The losses were considerable. When we were back in order, we were supported by twenty-five to thirty guns of the artillery of the Imperial Guard that the emperor sent to re-establish the combat at this point and this cannonade contributed to stopping the English.

General Durutte had left behind the division a regiment which had at most 800 men to serve as a support in case of need. This regiment having formed square, successfully repulsed the charges of the English cavalry: clear proof that if the divisions of I Corps had been formed in columns by regiment and by division, at a *peleton*[1] distance, these regiments at 100 to 200 paces apart, the squares, once formed, would certainly have repulsed the English dragoons, as did the regiment we have already cited.

Our cavalry division rendered a great service to I Corps. One asks why no one had given this division the order to support the I Corps' attack. If it had been found there, at the moment of the charge of the English dragoons, it would have immediately launched itself on them, would have repulsed them and allowed the divisions of I Corps to continue their attack. We were not very far from the Soignes forest when we were stopped by the English cavalry. This movement would have been decisive, for once established on the left flank of the English army, we would have cut their communications with the Prussians, which have forced these last into a retrograde movement and have made it impossible for them to have attacked us.

VI Corps, which had taken position a certain distance to the right of the Guard infantry and to the rear of I Corps, would have been able to support the advance of I Corps; as no one had yet noticed the Prussian columns.

On the return of our prisoners, we learnt that the attack of I Corps, although it had not succeeded, had nevertheless produced disorder in the rear of the English army and that this disorder was increased by the attack of the army's cavalry which captured, but was not able to retain, nor take off, the English artillery, which was in front of it. We were assured that the brilliant charges of our cavalry were ordered too early and that we did not have it available at the end of the day when it would have been so useful.

It was about 3 o'clock when I Corps suffered this check. The divisions, well reduced, sustained an aggressive musketry with the English skirmishers and attempted several times, without success, to seize la Haie Sainte.

From three to four o'clock we started to notice the movements of the Prussians on the right of our army. Sometime after, we received the fire of their scouts. My battalion tried to stop them – it succeeded – a strong fire of musketry lasted for half an hour, when General Labédoyère, the emperor's aide-de-camp, hurrying across the front of the army, came to announce that it was Marshal Grouchy who was deploying on our right. I pointed out to him what was already known by everyone else, that to the contrary, it was the Prussians that we had in front of us, that we had already killed and wounded several men and at the same moment the captain of voltigeurs of my battalion fell wounded by a ball to the thigh. I had him placed on my horse, for the Prussians were beginning to appear in force and I sent him to the army's ambulances.

We did not know what was happening with II Corps.

The Prussian army started to deploy to turn the right of the French army and take it in the rear; VI Corps, a division of the Young Guard and some cavalry opposed them. I cannot give details on what happened on this part of the battlefield. It was evident that the Prussian army manoeuvred to threaten our army's retreat.

The fighting with I and II Corps was always hard.

When the English army saw the progress of the Prussians on our right flank, it prepared to make a general attack on our whole line. It was about 7pm.

Then we saw arrive on the main road the emperor himself leading several regiments of the Middle Guard to make a new attack on La Haye Sainte. His intention, it was said, was to force this point on the English centre. But unfortunately, this last effort was no more successful than the first. The Guard lost many men. The emperor, losing all hope of success on this point, returned to his first position. He was sombre, but calm and firm. He ordered the Old Guard to form several squares to the right and left of the road. Towards eight o'clock, the English army having advanced, the weak battalions or detachments of the different regiments which still held on our line retired in disorder. The emperor had hoped that they would stop close to the squares of the Old Guard; but they continued their retreat mixed up with the cavalry and artillery and this retreat soon changed into a terrible rout.

General Durutte, noticing the disorder which reigned to our left, concentrated two weak regiments of his division, around 1,000 men, supported their left on the road with the intention of forming a rearguard with which to receive those that were retreating. Arriving close to a small steep-sided track, which our weak column would not be able to cross without breaking up, the general, wanting to avoid this inconvenience, stopped us and ordered us to wait while he went to find an easier passage. He had hardly left, than Marshal Ney arrived with us; he was animated and his horse covered in mud and blood: he had part of a sword in his hand and addressed these few words to us that I remember clearly. 'Come, come my brave comrades, I will go to show you how a marshal of France dies on the battlefield!' The two weak regiments replied with shouts of '*Vive l'Empereur! Vive le Maréchal Ney!*' The small column had not gone 200 paces towards ground that hid from us the English army, the whole of which we then saw marching forwards. At the same moment, cannon shots of canister and a furious cavalry charge had soon killed and wounded more than half our column. An English officer and dragoon threw themselves at our eagle to capture it, seriously wounding the *Porte-Aigle*. I only just had the time to snatch the eagle from his hands and to throw myself into the sunken lane following Marshal Ney who, by a miracle, had not received a single wound. He joined a square of the Old Guard at the gallop and I entered with him. English dragoons pursued us into the sunken lane; but one of their horses having fallen, it stopped the pursuit by the others for a short time.

Meanwhile, General Durutte had retraced his steps to re-direct his two weak regiments, completely ignorant that Marshal Ney had led them against the enemy: he fell into the middle of the English cavalry and was mercilessly sabred; a sabre blow struck him on the right wrist and others horribly cut his face; covered in blood, the English abandoned him behind them, but his horse, which he could not control, for he had almost lost consciousness, followed the charge and the main road where he happily got mixed up in the fugitives; the general, recognised by a sergeant of cuirassiers, finally arrived at Genappe where his hand was amputated at the wrist. The Old Guard were retreating to the right and left of the main road: it was a terrible rout. The crowding at Genappe was such that it was impossible for the artillery to cross there, it almost entirely remained on the road with a considerable number of caissons of all types; it was a terrible spectacle!! The moon lit up the rout of our army which had been so fine in the morning and so completely disorganised, destroyed in the evening of this fatal day.

We have spoken in detail of that which concerned I Corps; it is not possible to do the same for the other army corps, even though our division was not far off during this sad battle.

Towards 4am this mass of fugitives reached the junction of the road to Charleroi; some went towards Charleroi; the others on Marchienne au Pont. All continued their retreat by Philippeville and Avesnes and Laon where part of the army concentrated.

The emperor stopped for a short time at Charleroi where the Old Imperial Guard had re-assumed part of its usual order. The emperor then headed, on horseback, for Philippeville, where he rested for about three hours; and we saw him, for the last time, leaving in a vehicle for Paris. He was accompanied by General Bertrand and two other generals. In the evening, the troops which had taken this direction re-started their march. It was only at Laon that the army concentrated; then it was directed on Soissons, where it completed its re-organisation as far as it was possible. The battalion had at Laon about 200 men, the regiment 400. The regiment thought it had lost its eagle, but when the *chef de bataillon* rejoined them, and presented the eagle to them, there were shouts of indescribable joy; they thought he had been killed in the evening of the 18th and that the enemy had captured the eagle. This devotion to the flag was very honourable and characterised well the spirit of the French soldier.

At Soissons the strength of the regiment was very much the same. The army retreated to Paris in two columns. I cannot say what its strength was. The losses in killed, wounded and prisoners were considerable. We could also include a good number of deserters who returned to their families.

The morale in I, II and VI Corps, the cavalry and in the Imperial Guard was good. All these troops would have fought well if it had been judged useful to deliver battle at Paris. The two army corps (III and IV) and the cavalry of Marshal Grouchy were still very fine; I saw them arrive at Paris and all this part of the army blamed severely and with justice the conduct of this marshal during the day of the 18th. If he had made a movement from Vavres [*sic*] where he unfortunately remained stationary, to approach the army that fought at Waterloo, all could have been saved. This was a true fatality.

Jacquinot's 1st Cavalry Division

Colonel Louis Bro

Mémoires du Général Bro (1796–1844) (Paris: Plon, 1914), pp. 148–50.

During the 1815 campaign Bro commanded the 4th Lancers which were part of the 2nd Brigade (Gobrecht) of the 1st Light Cavalry Division commanded by General Jacquinot. This division was part of I Army Corps (d'Erlon).

Bro was born in 1781. Already inspired by the revolution and the wars which followed and seriously considering a career in arms, Bro was conscripted in 1801; his father's connections helped to get him into the 1st Hussars. Hardly in uniform, he found himself bound for Saint-Domingue (modern Haiti), as part of the expedition against the rebel slaves led by the famous Toussaint. Arriving in February 1802, Bro was promoted to brigadier *(cavalry corporal). The campaign against the rebels was short and successful. In a second campaign he was seriously wounded, and after the capitulation to the British the small French force was repatriated to France which he reached in July 1804. He was given leave for his wound to heal. Recovered, his father attempted to have him taken into the guard, but with insufficient experience he was refused. Instead, Bro was commissioned and became aide-de-camp to General Augereau, who commanded at Brest. In this capacity he worked for Donzelot, who was to command a division at Waterloo, and a fellow aide-de-camp, the famous Marcellin Marbot. As* adjoint *to the 7th Corps headquarters he missed the 1805 campaign against Austria, but marched into Prussia the following year and was present at the battle of Jena after which, in January 1807, he was promoted captain in the 7th Hussars. He was present with his regiment at Eylau, Heilsberg and Friedland after which he was promised the Légion d'Honneur by Napoleon himself. During his time with the 7th Hussars the regiment was commanded by Edouard Colbert, who was to command the Red Lancers of the Guard at Waterloo, and served in the brigade commanded by General Jacquinot, who commanded a cavalry division at that battle. In 1809 he was present at Wagram, where he was wounded and after the battle he became aide-de-camp to General Colbert, his former colonel, and went into garrison at Magdeburg. At the end of 1811, he was nominated to be* chef d'escadron *in the hussars, but chose to stay captain in order to join the prestigious Guard Chasseurs à Cheval with whom he took part in the invasion of Russia. He was present at Borodino, but the Guard remained in reserve throughout and saw little of the battle. In 1813, still with the chasseurs of the Guard, he fought at Lützen, Bautzen, Dresden, Leipzig and Hanau. On return to France he was promoted to* major en second *(lieutenant colonel) and sent to Paris to organise and command a*

*newly-raised provisional regiment, with which he made a famous charge at Montereau
and for which he was awarded the* Légion d'Honneur. *His regiment broken up, he
was attached to the headquarters of Roussel d'Urbal as* adjutant commandant, *with
whom he fought to the end of the campaign. Put on the inactive list after the First
Restoration, on Napoleon's return he was at first assigned as chief-of-staff of the 3rd
Cavalry Division, but then given command of the 4th Lancers (as colonel) with whom
he fought at Waterloo. Wounded at this battle, he returned home to recover. He was
able to recover sufficiently to give his farewells to his regiment before it was disbanded.
His rank as colonel was not endorsed by the Second Restoration and he was once more
listed as inactive. He served once more after the July Revolution and his rank as colonel
confirmed, he commanded the 1st Lancers. He led them into Belgium in 1831 and after
this campaign was promoted* maréchal de camp. *He commanded a brigade in Algeria
before returning to France in 1837 and commanding the departments of Hérault and
then Dordogne before becoming inspector of cavalry in the north. He briefly commanded
a cavalry brigade before being promoted once more to lieutenant general in 1841 but,
dissatisfied with the state of the army, he immediately retired. He died in 1844.*

*Bro gives an interesting account of his regiment's counter-attack against the
charging British cavalry in which he was wounded and forced to leave the battlefield.
He also describes the death of General Ponsonby.*

On the 18th we were given Mont-Saint-Jean as the objective. At eleven o'clock
in the morning Napoleon stopped after an inspection at the farm of Caillou,
dictated this order for the left: 'Once the army is ranged in order of battle,
towards one o'clock in the afternoon, at the moment when the emperor gives the
order to Marshal Ney, the attack will commence to seize the village of Mont-
Saint-Jean where there is an intersection of roads. To this end, the twelve-
pounder batteries of II Corps and those of VI Corps will join those of I Corps.
These eighty guns will fire on the troops at Mont-Saint-Jean and Count d'Erlon
will start the attack by advancing his left division and supporting it, according
to circumstances, by the [other] divisions of I Corps. II Corps will advance to
guard the flank of Count d'Erlon. The companies of *sapeurs* are to be prepared to
barricade Mont-Saint-Jean immediately.'

Of the terrible battle of Waterloo, this is what I saw and will see until my death:

At one o'clock in the afternoon, Donzelot's division, preceding the batteries,
marched on the château of Goumont [he must mean La Haye Sainte], repulsed
a Belgian division and got scattered in rough terrain. The English corps of Picton
attacked its left flank. Marcognet's division rushed forward, but was not able to
save a battery that had been taken by the troop of Ponsonby who charged at the
head of the Scots Greys. Our infantry, cut to pieces, broke up. Drouet d'Erlon
ordered the cavalry to charge. The water-logged ground did not allow us to
manoeuvre easily. I set off my 4th Lancers. To the right of a small wood, we noticed

the English cavalry, which, promptly reformed, threatened to outflank the 3rd Chasseurs. I took the head of the squadrons shouting, 'Come on my children, we need to overturn this rabble!' The soldiers answer me, 'Forward! *Vive l'empereur*! *Vive l'empereur*!' Two minutes later, the shock took place. Three enemy ranks were overturned. We crashed into the others! The melee became terrible. Our horses crushed dead bodies, and the shouts of the injured arose from all parts, for a moment I found myself lost in the powder smoke. In a clear moment, I noticed some English officers surrounding *sous-lieutenant* Verrane, the eagle bearer. Rallying several troopers, I went to his support. *Maréchal de logis* Orban killed General Ponsonby with a thrust of his lance. My sabre cut down three of his captains. Two others fled. I turned to the front to save my adjutant-major. I had emptied my second pistol when I suddenly felt my right arm paralysed. From the left hand, I knocked down the attacker who had defied me . . . A dizzy spell forced me to grab the mane of my horse. I had the strength to say to Major Perrot, 'Take command of the Regiment!' General Jacquinot appeared; on seeing the blood covering my clothing, he supported me and said, 'Retire!' The frustration of leaving my squadrons made me shed tears.

Remaining on horseback, I was able to reach the main ambulance at Montplaisir. M. Robert, the head doctor, wished to bandage my wound himself. He found the flesh of the right arm above the elbow, was cut to the bone and the bone grazed. I had lost a lot of blood and finding myself weak from this loss, I was obliged to rely on my servant to hold me upright.

The emperor had ordered that the wounded should be taken to Charleroi. Unable to offer any service to the war and authorised to move to the rear, I hired a carriage which was part of Count Drouet d'Erlon's suite. At five o'clock in the evening, when the cannonade was raging, we arrived before Genappe. A long convoy of artillery blocked the road. I learnt in this place that the French army was retreating. Two cavalrymen told us in passing that Napoleon had been killed in a square of the Guard. This news caused me an inexplicable uneasiness. Prevented from flying to the support of my brothers in arms and not wanting to fall as a prisoner into the hands of the enemy, I directed my carriage towards Nivelles by a back road which then served, being very sunken, as a bed for the water that had fallen the preceding days. From Nivelles, a local led me to Binch . . .

Colonel Jean-Baptiste-Antoine-Marcellin Baron de Marbot

The Memoirs of Baron Marbot (London: Longmans, 1892), Vol. II, pp. 456–8.

During the Waterloo campaign, Colonel Marcellin Marbot commanded the 7th Hussars. The regiment belonged to the 1st Brigade (Bruno) of the 1st Light Cavalry Division (Jacquinot), attached to I Army Corps (d'Erlon).

Marbot was born in 1782. His father had served in the Royal Guard and reached the rank of général de division when he died at the siege of Genoa in 1800. At the end of 1799, Marbot entered the 1st Hussars, and saw action against the Austrians. Having quickly been promoted maréchal des logis (sergeant) he was commissioned in the same regiment by the end of that first year. After a short time with the 25th Chasseurs à Cheval and then at the cavalry school at Versailles, in 1803 he became aide-de-camp to General (later Marshal) Augereau, serving with whom he was promoted lieutenant in 1804. In the campaigns of 1805–07 he served at Austerlitz, Jena, Eylau, where he was wounded, and Friedland, promoting to captain early in 1807. He became aide-de-camp to Marshal Lannes in 1808 and went to Spain where he was wounded twice, most notably at the siege of Saragossa. He moved with Lannes back to Germany for the campaign against Austria in 1809 and was wounded at Essling. Promoted to chef d'escadron in June of that year he ended the campaign as aide-de-camp to Marshal Masséna and was wounded at Znaïm. He accompanied Masséna to Portugal in 1810–11 and was wounded twice more before joining the 1st Chasseurs à Cheval in 1811 and the 23rd Chasseurs the following year. He served with this regiment in the invasion of Russia and was promoted colonel of the regiment during the retreat. During this campaign he received two further wounds. He commanded this regiment in the campaign of Germany in 1813. He was wounded at Leipzig. In October 1814 he was placed as the colonel of the 7th Hussars, who he subsequently led during the 1815 campaign. After Waterloo, Marbot had to leave France and he spent his exile in Germany writing his memoirs. He also wrote a critique of Rogniat's Considérations sur l'Art de la Guerre, which was so admired by Napoleon that he left Marbot 100,000 francs in his will! He returned to France in 1818 and, recalled to service in 1829, he became colonel of the 8th Chasseurs. The following year he became aide-de-camp to the Duke of Orleans and made lieutenant general. He received his final wound in Algiers aged nearly sixty! He finally retired in 1848 and died in 1854.

Marbot's memoirs end with Napoleon's first abdication in 1814 so we have no detailed account by him of the Waterloo campaign. However, two letters give some interesting detail on his role at Waterloo.

In a letter written on 26 June, just eight days after the battle, he writes from Laon where the army was rallying. Although it tells us very little of the battle, it offers an interesting insight into the state of the army after the battle.

I cannot get over our defeat. We were manoeuvred like so many pumpkins. I was with my regiment on the right flank of the army almost throughout the battle. They assured me that Marshal Grouchy would come up at that point; and it was guarded only by my regiment with three guns and a battalion of infantry – not nearly enough. Instead of Grouchy, what arrived was Blücher's corps. You can imagine how we were served. We were driven in, and in an instant the enemy was on our rear. The mischief may have been repaired, but no one gave any orders. The big generals were making bad speeches at Paris; the small ones lose their heads, and all goes wrong. I got a lance wound in the side; it is pretty severe, but I thought I would stay to set a good example. If everyone had done the same we might yet get along; but the men are deserting, and no one stops them. Whatever people might say, there are 50,000 men in this neighbourhood who might be got together; but to do it we should have to make it a capital offence to quit your post, or to give leave of absence. Everybody gives leave, and the coaches are full of officers departing. You may judge if the soldiers stay. There will not be one left in a week, unless they are checked by the death penalty. The Chambers can save us if they like; but we must have severe measures and prompt action. No food is sent to us, and so the soldiers pillage our poor France as if they were in Russia. I am at the outposts before Laon; we have been made to promise not to fire, and all is quiet.

In a letter written fifteen years later to ex-Marshal Grouchy, he enters into more details on the battle. Grouchy was working hard to counter the accusations of Napoleon that he was responsible for the loss of the battle of Waterloo and was no doubt seeking evidence from Marbot to help his case. In particular, Marbot describes his role on the right flank of the army which seems to confirm Napoleon's claim that he was truly expecting the marshal to arrive in time to take a decisive role in countering the arrival of the Prussians. However, we must take a cautious approach in taking Marbot's word for this. His memoirs are not generally accepted as the unadulterated truth (showing a tendency to stretch the truth in order to tell a good story) and as an ardent supporter of Napoleon, he seems inclined to support the emperor's claims about the battle. For example, he describes skirmishing with the advanced Prussian cavalry and yet Prussian accounts are all adamant that they approached the battlefield unobserved and without any contact with the French. Marbot's account clearly supports Napoleon's claim that he was expecting Grouchy to arrive on the battlefield, but some historians believe that his account was deliberately falsified to give credence to Napoleon's version of events.

Taken from Bernard Coppens and Patrice Courcelle, *Les Carnets de la Campagne* No.4, *LaPapelotte* (Brussels: Éditions de la Belle Alliance, 2000)

My General,

I have received your letter in which you desire to know the reconnaissance marches directed by me on the Dyle on the day of Waterloo. I hurry to respond to the questions that you have addressed to me on this subject.

The 7th Hussars, of which I was colonel, was part of the light cavalry division attached to the 1st Corps, forming, on the 18th June, the right of the portion of the army that the Emperor commanded in person. At the start of the action, towards eleven in the morning, I was detached from the division with my regiment and a battalion of infantry placed under my command. These troops were deployed *en potence* to the extreme right, behind Frischermont facing the Dyle.

Detailed orders were given to me, on behalf of the emperor, by his aide-de-camp, Labédoyère, and an orderly officer whose name I do not remember. They instructed me to always leave the main body of my force in view of the battlefield, to move two hundred infantrymen into the Frichermont wood, a squadron at Lasne, pushing its posts as far as Saint-Lambert; another squadron, half at Couture and half at Beaumont, sending reconnaissances as far as the [River] Dyle, to the bridges of Moustier and Ottignies. The commanders of these various detachments were to maintain small posts a quarter of a league [about a kilometre] apart, forming a continuous chain to the battlefield, in order that, by means of a hussar galloping from post to post, the officers on reconnaissance could quickly warn me of their junction with the advance guard of Marshal Grouchy, who was to arrive from the direction of the Dyle. Finally, I was to send the information gathered on these reconnaissances directly to the emperor. I executed the order that was given to me.

It is impossible for me, after a time lapse of fifteen years, to fix exactly the hour at which the detachment directed towards Moustier reached this point, especially since Captain Éloy, who commanded it, had received the order from me to scout further on and to march with the greatest caution. But in mentioning that he left the battlefield at eleven o'clock and that he had no more than two leagues [about 8km] to cover, you can presume that he did this in two hours, which fixes his arrival at Moustier at one o'clock in the afternoon. A note from Captain Éloy, which was quickly relayed to me by intermediate posts, informed me that he had found no troops at Moustier, nor at Ottignies, and that the local inhabitants had assured him that French troops were on the right bank of the Dyle crossing the river at Limal, Limelette and Wavre.

I sent this note to the emperor with Captain Kouhn, who worked as the adjutant-major. He returned accompanied by an *officier d'ordonnance*, who told me from the emperor to leave a line of outposts established from Moustier, and to order the officer scouting the defile of Saint-Lambert to pass through it and to push as far as possible in the direction of Limal, Limelette and Wavre. I sent this order and even my map to the commander of the detachment at Lasne and Saint-Lambert.

One of my platoons, being a quarter of a league beyond Saint-Lambert, encountered a platoon of Prussian hussars from which it took several prisoners, including an officer. I warned the emperor of this odd capture, and sent the prisoners to him.

I was soon certain of the opposite. The head of the Prussian column was approaching, but very slowly. Twice I threw back into the defile some hussars and lancers which preceded it. I tried to gain time by holding up the enemy as much as possible, who was only able to pass along the sunken and muddy tracks along which they were travelling with great difficulty; and when, finally, constrained by their superior forces I retreated, the adjutant-major, who I had ordered to inform the emperor of the positive arrival of the Prussians in front of Saint-Lambert, returned to tell me that the emperor directed that the head of Grouchy's column, which at this moment should be crossing over the bridges of Moustier and Ottignies as they were not crossing at Limal and Limelette, should be informed of this.

I wrote to this effect to Captain Éloy, but he, having vainly waited without seeing any troops, and hearing the cannon towards Saint-Lambert, feared being cut off. He thus retired successively on his small outposts and re-joined the main body of the regiment which had remained in view of the battlefield, at the same moment as the squadrons which were returning, pressed by the enemy, from Saint-Lambert and Lasne.

The terrible combat that was taking place beyond the Frischermont wood by the troops that I commanded and those who had come to support them, absorbed all my attention so I cannot specify the exact time; but I think that it would be close to seven o'clock in the evening; and as Captain Éloy, retired at the trot and could not have taken more than an hour to return, I estimate that it was towards six o'clock that he would have left the Moustier bridge, on which he had remained for five hours. It is thus very surprising that he had not seen your aide-de-camp, at least if he was not mistaken on the name of the place where he reached the Dyle.

Such is the summary of the movements that the regiment that I commanded made during the battle of Waterloo on the right flank of the French army. The march and the direction of my reconnaissances were of such high importance on this memorable day, that Marshal Davout, Minister of War, ordered me at the end of 1815 to record the circumstances in a report which I had the honour to address to him and which should still be found in the war archives.

The facts that I have narrated has resulted in me being convinced that the emperor awaited the corps of Marshal Grouchy on the battlefield of Waterloo. But on what hope was this based? I do not know, and I cannot judge, limiting me to the account of what I saw for myself.

The report that Marbot claims to have written would have provided vital evidence in the case for or against Grouchy's account of why he was unable to intervene at Waterloo, and to counter the accusations made by Napoleon that blamed him for the loss of the battle. Given that much correspondence from the campaign went missing, it is of perhaps no surprise that Marbot's report also seems to have disappeared and the many admirers of Napoleon feel they can continue to point the finger of blame at Marshal Grouchy.

Chef d'Escadron Victor Dupuy

Souvenirs Militaires de Victor Dupuy, Chef d'Escadron de Hussars 1794–1816 (Paris: Calmann Levy, 1892), pp. 289–92.

During the Waterloo campaign, Victor Dupuy served as a squadron commander in the 7th Hussars (Marbot). The regiment belonged to the 1st Brigade (Bruno) of the 1st Light Cavalry Division (Jacquinot), attached to I Army Corps (d'Erlon).

Victor Dupuy was born in 1777 and was only twelve on the outbreak of the revolution. Despite this he joined one of the first volunteer battalions at fourteen. However, on trying to join a regular battalion he was turned away because of his age and instead went to the école de Mars *which was run by the Jacobins and provided a company of National Guards. Whilst serving with these in Paris he was wounded by a musket ball in his right thigh. Now eighteen and worried that he would be conscripted into the infantry, he volunteered for the 11th Chasseurs à Cheval. He fought with them in the Army of the Danube and then the Army of the Rhine. He served at Austerlitz and Znaïm in the 1805 campaign as adjutant and after fighting at Jena in the 1806 campaign he was commissioned in Berlin by Napoleon aged twenty-nine. He later fought at Heilsberg. At the beginning of the 1809 campaign he became aide-de-camp to General Jacquinot and fought at Wagram. He continued his service as aide-de-camp to Jacquinot during the invasion of Russia in 1812. After the battle of Borodino he was promoted to* chef d'escadron, *survived the retreat and served in the sacred squadron. In 1813 he fought at Lützen, Bautzen, Reichenbach and Dresden before being promoted to major in the 6th Hussars. He was captured at the affair of Altenburg and imprisoned in Hungary. He returned to France after Napoleon's abdication in 1814 as* chef d'escadron *in the 7th Hussars commanded by the famous Colonel Marbot. After Waterloo he retreated with his regiment and commanded it after Marbot was proscribed. After over seeing its disbandment he was put on the inactive list and under police surveillance in 1816. Although he formally retired in 1828 he re-entered service after the 1830 July Revolution, but would not accept an active command because of the length of his absence from duty and he finished his career as sub-prefect of Cognac. He finally retired in 1846 and died in 1857.*

Dupuy might be considered a more dependable witness than Marbot, his commanding officer. However, he supports Marbot's claim that his mission was to meet Grouchy rather than scout the Prussians.

Finally, I received the order to re-join the rear of the brigade. The weather was terrible; the rain fell in torrents. After having wandered about to find somewhere to put ourselves up, the two regiments established themselves in a large farm, where the men and horses could be sheltered.

We were mounted at 4am on the 18th, and towards 8am, after having refreshed our horses for a short time, we came to the battlefield. Our regiment was detached from the division and, with three squadrons of chasseurs, took position on the extreme right, having no enemy in front of us.

The struggle started to our left along the whole line. From midday, panic seized several regiments of infantry of I Corps and the *sauve qui peut* was uttered. They fled in the greatest disorder; I rushed over to them with a platoon of hussars to stop them. Seeing amongst them a standard-bearer with his eagle, I asked him to give it to me; he moved to give it to me, when the thought came to me, 'I do not wish to dishonour you, monsieur', I said to him, 'display your flag and move ahead, calling "*Vive l'Empereur*!" with me'. He did so immediately, the brave man! Soon the soldiers stopped and, in a short time, thanks to their efforts and ours, almost 3,000 men had been collected and about-faced.

The flight was so surprising that the enemy did not pursue them; but which troublemaker had called '*sauve qui peut*!'? No one knew. Until towards 4pm we remained peaceful spectators of the battle. At this time General Domon came to me; the fire of the English had almost ceased; he told me that the battle was won, that the enemy army was in retreat, that we were there to make a junction with Marshal Grouchy's corps and that by the evening we would be in Brussels. He left.

A few moments after, instead of meeting Grouchy's troops, we received the attack of a regiment of Prussian uhlans. We repulsed them vigorously and chased after them, but we were forced to retreat by canister fired by six guns behind which the uhlans retired.

Colonel Marbot had been wounded by a lance thrust to the chest during the Prussian attack.

Attacked then by infantry, we reformed on the centre and started to retreat

In our retrograde movement, we encountered Marshal Soult, the *major-général* [chief of staff], who positioned us close to a brigade of the Guard to support it; enemy cannon fire caused us some casualties.

A little later, we received the order to move to the rear to oppose some Prussian skirmishers.

Until then, we thought we had won the battle at other parts of the line; but as we arrived on the main road, seeing it covered in fleeing men, we were disabused of this. At first we tried to rally them, but this was impossible, it was necessary to retreat also, but at least we did it in order, marching several hundred paces from the road until night and the difficulties of the route forced us to move back onto it and to march all mixed up with the fugitives of all arms. Our defeat had not been calculated in advance; caissons unharnessed, of which the shafts were set one into the other having passed here and there across the main road to hinder our march and to stop our materiel and baggage. There were large ditches on the sides; it was often necessary to dismount several of our men to pull down the embankments in order to thus make a passage.

After having marched all night, during which several of us got lost, the brigade, having left the Charleroi road, took that to Marchiennes where, almost complete, it crossed the Sambre.

It is useless to consider how the results of this terrible day might have been different! . . . The disorder was already in the English army when the Prussians, having slipped away from Marshal Grouchy, arrived on the battlefield and seized back the victory that had escaped the English. Without this skilful march, the Waterloo bridge that was built on the Thames would have been on the Seine! Ah! Or at least, if justice had been done, one would have seen a statue of a Prussian general on this monument! . . . We have only those to Austerlitz and Jena!!! No one has a right to claim *la gloire*!!!

The French Army at Waterloo Order of Battle

Commander-in-Chief
The Emperor Napoleon I

Commander of the Right Wing Marshal Ney, Prince of Moskwa
Chief of Staff Marshal Soult, Duke of Dalmatia
Chief Staff Officer Lieutenant General Count Bailly de Monthyon
Commander of Artillery Lieutenant General Ruty
Commander of Engineers Lieutenant General Baron Rogniat

IMPERIAL GUARD (Lieutenant General Count Drouot)

INFANTRY OF THE GUARD
Old Guard
1st and 2nd Regiments Grenadiers (4 bns)
1st and 2nd Regiments Chasseurs (4 bns)

Middle Guard[1]
3rd and 4th Regiments Grenadiers (3 bns)
3rd and 4th Regiments Chasseurs (4 bns)

Young Guard (Lieutenant General Count Duhesme)
1st and 2nd Regiments Tirailleurs (4 bns)
1st and 2nd Regiments Voltigeurs (4 bns)

CAVALRY OF THE GUARD
Light Cavalry (Lieutenant General Count de Lefebvre-Desnoëttes)
Guard Lancers
Guard Chasseurs à Cheval

Heavy Cavalry (Lieutenant General Count Guyot)
Grenadiers à Cheval
The Empress Dragoons
Gendarmerie d'Élite

ARTILLERY OF THE GUARD (Lieutenant General Baron Desvaux de St Maurice)
13 Foot Batteries
3 Horse Batteries
Engineers of the Guard (1 coy)
Sailors of the Guard (1 coy)

I CORPS (Lieutenant General Drouet d'Erlon)

1st Division (*Maréchal de Camp* Baron Quiot du Passage)
1st Brigade (Colonel Charlet) 54th and 55th Line (4 bns)
2nd Brigade (*Maréchal de Camp* Bourgeois) 28th and 105th Line (4 bns)

2nd Division (Lieutenant General Baron Donzelot)
1st Brigade (*Maréchal de Camp* Schmitz) 13th Light and 17th Line (5 bns)
2nd Brigade (*Maréchal de Camp* Baron Aulard) 19th and 51st Line (4bns)

3rd Division (Lieutenant General Baron Marcognet)
1st Brigade (*Maréchal de Camp* Nogues) 21st and 46th Line (4 bns)
2nd Brigade (*Maréchal de Camp* Grenier) 25th and 45th Line (4 bns)

4th Division (Lieutenant General Count Durutte)
1st Brigade (*Maréchal de Camp* Pégot) 8th and 29th Line (4bns)
2nd Brigade (*Maréchal de Camp* Brue) 85th and 95th Line (4 bns)

1st Cavalry Division (Lieutenant General Baron Jacquinot)
1st Brigade (*Maréchal de Camp* Baron Bruno) 7th Hussars and 3rd Chasseurs à Cheval
2nd Brigade (*Maréchal de Camp* Gobrecht) 3rd and 4th Lancers

I Corps Artillery (Colonel Desalle) 5 Foot Batteries and 1 Horse Battery

II CORPS (Lieutenant General Count Reille)

5th Division (Lieutenant General Baron Bachelu)
1st Brigade (*Maréchal de Camp* Baron Husson) 2nd Light and 61st Line (6 bns)
2nd Brigade (*Maréchal de Camp* Baron Campi) 72nd and 108th Line (5 bns)

6th Division (Lieutenant General Prince Jérôme Bonaparte)
1st Brigade (*Maréchal de Camp* Baron Bauduin) 1st Light and 3rd Line (5 bns)
2nd Brigade (*Maréchal de Camp* Baron Soye) 1st and 2nd Line (6 bns)

9th Division (Lieutenant General Count Foy)
1st Brigade (*Maréchal de Camp* Baron Gauthier) 92nd and 93rd Line
2nd Brigade (*Maréchal de Camp* Baron Jamin) 100th Line and 4th Light (6 bns)

2nd Cavalry Division (Lieutenant General Baron Piré)
1st Brigade (*Maréchal de Camp* Baron Huber) 1st and 6th Chasseurs à Cheval
2nd Brigade (*Maréchal de Camp* Baron Wathier) 5th and 6th Lancers

II Corps Artillery (Colonel Pelletier) 5 Foot Batteries and 1 Horse Battery

VI CORPS (Lieutenant General Mouton, Count de Lobau)

19th Division (Lieutenant General Baron Simmer)
1st Brigade (*Maréchal de Camp* Baron de Bellair) 5th and 11th Line (5 bns)
2nd Brigade (*Maréchal de Camp* Thévenet) 27th and 84th Line (4 bns)

20th Division (Lieutenant General Baron Jeanin)
1st Brigade (*Maréchal de Camp* Bony) 5th and 10th Line (4 bns)
2nd Brigade (*Maréchal de Camp* Count Tromelin) 107th Line (2 bns)

3rd Cavalry Division (Attached from III Corps) (Lieutenant General Baron Domon)
1st Brigade (*Maréchal de Camp* Baron Dommanget) 4th and 9th Chasseurs à Cheval
2nd Brigade (Colonel de Grouchy) 12th Chasseurs à Cheval
1 Horse Battery

5th Cavalry Division (Attached from 1st Cavalry Corps) (Lieutenant General Baron Subervie)
1st Brigade (*Maréchal de Camp* Count Colbert) 1st and 2nd Lancers
2nd Brigade (*Maréchal de Camp* Merlin) 11th Chasseurs à Cheval
1 Horse Battery

VI Corps Artillery (Colonel Noury) 4 Foot Batteries

III CAVALRY CORPS (Lieutenant General Kellerman, Count Valmy)

11th Cavalry Division (Lieutenant General Baron l'Héritier)
1st Brigade (*Maréchal de Camp* Baron Picquet) 2nd and 7th Dragoons
2nd Brigade (*Maréchal de Camp* Guiton) 8th and 11th Cuirassiers
1 Horse Battery

12th Cavalry Division (Lieutenant General Baron Roussel d'Hurbal)
1st Brigade (*Maréchal de Camp* Baron Blancard) 1st and 2nd Carabiniers
2nd Brigade (*Maréchal de Camp* Donop) 2nd and 3rd Cuirassiers
1 Horse Battery

IV CAVALRY CORPS (Lieutenant General Count Milhaud)

13th Cavalry Division (Lieutenant General Watier)
1st Brigade (*Maréchal de Camp* Baron Dubois) 1st and 4th Cuirassiers
2nd Brigade (*Maréchal de Camp* Baron Travers) 7th and 12th Cuirassiers
1 Horse Battery

14th Cavalry Division (Lieutenant General Baron Delort)
1st Brigade (*Maréchal de Camp* Baron Farine) 5th and 10th Cuirassiers
2nd Brigade (*Maréchal de Camp* Baron Vial) 6th and 9th Cuirassiers
1 Horse Battery

Notes

Introduction

1. Lieutenant Gawler, 52nd Light Infantry.

Chapter 1: Using Eyewitness Accounts

1. Ensign Leeke, 52nd Light Infantry.

Chapter 2: Napoleon's Own Accounts

1. Adolf Hitler.
2. *Mémoires de Fleury de Chaboulon, ex-secrétaire de l'Empereur Napléon et de son Cabinet, pour server à l'histoire de la vie privée, du retour et du règne de Napoléon en 1815* (Paris: Edouard Rouveyre, 1901), Vol. II, pp. 161–2.

Chapter 3: Napoleon's Household

1. A *prolonge* was a long rope that a number of nations used to manoeuvre a gun without having to limber it up. The British did not use these and therefore did not have to waste time detaching them before leaving their guns with the limbers.

Chapter 4: Imperial Headquarters

1. Margerit, *Waterloo, l'Europe contre la France* (Éditions Gallimard, 1964), p. 169.
2. See Note 1 to Chapter 3 above.
3. There was no Bonnet serving with the 1st *Légère* at Waterloo. The officer responsible for this episode was Lieutenant Legros.

Chapter 5: I Army Corps

1. A *peleton* was the tactical unit of a company and does not accurately translate as 'platoon' which in modern armies is only part of a company, there normally being three or even four platoons in a modern company. In the French

army a company was a purely administrative organisation and the *peleton* a company-sized tactical organisation.

Appendix

1. Whilst it is true that the 3rd and 4th Grenadiers and Chasseurs were officially part of the Old Guard, nearly all French accounts, and even many British, refer to them as Middle Guard, as this is clearly how they were perceived in the French army and, it appears, even in the Guard itself. Indeed, one British officer claims that having asked a wounded French soldier to which unit he belonged, he replied that he was in the Middle Guard.